D0086613

CRITICAL INSIGHTS

Death of a Salesman

CRITICAL INSIGHTS

Death of a Salesman

by Arthur Miller

WITHDRAWN

BETTY SUE JESSUP LIBRARY
PIEDMONT VIRGINIA COMMUNITY COLLEGE

Editor
Brenda Murphy
University of Connecticut

Salem Press
Pasadena, California   Hackensack, New Jersey

Cover photo: Time & Life Pictures/Getty Images

Published by Salem Press

© 2010 by EBSCO Publishing
Editor's text © 2010 by Brenda Murphy
"The *Paris Review* Perspective" © 2010 by Elizabeth Gumport for *The Paris Review*

All rights in this book are reserved. No part of this work may be used or reproduced in any manner whatsoever or transmitted in any form or by any means, electronic or mechanical, including photocopy, recording, or any information storage and retrieval system, without written permission from the copyright owner except in the case of brief quotations embodied in critical articles and reviews or in the copying of images deemed to be freely licensed or in the public domain. For information address the publisher, Salem Press, P.O. Box 50062, Pasadena, California 91115. For copyright information, contact EBSCO Publishing, 10 Estes Street, Ipswich, MA 01938.

∞ The paper used in these volumes conforms to the American National Standard for Permanence of Paper for Printed Library Materials, Z39.48-1992 (R1997).

Library of Congress Cataloging-in-Publication Data

Death of a salesman, by Arthur Miller / editor, Brenda Murphy.
p. cm. — (Critical insights)
Includes bibliographical references and index.
ISBN 978-1-58765-610-1 (alk. paper)
1. Miller, Arthur, 1915-2005. Death of a salesman. I. Murphy, Brenda, 1950-
PS3525.I5156D4337 2010
812′.52—dc22

2009026317

PRINTED IN CANADA

Contents

The Play and Author

Critical Contexts

Critical Readings

Resources

About This Volume

Brenda Murphy

This volume in the *Critical Insights* series offers a diverse and far-ranging selection of criticism on Arthur Miller's major play *Death of a Salesman* (1949), the most significant American play of the twentieth century. The volume is divided into two parts, the first composed of essays that were commissioned specifically for this volume and the second of reprinted essays that not only are interesting and revealing studies in themselves but reflect the play's critical history as well.

As background for the individual critical studies, the editor's "On *Death of a Salesman*" and Elizabeth Gumport's *Paris Review* perspective present a general critical context for the play, and Carl Rollyson provides a brief biography of Arthur Miller. These essays are followed by new articles that illuminate *Death of a Salesman* from several different perspectives. Jon Dietrick offers a close analysis of *Salesman* in the context of literary Naturalism and monetary theory. Joshua E. Polster provides the too often ignored historical context of the 1930s theaters of social protest, seeing *Salesman* as the culmination of the social drama movement in the United States. Neil Heims takes a new approach to the much-debated issue of the nature of tragedy in *Salesman*. Amy Sickels provides a broad overview of some of the issues that have interested the play's critics in the sixty years since its premiere.

The essays reprinted in the second section reflect the wide variety of critical and theoretical perspectives that have been trained on *Death of a Salesman*. Setting the stage for a good deal of criticism to come, in his 1970 essay Chester Eisinger writes of the play's antithesis between dream and reality and the competing dreams of the Loman family. Irving Jacobson presents an early exploration of the play in terms of Willy Loman's need to, in Miller's words, "make of the world a home," arguing that Willy is not a modern Everyman but rather "an anomaly, a bourgeois romantic." In more recent criticism, Kay Stanton's provocative analysis of Miller's treatment of women argues that the male-oriented American Dream presented in the play requires "unacknowledged dependence upon women as well as women's subjugation and exploitation," and suggests that Linda Loman, as "common woman," has greater tragic nobility than Willy. From a postmodern perspective, Granger Babcock interrogates the prevailing notion of Willy Loman as liberal subject, arguing that he represents Deleuze and Guattari's idea of the "desiring machine." Fred Ribkoff addresses the dynamics of shame, guilt, empathy, and the search for identity in *Salesman*, arguing that Biff Loman's confrontation with feelings of shame enables him to "find himself, separate his sense of identity from that of his father, and empathize with his father." In a brief but illuminating close reading, Terry W. Thompson demonstrates the deep resonance and the ironic implications of Willy's casual comparison of Biff to Hercules. Through her analysis based on Deborah Tannen's study of gender-associated linguistic patterns, Heather Cook Callow offers the intriguing argument that it is not Willy's failure to succeed, but "the curiously androgynous nature of his goals and methods that adds fuel to critics' dispute over his right to the title of American Everyman." Lois Tyson gives a provocative reading of *Salesman* based on the question, "How do psychology and ideology intersect in this drama to make the traditional Americanist separation of psyche and socius an untenable theoretical construct?" Matthew Roudané gives a deeply informed overview reading of *Salesman* both as literary work and as production. Finally, based on his unequaled knowledge of *Salesman*'s composition and Miller's life and work, Christopher Bigsby gives a richly layered reading of the play in the context of American culture. A chronology of Miller's life, a list of his major works, and a bibliography complete the volume.

THE PLAY AND AUTHOR

On *Death of a Salesman*

Brenda Murphy

Death of a Salesman is perhaps the greatest dramatic work by an American. From the time of its premiere on February 10, 1949, it was recognized as a play of artistic quality that was rarely seen in the contemporary theater. As one newspaper critic commented at the time, the New York audience had "waited for *Death of a Salesman* with the expectation of seeing a masterpiece" because "whoever you met that had caught the show out of town had clearly seen a masterpiece already, and behaved as if he had seen a ghost." Few things in Broadway history, he commented, "have had so sensational a build-up: fewer still—which is far more wonderful—have been so breathlessly received when they arrived."[1]

In a time when Broadway averaged more than a premiere a week and theater criticism tended toward the jaded and cynical, the immediate response to *Salesman* was almost universally rhapsodic. The reserved *New York Times* critic called it "a superb drama,"[2] and even the show-biz *Variety* reviewer said that *Salesman* was "in a class by itself. All the superlatives a tub-thumper ever dreamed up apply perfectly to this opus."[3] The recognized intellectual leader of American theater critics, Harold Clurman, called the premiere "a cardinal event not only of this season but of many a long year in the American theatre."[4]

Death of a Salesman won the Pulitzer Prize, the New York Drama Critics' Circle Award, the Donaldson Award, and Tony Awards for best play, best direction, best scene design, and best supporting actor. Not a mere critical success, the play was embraced by audiences and readers throughout the world. It ran for 742 performances on Broadway. The published script was a best seller, and it was the only play ever to be a Book-of-the-Month Club selection.

What was so special about this play that it inspired such reactions from such diverse critics and audiences? Why has it continued for sixty years to be the touchstone of American drama, the iconic play by which the world defines American values? In theatrical terms, there were a number of things about Miller's play, and about that first production by director Elia Kazan, designer Jo Mielziner, and actors Lee J. Cobb, Mildred Dunnock, Arthur Kennedy, and Cameron Mitchell, that contributed to making it the theatrical watershed that it was.

First is the genre itself. In the 1940s, the American theater audience had become used to a sophisticated but straightforward realism in its theater, whether in portraying the working-class characters of Clifford Odets, the middle class of Lillian Hellman, or the society people of Philip Barry. The goal was to produce the illusion that the audience was simply looking through a "fourth wall" at real life being lived out on the stage before them. Working with Tennessee Williams on *The Glass Menagerie* (1945) and *A Streetcar Named Desire* (1947), Kazan and Mielziner had begun to change that expectation, disrupting some of the conventions of dramatic realism to produce a theatrical idiom, a combination of realism and expressionism that conveyed some of the protagonist's subjective experience while the overall production maintained its premise of portraying objective reality.

In *Salesman*, Miller envisioned a much more radical challenge to the audience's expectations. His working title for the play, "The Inside of His Head," was based on the image "of an enormous face the height of the proscenium arch which would appear and then open up, and we would see the inside of man's head . . . a mass of contradictions,"[5] which was Willy Loman. After seeing the production of Williams's *Streetcar*, and its techniques for portraying "objectively real" events through the nightmarishly distorted perspective of Blanche DuBois, Miller conceived of a way to represent Willy Loman, a character who "is literally at that terrible moment when the voice of the past is no longer distant but quite as loud as the voice of the present," on the stage. In *Salesman*, "the structure of events and the nature of its form are also the direct reflection of Willy Loman's way of thinking at this moment of his life. . . . The way of telling the tale, in this sense, is as mad as Willy and as abrupt and as suddenly lyrical." In order to do this, Miller made use not of flashbacks, but of "daydreams," in which there is "a mobile concurrency of past and present . . . because in his desperation to justify his life, Willy Loman has destroyed the boundaries between now and then."[6]

In representing Willy's world, Miller created a dramatically complex blending of realism and expressionism, a modernist theatrical idiom that overtly portrays a character's subjective perception of reality, the theatrical equivalent of fiction's stream of consciousness. As Miller put it, "*Death of a Salesman* was conceived literally on two dimensions at the same time. On one level there are autonomous characters while on another there are characters who exist as symbols for Willy Loman."[7]

Not only does *Salesman* represent the events of the present simultaneously with the events of the past as they are filtered through Willy's consciousness; it combines characters who are meant to be seen as pure constructs of Willy's troubled imagination, such as Ben and The Woman, with characters who are meant to be "real people" in the play's present *and* younger constructs of themselves in Willy's memory, colored by his idealization of them and his guilt at having let them down, in the play's past. An enormous challenge for director, designer, and actors, the play created the new theatrical idiom of subjective realism, which became known as "the American style" and was imitated extensively in mid-twentieth-century theater throughout the world.

At the same time that *Death of a Salesman* was seen as a groundbreaking modernist play, it was also recognized as one of the few authentic tragedies of the twentieth century. Several of the opening-night newspaper critics saw immediately that Miller had written what one called "a soaring tragedy,"[8] using what another called "the same materials used by the Greek tragedians of the Golden Age."[9] In the wake of the premiere, a debate about the play's relationship with classical tragedy began, which has continued among scholarly critics to this day.

Can the play be a classical tragedy if Willy Loman has no moment of "recognition," in Aristotle's terms, no process of learning and transcendence as a result of his experience? Is Willy Loman a significant enough figure to rise to the status of tragic hero? These are objections that Miller anticipated, and he headed off the debate early with a brief article he published in *The New York Times* called "Tragedy and the Common Man," an article that became one of the classic essays on drama from the twentieth century. In his essay, Miller flatly asserted that "the common man is as apt a subject for tragedy in its highest sense as kings were."

Perhaps more important, Miller turned several of the conventional assumptions about tragedy on their heads in his essay, locating good not in a higher supernatural or social order but in the individual's right to personal freedom and self-actualization, evil not in the violation of a higher order but in oppression of the individual by just such external forces. Rather than the resignation and submission to a higher authority that characterizes the ending of the traditional tragedy, Miller insisted that "in the tragic view the need of man to wholly realize himself is the only fixed star" and it is from the "total questioning of what has previously been unquestioned" that "we learn."[10] Miller's statement has provoked a significant and enduring critical debate, not only about his play, but about drama in the twentieth century.

While the extensive critical analysis devoted to *Salesman* is one good index of its cultural significance, it is important to remember that a play's most vital existence is on stage enacted by actors in front of an audience. *Death of a Salesman* has had a long and vigorous life in the world theater. Its American production was quickly followed by major productions in England, Germany, Austria, Italy, Ireland, South Africa, Spain, Australia, Mexico, Korea, Israel, the Soviet Union, Canada, and France, and later Japan, Taiwan, and, in a famous production directed by Miller in 1983, Beijing.

At this point, *Salesman* has been performed throughout the world and is taught in schools and acted in community and professional theaters in many countries besides the United States. Willy Loman has become a universal synonym not only for the salesman but also for the contemporary Everyman with big dreams. A recent Google search for "Willy Loman" resulted in more than 170,000 hits. Articles in business journals have titles like "Overcoming the Willy Loman Syndrome," "Leadership Lessons from Willy Loman," and "It's Wired Willy Loman!" It is clear that play and character have entered deeply into contemporary global culture, and they show no signs of leaving anytime soon.

Notes

1. Louis Kronenberger, "The Theater," *Town and Country* 17 (1949): 65.
2. Brooks Atkinson, "*Death of a Salesman*, a New Drama by Arthur Miller, Has Premiere at the Morosco," *New York Times*, 11 February 1949.
3. *Variety* clipping, Arthur Miller scrapbook, Harry Ransom Humanities Research Center, University of Texas at Austin.
4. Harold Clurman, *Lies Like Truth* (New York: Macmillan, 1958) 72.
5. Arthur Miller, *The Theater Essays of Arthur Miller*, ed. Robert A. Martin and Steven R. Centola (New York: Da Capo, 1996) 135.
6. Miller, *Theater Essays*, 138–39.
7. Christopher Bigsby, *Arthur Miller and Company* (London: Methuen, 1990) 59.
8. Howard Barnes, "A Great Play Is Born," *New York Herald Tribune*, 11 February 1949: 14.
9. Robert Coleman, "Death of a Salesman Is Emotional Dynamite," New York *Daily Mirror*, 11 February 1949. Rpt. Rachel Coffin, ed. *New York Theater Critics Reviews* 10 (1949): 360.
10. Miller, *Theater Essays*, 6, 4.

Biography of Arthur Miller

Carl Rollyson

Biography

Arthur Miller grew up in New York City with an older brother and a younger sister. His father was a prosperous businessperson until the Crash of 1929, after which the family suffered through the Depression, a period that had a major impact on Miller's sense of himself, his family, and his society, and one that figures prominently in many of his dramas, essays, and stories. During the Depression, Miller drove trucks, unloaded cargoes, waited on tables, and worked as a clerk in a warehouse. These jobs brought him close to the kind of working-class characters who appear in his plays. His observations of his father's fall from financial security and of the way the people immediately around him had to struggle for even a modicum of dignity placed Miller in a position to probe individuals' tenuous hold on their place in society.

Although Miller had been a poor student in school, he was inspired by Fyodor Dostoevsky's implacable questioning of individual impulses and societal rules in *The Brothers Karamazov* (1879–1880), and eventually he was able to persuade the University of Michigan to admit him. Almost immediately he began to write plays that would receive several Hopwood awards. If Miller was not exactly a Marxist during his college years (1934–1938), he was certainly a radical insofar as he believed that American society had to be changed and made fair for the masses of people who had been ruined by the Depression.

His early student plays contain sympathetic portrayals of student militants and union organizers as well as compassionate characterizations of small business owners and professional people caught in the economic and political tyranny of capitalism. In the fall of 1938, after his graduation from the University of Michigan with a bachelor of arts degree in English language and literature, Miller joined the Federal Theatre Project in New York City, for which he wrote numerous radio plays and scripts until 1943. Some of these works express his irrepressible interest in social and political issues. In 1940, Miller married Mary Grace Slattery, and a daughter, Jane, was born in 1944. The couple divorced in 1956.

From Miller's earliest student plays to *Death of a Salesman*, there is an evolution in his treatment of individuals in conflict with their society, a gradual realization of conflicts within individuals that both mirror the larger conflicts in society and define a core of singularity in the characters themselves. Undoubtedly, Miller's intense involvement in public affairs in the 1940s and 1950s—his support of various liberal and radical causes and his subsequent testimony about his political commitments before the House Committee on Un-American Activities in 1956 are two examples—reflected and reinforced his need to write social plays.

Miller's marriage to Marilyn Monroe in 1956, far from being the perplexing and amusing sideshow the press made of it, had a significant impact on his writing, not only by encouraging him to focus on female characters in ways he previously had not, but also by stimulating him to enlarge on and reconsider the theme of innocence, which he had adumbrated in earlier plays. After his divorce from Monroe in 1961, he wrote some of his finest plays and continued to participate in local, national, and international affairs—including two terms as international president of PEN, the worldwide writers' organization. He was a delegate to the Democratic conventions of 1968 and 1972. Miller married Ingeborg Morath, an Austrian-born photojournalist, in 1962, and the couple collaborated on several travel books. After serving as a lecturer at the University of Michigan in the mid-1970s, Miller retired to a large Connecticut estate, where he continued to write and indulged in such hobbies as carpentry and gardening. In 1997, he petitioned the Czech government to halt arrests of dissident writers. His international reputation expanded during the 1980s, when he directed *Death of a Salesman* in Beijing. Throughout the 1990s, Miller continued to receive numerous awards for distinguished achievement. In early 2002, his wife died; three years later Miller died at his home in Roxbury, Connecticut.

Achievements

Arthur Miller has been acclaimed as one of the most distinguished American dramatists since Eugene O'Neill, the father of modern American drama. Because of his direct engagement with political issues and the theoretical concerns of contemporary drama, he was frequently a significant spokesperson for his generation of writers. His reputation seems secure both nationally and internationally, and his plays continue to be performed live and through screenplay adaptations all over the world.

Miller successfully synthesized diverse dramatic styles and movements in the belief that a play should embody a delicate balance between the individual and society, between the singular personality and the polity, and between the separate and collective elements of life. Miller was a writer of social plays whose concern with the moral problems in American society led him to probe the psychological causes of behavior. He built on the realist tradition of Henrik Ibsen in his exploration of the individual's conflict with society but also borrowed Symbolist and expressionist techniques from Bertolt Brecht and others. He based his plays on the assumption of an comprehensible objective reality as well as a subjective reality that makes life problematic and ambiguous. Therefore, all attempts to interpret his work from either an exclusively political or an exclusively psychological standpoint fail, for Miller regarded his plays as indissoluble amalgamations of inner and outer realities.

Miller's achievement as a dramatist has been recognized with numerous awards. These include the New York Drama Critics' Circle Award for *All My Sons* in 1947 and for *Death of a Salesman* in 1949; the Pulitzer Prize in 1949 for *Death of a Salesman*; and the Antoinette Perry (Tony) Award in 1949 for *Death of a Salesman* and for *The Crucible*. In 1956, Miller received an honorary doctor of humane letters degree from the University of Michigan, and he was elected to the National Institute of Arts and Letters in 1958. During the 1990s, he received the William Ingle Festival Award for distinguished achievement in American theater and the Edward Albee Last Frontier Playwright Award. In 1998, Miller was named Distinguished Inaugural Senior Fellow of the American Academy in Berlin. He received the Tony Award for Best Revival of a Play (*Death of a Salesman*) in 1999 and a National Endowment for the Humanities fellowship and the John H. Finley Award for Exemplary Service to New York City in 2001.

From *Critical Survey of Drama, Second Revised Edition* (Pasadena, CA: Salem Press, 2003): 2346-2358. Copyright © 2003 by Salem Press, Inc.

Bibliography

Bigsby, Christopher, ed. *Arthur Miller and Company*. London: Methuen, 1990. A series of impressions on Miller's works from noted writers and theater personalities. Presents a variety of insights into Miller and his work.

___________, ed. *The Cambridge Companion to Arthur Miller*. Cambridge: Cambridge University Press, 1997. Contains a detailed chronology, an essay on the tradition of social drama, and chapters on the early plays, the major plays, and Arthur Miller in each of the decades from the 1960s through the 1990s. Following chapters discuss Miller's involvement with cinema, his fiction, and his relationship with criticism and critics. Includes a bibliographic essay and an index.

Bloom, Harold, ed. *Arthur Miller*. New York: Chelsea House, 1987. This volume consists of essays on Miller's major drama from *All My Sons* to *The American Clock*, a brief introduction discussing Miller's significance, a chronology, a bibliography, and an index. Includes important early essays (Raymond Williams and Tom F. Driver on the playwright's strengths and weaknesses) and later criticism by Neil Carson, C.W.E. Bigsby, and E. Miller Buddick.

___________, ed. *Arthur Miller's Death of a Salesman*. New York: Chelsea House, 1988. Contains critical discussions published between 1963 and 1987, a chronology of Miller's life, a comprehensive bibliography of books and articles, and an index. In spite of reservations about Miller's importance as a writer, Bloom explains in his introduction how the play "achieves true aesthetic dignity" and discusses the particular merits of the essays in this collection.

Brater, Enoch. *Arthur Miller: A Playwright's Life and Works*. New York: Thames & Hudson, 2005. A basic introduction to Miller and some of his best-known plays. Includes seventy black-and-white photos.

___________, ed. *Arthur Miller's America: Theater and Culture in a Time of Change*. Ann Arbor: University of Michigan Press, 2005. A collection of essays by Miller scholars.

Gottfried, Martin. *Arthur Miller: His Life and Work.* Cambridge: Da Capo, 2003. The first full-length biography of Miller, this profile discusses the playwright's work in the context of his life.

Koon, Helene Wickham, ed. *Twentieth Century Interpretations of Death of a Salesman.* Englewood Cliffs, NJ: Prentice-Hall, 1983. These essays from the 1960s and 1970s emphasize the play's cultural significance, its status as a modern classic, and its style and point of view. The introduction provides a brief biography, and discussions of Miller's major themes, the play's relationship to classical tragedy, and Miller's manipulation of time. Includes a brief bibliography and chronology of events in Miller's life and times.

Koorey, Stefani. *Arthur Miller's Life and Literature.* Metuchen, NJ: Scarecrow Press, 2000. A bibliographic resource to primary and secondary sources.

Martine, James. *Crucible: Politics, Property, and Pretense.* New York: Twayne, 1993. An in-depth analysis of *The Crucible* from a number of viewpoints, including the historical context of McCarthyism, the play's place in Miller's oeuvre, and how the play fits into the genre of tragedy.

Murphy, Brenda. *Miller: Death of a Salesman.* New York: Cambridge University Press, 1995. This comprehensive treatment of Miller's play discusses its Broadway production, productions in English and in other languages, and media productions. Also provides a production chronology, a discography, a videography, and an extensive bibliography and index.

Schlueter, June, and James K. Flanagan. *Arthur Miller.* New York: Frederick Ungar, 1987. Contains a comprehensive narrative chronology, a thorough first chapter on Miller's literature and life to 1985, chapter-length discussions of his major plays (including *The Archbishop's Ceiling*), and a concluding chapter on his later one-act plays. Extensive notes, a bibliography of Miller's work in all genres, a select secondary bibliography of books and articles, and an index.

The *Paris Review* Perspective

Elizabeth Gumport

Written in 1949, Arthur Miller's *Death of a Salesman* debuted to rapturous acclaim: the play received both the Pulitzer Prize for drama and the Tony Award for best play, and an early *New York Times* review said Miller's work caused "critical appraisers to toss their hats as one into the air." A more recent *Times* review, written over thirty years after the play's opening night, echoed that earlier ecstasy, calling *Death of a Salesman* a "thunderous thing" at which we must "marvel." Still one of the most frequently performed dramas in America, the play's thunder continues to reverberate because it sounds at once timeless—coming down from on high, the sound of gods who have been angered—and fiercely contemporary.

Death of a Salesman—written on the heels of *All My Sons*, Miller's first commercial success, in which he began to explore the father-son dynamics so central to *Salesman*—was conceived during America's postwar boom, a time of rapid economic growth and correspondingly high expectations. Yet although the play's trappings are modern, with its packages of stockings and General Electric refrigerators, the architecture of Arthur Miller's play is wholly classical. He begins the play a Sophoclean figure, sorely lacking in self-knowledge and unable to see himself clearly. His blindness is introduced in the first moments of the play. "I suddenly couldn't drive anymore," Willy tells Linda. "Maybe it's your glasses," she offers. "You never went for your new glasses." "No," Willy answers, "I see everything." What he sees, however, is not the world as it is but a world of his own making, one he has fashioned through mad faith. To his family, to his business associates, and to himself, he insists on the value of the individual, arguing that commercial exchange depends on the men who make those exchanges. These men, Willy maintains, must be cherished, yet it is this ravening certitude in a system that does not, and cannot, exist that ensures his obliteration.

Willy is the first word spoken onstage: Linda calls out to her husband, and the following action is an echo of that call, the futile pursuit of a man who eludes even himself. Miller emphasizes Willy's complicity in his own destruction. His fantasies are identified as a physical threat: "If I'd've gone the other way over the white line," he says, "I might've killed somebody. So I went on again—and five minutes later I'm dreamin' again." Thus death, in *Death of a Salesman*, is first introduced as the product of untrammeled desire; the dreamer is annihilated by his own dreams. By the end of the play, the distinction between dream and threat collapses entirely. Willy gets in his car and goes the other way over that white line. Here Miller both adheres to and advances the classical formula. In the tragic tradition, Miller believed, the hero proves "a moral world at the cost of his own life." His crime is "a civilizing crime," an act that unifies and restores the community. His blood, like blood let in ritual sacrifice, redeems the survivors and binds them together. In *Death of a Salesman*, this redemption manifests itself literally: his life insurance policy redeemed, Willy's mortgage is paid off. It is a small world, a world lower than the one inhabited by kings and gods, and one in which moral balance is inextricably bound to account balance.

Willy's death, however, is not brought about by any Oedipus-like revelation: he dies not because he sees, but because he does not. His death is not a rejection of but a cleaving to the laws and ideals that governed his life. (These laws and ideals outlast the man who cherished them. Standing at his father's grave, Happy declares, "He had a good dream. . . . He fought it out here, and this is where I'm gonna win it for him." One narrator is gone, but the narrative remains.) The play ends just as it began: "Willy!" Linda cries again, just as we hear a car engine start up. The repetition of Willy's name indicates the lack of progress; we began calling out to him, and we end calling out to him still. *Death of a Salesman*, ultimately, provides the blueprint for contemporary tragedy, its structure defined not by the epiphanic moment and its aftermath but by the absence of epiphany, the deep persistence of darkness.

Formally, too, Miller's play was groundbreaking. Originally conceived of as a monodrama entitled "The Inside of His Head"—a version in which we would not, presumably, have watched the images Willy projects onto the world, but stood inside the magic lantern itself—the play synthesizes the American tradition of social realism with the kind of European expressionism associated with Bertolt Brecht and Samuel Beckett, which gestured toward the futility of human connection and linguistic expression in modern society. The traditional tropes of realism, Miller knew, were too small to contain the content of his play: "in Willy," Miller wrote, "the past was as alive as what was happening at the moment, sometimes even crashing in to completely overwhelm his mind." The style of the time demanded what was "natural," but for his story, Miller believed, what was natural would have been monstrous. Willy's grief demanded urgent, keening release, in language that surpassed "the crabbed dramatic hints" of the real and entered into the realm of "superconsciousness." When he speaks, in other words, Willy speaks all our words, a medium at the séance that is our era.

Still, Miller's vision is neither nihilistic nor absurd: "I have," he once said, "a psychic investment in the continuity of life," and his plays share those stakes. Tragedy is not synonymous with defeat, and to announce the presence of death is not to renounce life. In the final stage directions, Willy's absence serves as the axis of community, drawing together those who stood apart. Biff gathers his mother into his arms, and "Bernard and Charley come together and follow them, followed by Happy." The moment is not a triumphant one—"the hard towers of the apartment buildings" still loom over the mourners as they depart—but it is one of unity, temporary though it may be.

Copyright © 2008 by Elizabeth Gumport

Works Cited

Calta, Louis. "Premiere Tonight for Miller Drama." *The New York Times*, February 10, 1949.

Miller, Arthur. "The Art of Theater No. 2." Interview with Olga Carlyle and Rose Styron. *The Paris Review* 38 (Summer 1966).

___________. *Death of a Salesman*. New York: Penguin Books, 1976.

___________. *Timebends: A Life*. New York: Penguin Books, 1987.

Rich, Frank. "Theater: Hoffman, 'Death of a Salesman.'" *The New York Times*, March 30, 1984.

CRITICAL CONTEXTS

"The Jungle Is Dark and Full of Diamonds": Natural Value and the Logic of Naturalism in *Death of a Salesman*

Jon Dietrick

When Willy Loman's brother Ben, in the second act of *Death of a Salesman*, contrasts the present and substantial value of a diamond with the continually deferred value of Willy's sales "appointments," the attentive reader or audience member perhaps will notice that this advice comes from a character who is himself not quite present or substantial. As a phantom or a delusion or a memory that holds out the promise of a "natural" money as well as an essential, natural self (for Ben is Willy's only source of knowledge about his father, about "the kind of stock" the Lomans "spring from"), Ben manifests precisely the characteristics of money that both tantalize and terrify the Lomans (34). Historically, the increasingly arbitrary relationship between money's physical material and its "face value"—the move, in Marc Shell's phrase, from "the electrum money of ancient Lydia" to "the electronic money of contemporary America"—has made money function as a symbol of a more general disjunction between appearance and reality, seeming and being, "material" and "intellectual currency" (1). One "solution" to this problem has been the fantasy of a *natural* value. This notion informed the debates surrounding gold or silver and its relation to money that raged throughout the nineteenth century in America, and resurfaced during the Depression.[1] As Ben's diamonds do for Willy, so does gold (or silver) money promise to eliminate the troubling gulf between substance and sign, or between the often-unreliable signs we must use to navigate the world and what we perceive to be the "reality" of that world.

In *The Gold Standard and the Logic of Naturalism*, Walter Benn Michaels locates in American literary naturalism this anxiety over issues of material reality and representation. The "logic" of naturalism Benn Michaels elaborates is based on the repression of money as free-floating signifier, which expresses itself in various (and always unsuccessful) strategies of "escape" from the money economy. An aesthetic expression of both the desire for and the impossibility of this escape, naturalism obsesses over the ontological and epistemological questions raised by money, becoming "the working out of a set of conflicts between pretty things and curious ones, material and representation, hard money and soft, beast and soul" (173).

Of course it would be a mistake to view *Death of a Salesman* as an unproblematically naturalist play. Influenced both by the highly naturalistic theatre of the 1930s and by the Depression milieu that gave birth to those plays, Miller's watershed play is naturalistic in its portrayal of humans subject to economic and ideological forces; at the same time, the naturalism of the play is complicated by its almost postmodern treatment of distinctions such as present and past, action and "talk," hard value and soft currency, a treatment that resists naturalism's "hard" distinction between signs and the real. In *Death of a Salesman*, Miller elaborates his own vision of the relation of economic to psychic life by dramatizing the attempted "escape" from the money economy Benn Michaels locates as the obsession of naturalism—the doomed attempt to, in the critic's words, "stage the disappearance of money" (144). The distinctions that obsess the characters of the play—between saying and doing, seeming and being, technology and nature—are themselves rooted in money and the commodification of life in America. Ultimately, however, the play demonstrates how the increasing commodification of American life complicates those very distinctions.

One of the most salient aspects of *Death of a Salesman* is the play's exploration of the tricky distinction between saying and doing, talk and action. Often taken as evidence of what Richard Hofstadter famously delineated as the business world's general hostility toward intellectuals and almost religious dedication to "practicality," the American businessman, at least in the twentieth century, appears on the literary and cultural scene as a self-described "man of action" with no time for "idle talk."[2] While this strictly instrumentalist conception of language has long been associated with businessmen generally, the salesman, in particular, has reason to possess a somewhat more complicated attitude toward language. The fact that the salesman, more than perhaps any other businessman, makes his living *by talking* leads to a profound ambivalence toward language that complicates the distinction between discourse and action. The salesman, in Miller's play, represents at once a heightened understanding of the dialectical inseparability of "talk" and "action" and a deep anxiety caused by this knowledge.

The very insistence on a hard distinction between talk and action reveals an anxiety over the unavoidable ambiguity and misdirection of language. It has become axiomatic that Willy Loman mistakes saying for doing; a look at the attitudes toward the spoken word of the major characters in the play, however, reveals something more complex. Linda clearly sees Willy's excessive "saying" as indicative of a lack of doing: as she explains to Biff and Happy, "Instead of walking he talks now" (352). In Linda's formulation, language (Willy's "talking") denotes the absence of reality—it *takes the place of* action. It is true that at times Willy seems to possess an almost boundless faith in the ability of one's words to have a real impact on the world, merely through their utterance. At the same time, however, Willy recognizes his profuse talking as a liability. Searching for reasons for his failure at sales, Willy tells Linda, "I don't know why—I can't stop myself—I talk too much" (346). In fact at other times in the play Willy tries his best to limit or outright prevent the talk of other characters in the play. After the first memory-scene involving the "Woman" with whom Willy has a sexual affair in Boston, the stage directions tell us that Willy attempts to silence Linda by "*put[ting his] hand gently over her mouth*" (28).[3] A moment later, unwilling to face unpleasant truths about Biff, he tells first Bernard and then Linda to "Shut up!" (28). Later in the first act, he again commands Bernard to "Shut up!" (36). The situation is clearly more complicated than Willy's simply mistaking "talk" for "action." Rather, Willy seems to glean something about the slipperiness of this very distinction, and tries to control reality through controlling speech.

Willy's complicated attitude toward "talk" and its relation to "action" is intimately related to his profession. The salesman by definition complicates any easy distinction between saying and doing. He engages in speech that is what philosopher John L. Austin has called "performative"—he performs actions through the uttering of words, thus complicating the distinction between signification and the real (5). Furthermore, Willy's anxiety about the slipperiness of the talk/action distinction is a manifestation of his anxiety concerning money as it both symbolizes and exacerbates a troubling disparity between signs and the real (or between "talking" and "walking"). As a commission salesman Willy would understandably possess a heightened anxiety concerning this aspect of money. As we learn late in the first act, Willy has recently been denied a salary and put on "straight commission," as Linda tells Biff and Happy, "like a beginner, an unknown" (351). In fact, in an important sense a salesman is a kind of perpetual beginner, and perpetual unknown. For the salesman working for commission, neither past nor future matters. He is worth exactly what he is making in commission *in the present*, and neither past glories nor promises of future potential matter at all. Willy's loss of salary thus amounts to a kind of negating of his past and future. Working for straight commission, Willy is worth only what he is earning in sales now—which, we learn, is nothing. Given the denial of his past with the company and lack of faith in his future potential that the taking of his salary symbolizes, it is not surprising that Willy feels "kind of temporary" about himself (63). His only escape from the painful, commodified present is to reconstruct memories and project into the future—two processes that become impossible when Biff arrives, thus exacerbating the threat Biff poses to Willy's sense of identity. Willy would value himself—and Biff—either by what he imagines they once were or by what he imagines they could potentially be in the future. In doing so, he belies an anxiety concerning his (and Biff's) valuelessness in the present.

Contrasted with the garrulous Willy is Charley, whose very existence provides a constant critique of Willy's equation of business success with a certain type of speaking. Described in the stage directions as "*laconic*" and "*slow of speech*," Charley seems wholly lacking in the qualities Willy associates with business success; yet it is Charley and not Willy who makes a modest success in business (347). Willy even tells Linda, in a moment of self-doubt, that unlike himself, Charley is "respected" because he is "a man of few words" (346). And like Linda, Charley seems to appreciate doing over saying. When Willy shows surprise that Bernard is about to argue a case in front of the Supreme Court and yet "didn't even mention it" in his conversation with Willy, Charley replies, "He don't have to [mention it,] he's gonna do it," echoing the view of language expressed in Linda's comment—as that which *replaces* reality, or that which denotes its absence: one talks *instead of* walking (363).

Less obvious perhaps than Charley's easy distinction between talk and action is the fact that his comment about Bernard at the same time inadvertently equates speech (arguing in front of the Supreme Court) with *doing*. It is an irony lost to most critics of the play that Bernard—the character who would correct Biff's mistaking of language for action by telling him that writing the words "University of Virginia" on his shoes will not lead to his going there (23)—emerges by the end of the play as one who makes his living by using language to affect reality. In fact the lawyer's speech shares much with the salesman's: both are meant to persuade; both rely heavily on extra-verbal factors such as appearance, intonation, and body language; both are essentially performative.[4]

Willy's brother Ben complicates the distinction between talk and action even further. Like Charley, Ben seems to label as impotent Willy's brand of "talk," preferring things of value you can "[l]ay your hand[s] on" over what he seems to view as Willy's pie-in-the-sky rambling (360). In this sense Ben's view of language is in accord with Linda's and Charley's, viewing it as absence, as the opposite of "concrete" reality. But Ben also appreciates (and possibly fears) the power of effective "talk" of the sort Bernard is eventually engaged in as an attorney. Attempting to enlist Willy in his Alaska adventures, Ben clearly recognizes no place in his business enterprises for "talk" of either sort: "You've got a new continent at your doorstep, William. Get out of these cities, they're full of talk and time payments and courts of law. Screw on your fists and you can fight for a fortune up there" (359). Ben's aversion to "talk and time payments and courts of law" is unsurprising considering the lawless land-grabs and exploitative labor practices we assume he is pursuing in Africa and Alaska. In Ben's rhetoric, language denotes both power and its absence: the ineffective "talk" of Willy represents a failure to act, while the effective "talk" of courts of law threatens to subject his business practices to ethical and legal analysis.

At the same time, Ben is a sophisticated user of language in his own right. If Ben's philosophy of "screwing on one's fists" and fighting for "a fortune" represents in this play the ruthless realities of capitalism, Ben is adept at obfuscating those realities when it suits him. Asked by Willy for the "secret" of his success, Ben replies each time with a carefully edited rags-to-riches narrative: "when I was seventeen I walked into the jungle, and when I was twenty-one I walked out. (*He laughs.*) And by God I was rich" (349). The violence and deceit that, as we learn from his rough play with Biff,[5] were essential to Ben's acquiring his fortune in "the jungle" are here omitted, with the phrase "by God" hinting at both an explanation of and justification for Ben's wealth.[6] Ben's use of "God" to obfuscate the realities of capitalism and justify the acquisition of wealth after the fact has many precedents, from the American concept of "manifest destiny" to J. P. Morgan's apocryphal remark, in answer to a small child who asked why he had so much money while the child's family did not, that God wanted Morgan to be rich. Ben clearly knows how to weave a narrative that places his own success in the best light, demonstrating that despite his statements to the contrary, "talk" is an essential part of his "action."

Ben's complicating the talk/action distinction even as he employs it is part of his function in the play as the uncanny manifestation of Willy's deepest anxieties about the distinction between the real and the imaginary, action and talk—Benn Michaels' logic of naturalism. Ben appears in this play as ghost, past memory, and present hallucination at once—a walking example of what Miller wanted to portray in *Salesman* as "past and present concurrently, with neither one ever coming to a stop" (*Timebends* 131). Ben is an ephemeral being who at the same time represents a "hard" value you can "lay your hand on." A diamond, claims Ben, is "[n]ot like an appointment at all. A diamond is rough and hard to the touch" (134). As an operator of mines who alternately encourages and discourages Willy's turning himself into cash through suicide, Ben at once represents the naturalist obsession with "hard money" and its accompanying fears of an "insubstantial" value. This makes Ben the perfect tormentor of Willy, whose need to believe in a "hard" value is equaled by his fear that such value does not exist. Ben confirms both these tendencies: "The jungle is dark," he tells Willy, playing on his brother's fear of the absence of value in nature, but it is also "full of diamonds" (98). The ephemeral twenty thousand dollars Willy thinks (probably mistakenly) that his suicide would bring to his family is, says Ben, "something one can feel with the hand, it is there" (126). Willy's response shows the depth of his involvement in the logic of naturalism: "Oh, Ben, that's the whole beauty of it! I see it like a diamond, shining in the dark, hard and rough, that I can pick up and touch in my hand. Not like—like an appointment!" (126). Repressing money even as he chases after it, Willy here turns it into hard, "natural" value as opposed to soft currency.

In convincing Willy to treat his life as an abstraction and money as concrete reality ("something one can feel with the hand"), Ben personifies one of the earliest noted characteristics of money. A primary trope in Karl Marx's rendering of money is that of *monstrosity.* Paul Sheehan explains that for Marx, "Money's capacity for disfigurement, for warping perception and moral efficacy, makes it capable of turning reality into a grotesque distortion of itself" (98). For Marx, this tendency makes money a malevolent force: money leads to "the universal *confusion* and *exchange* of all things, an inverted world, the confusion and exchange of all natural and human qualities" (*Manuscripts* 98). This tendency of money to transform our reality into a mere abstraction and itself into the real—a tendency illustrated by our use of the accounting term "the bottom line" as a kind of shorthand for hard reality—is at the very heart of the Marxist critique. Furthermore, for Marx, money (in the form of finance capital) is monstrous in its apparent ability to self-generate, to breed itself *from* itself and to hide its own origins: capital "appears as a mysterious and self-creating source of interest—the source of its own increase," with the result that "the entire process of reproduction appears as a property inherent in the thing itself," and "in this form [finance capital] no longer bears the birth-marks of its origin" (*Capital* III, 385). In describing money as monstrous in this way Marx's texts echo one of the earliest known written descriptions of money, from Aristotle's *Politics* I, iii. There Aristotle condemns the practice of usury on the grounds that it "makes a gain out of money itself, and not from the natural use of it." The passage continues: "And this term Usury, which means the birth of money from money, is applied to the breeding of money, because the offspring resembles the parent."

As Ben represents money's monstrous ability to render the abstract concrete and the concrete abstract, so does he represent money's monstrous ability to seemingly self-generate, to hide "the birthmarks of its own origin." For Ben tantalizes the Loman men not only with the secret of success; he is also the family's only link to Willy's father and Biff's grandfather, and so to their own origins, to one version of their own "authentic" selves. Yet Ben's insistence on his own *self-making* refuses them access to those origins. Willy asks Ben to tell stories about his father so Biff and Happy can "know the kind of stock they spring from" (34). Yet in the one encounter between Ben and Biff that we witness, Ben turns violent during apparent play, tripping Biff and stopping just short of stabbing him in the eye with his umbrella, then admonishing his nephew, "Never fight fair with a stranger, boy. You'll never get out of the jungle that way" (49). The alternately warm and violent Ben, both a family member and a stranger, here appears as a monstrous and uncanny manifestation of the Lomans' deepest anxieties about money and the gulf it opens between appearance and reality, surface and essence.

Biff, like his father, is shown to have reason to be concerned about money. From the earliest moments of the play, Biff seems to be viewed by his father primarily in terms of how much money he is earning. The first fight we learn of between Biff and Willy is about money: "I simply asked him if he was making any money," explains Willy, who goes on to complain that after ten years of "tramping around," Biff "has yet to make thirty-five dollars a week" (9). Aside from his father's viewing him as a commodity, Biff is troubled by the existential implications of money, chief among which is what Shell notes as money's disassociation of appearance from reality, material value from "face" value (1). This manifests itself in the play as Biff's obsession with the authentic (with a "hard" or natural value) and the opposite, his preference for deceptive appearance over the real. Biff repeatedly accuses Willy of having "no character" or being "a fake" or even (redundantly) a "phoney little fake!" (40, 42, 88). Biff says he wants to find a woman "with substance" (17). Yet when Linda answers his question about her hair suddenly going gray with the explanation that it had been gray for a long time, that she "just stopped dyeing it," Biff seemingly chooses appearance over the real and asks her to "[d]ye it again" (39). In essence, Biff wants Linda's physical appearance to match his own timeless, unchanging idea of who/what she is.

Troubled as he is by the existential implications of money, Biff, like other protagonists in this study, enacts a (failed) strategy of "escape" from the money economy—firstly, in Biff's case, through his propensity to steal. In his study *The Philosophy of Money*, the sociologist Georg Simmel notes that both in what he calls "primitive" societies and among contemporary aristocracy, there is often "a distaste for exchange," with robbery and gift-giving looked at as the more honorable activities (97). The reason for this, Simmel hypothesizes, is an anxiety concerning the alienation from nature that characterizes economic exchange. Unlike the "objectivity" of economic exchange, theft and gift-giving represent "pure subjectivity in the change of ownership" (97). The stolen or freely given object is not reduced to money, not drained of its individual and irreplaceable qualities. Seen in this light, Biff's frequent stealing (of basketballs [18, 82], a football [20], lumber [36], and finally a pen [76]) represents an attempt to escape the alienating world of economic exchange and thus assuage his anxiety concerning reality and appearances, hard value and soft money.

A second manifestation of Biff's repression of money takes the form of Biff's efforts to escape the technological, commodified city and return to nature. Willy himself in fact repeatedly expresses his own sense of separation from nature: he bemoans the overdevelopment of his Brooklyn neighborhood, complaining to Linda that today, because of the surrounding apartment houses, you "[g]otta break your neck to see a star" in their backyard (350). Willy remembers when "[t]his time of year it was lilac and wisteria," but now buildings stand where once these flowers grew (340). While the fact that no seeds will grow in that same yard is surely a metaphor for Willy's dashed hopes for his sons, in a larger sense it also comments on Willy's sense of separation from the natural world, a feeling Biff apparently shares. By leaving the city and traveling west to work with horses, Biff is in one sense returning to nature. He tells Happy that in Texas "it's spring there now" and conjures images of mares giving birth to new colts (341). Biff's life on the farm represents a return to an experience of time as cyclical, one marked by the passage of seasons, which dictate to a certain degree one's labor (22). Conversely, the city is the place where time is sensed as linear and progressive: it is where you "build a future," where Hap slowly works his way up the corporate ladder, where flowers no longer grow in the backyard, where a man must "add up" to something, not be "ringing up a zero" (125, 126). This marking of the passage of time by natural events (the blooming of lilac, the birthing of the colts) contrasts sharply with a different sense of time, one embodied in Willy's remark that in "ten years" of trying to "find himself," Biff "has yet to make thirty-five dollars a week!" (Miller 16). Viewing these two senses of time across many cultures, E. P. Thompson has hypothesized an historical evolution from a preindustrial sense of "natural" time to a more Protestant sense of time as money, the latter either exacerbated or caused by the Industrial Revolution and the division of labor. Biff's move from country to city is, by this logic, more than just geographical and represents an attempt to escape the commodification of life implied in Willy's remark about his meager earnings.

By associating these two senses of time with the city and the country, the east and the west, Miller's play seems to be partaking in yet another manifestation of the American pastoral, with Texas standing in as the western "green world" where one may escape the pressures of the "civilized" eastern metropolis.[7] But a closer look reveals something more complicated, for both Willy and Biff are caught between what country and city symbolize in this play in a way that reveals how both are ensnared within the logic of naturalism associated with money. Texas in fact seems to offer Biff only an escape from the commodified city, for as he explains to Hap, each time he leaves, something draws him back to New York:

> Texas is cool now, and it's spring. And whenever spring comes to where I am, I suddenly get the feeling, my God, I'm not gettin' anywhere! What the hell am I doing, playing around with horses, twenty-eight dollars a week! I'm thirty-four years old, I oughta be makin' my future. That's when I come running home. And now, I get here, and I don't know what to do with myself. (*After a pause.*) I've always made a point of not wasting my life, and every time I come back here I know that all I've done is to waste my life.
>
> (341)

What Thompson and Weber identify as the Protestant idea of time as money, as something to be spent or wasted, appears in this passage as a kind of serpent invading Biff's western Eden. Biff exists in a kind of restless stasis. Repeatedly, he attempts to escape the commodified world of the city by moving physically west and working close to the land. But as we have seen, Biff essentially takes the city with him in the form of an internalized set of values that sees the future as something one "builds" and the value of a person's life measured in how much he earns. Similarly, upon returning to the world of money symbolically associated with cities and the east, Biff rejects what he sees as a "measly manner of existence" and longs to be back on a western farm.

In *The Country and the City*, Raymond Williams uncovers the way much if not all of our notions of "country" and "city" are the product of capitalist discourse, with its "abstracted economic drives, its fundamental priorities in social relations, its criteria of growth and of profit and loss" (302). This discourse clearly finds voice in Biff's tangled relationship between country and city, where, ironically, the arrival of spring sends Biff running back to the city, and where it is never clear which life—his life on a farm or his life in the city—he considers "wasted." Where the arrival of spring brings Willy to thoughts of lilac and the country, of regeneration through nature, the same season sends Biff back to the city to find another sort of regeneration, an economic one that is as "real" to him as "nature": to "make" his "future." Similarly, where thoughts of physical labor lead to Willy's anxiety over a perceived lack of seriousness or masculinity in his own profession, Biff now redefines his physical labor on a western farm as "playing around" and associates serious work with the "mental" talk-based labor of sales. In this way *Salesman* ultimately complicates, rather than reinforces, the distinction between country and city, technology and nature. If the play alerts us to a problem, that problem cannot be isolated as a specifically urban or technological one; rather, the capitalistic economic values the play investigates appear in both country and city—where do they seem more prevalent than in Ben's "jungle"? New York City is where one can "build a future," yet Willy spends all his work time in the "New England Territory," itself a term that calls to mind the conflicting images of an open frontier and industrial cities like Boston, Hartford, and Providence. The tangled distinction between country and city in the play is ultimately another manifestation of the logic of naturalism, with its fetishization of "hard," natural value and its anxiety over signification.

The distinction between country and city, nature and technology is further complicated by Willy's profession. Several cultural historians have noted the salesman's unique relation to the technological world. For Earl Shorris, periods of rapid economic expansion tend to position the salesman as "the Prometheus of the machine age," bringing "dozens of basic new ideas to the American public" (68). But in his cultural history of the salesman, Timothy Spears sees the figure's relation to technology as more ambivalent. At least in the nineteenth century, the American "commercial traveler" was "the aggressive, logical consequence of the expanding national market system, a figure who from an economic standpoint remained inseparable from the growth of the railroad and other developments that strengthened the 'visible hand' of business." At the same time, however, the traveling salesman remained somewhat freer to improvise than did other American businessmen: his relation to that expanding national and technological market "did not wholly determine the development of his sales techniques nor make him the pawn of institutional forces. In fact, it often provided him with a modicum of freedom, although not without some cost" ("Preface" xi). In one sense, the salesman is both a commodity and a piece of technology; in another sense, the salesman (especially the traveling salesman) escapes, to a degree, the confining, "rationalized" workplace he helps to create. The salesman working for commission is freer, in a sense, than the salaried worker; at the same time, he makes of himself that purely instrumental thing: a commodity. From the individual buyer's viewpoint, the salesman is both the tool of the market and the one human element in what otherwise faces the consumer as a vast, depersonalized marketplace. From the salesman's viewpoint, technology—in the form of the mass-produced goods he sells and the technologies of transportation (trains, automobiles, hotel rooms) and communication that make his job possible—is a paradox he lives with daily. As a human being in an increasingly streamlined marketplace, the salesman fears being replaced by technology and strives to "modernize" his profession, to turn selling into a science, himself into a kind of selling machine. As a piece of technology himself, he fears being replaced by new technology, which is of course the fate of all technology by its very nature. The "Prometheus of the machine age" is both humanized technology and technologized humanity, a portent of the future and a superannuated relic of the past. He is at once too human and too much a piece of technology.[8]

This tangled relationship to technology is represented with particular force early in the second act of the play, when Willy goes to see his boss, Howard Wagner, in an attempt to gain a salaried position in New York. Here, Willy tries to establish a personal connection with Howard by bringing up the warm relationship he once had with Howard's father—to establish a relationship on a more "essential" ground than as an employee talking to his boss. Initially, Howard is too preoccupied with a new piece of technology even to notice Willy. Howard describes the new wire-recording machine in a way that belies his own paradoxical relation to technology: this "most terrific machine [he] ever saw" has kept him "up all night" and is "driving [him] crazy" (76). Offering a more "fascinating relaxation," the recorder will, he tells Willy, replace his camera, his bandsaw, and "all [his] hobbies" (78). An office machine that has also become a family toy, the wire-recorder embodies the role of technology in breaking down boundaries between work and home. Willy is forced to listen to Howard's son recite the state capitals. Howard's wife, whom the stage directions characterize as "*beaten*," is forced by Howard the manager/husband to speak into the machine, as a piece of technology becomes that which *compels* speech: "Well, talk," commands Howard, "it's turning." His son announces mechanically that it is "nine o'clock, Bulova watch time" and thus time to go to bed, illustrating E. P. Thompson's thesis of the replacement of "natural" time with clock time in a way that also emphasizes the ominous role of corporate power in this process (it is *Bulova* watch time). At the same time, Howard points out that by using the recorder to tape his favorite radio shows, he gains a kind of control over time: "You can come home twelve o'clock, one o'clock, any time you like, and you get yourself a Coke and sit yourself down, throw the switch, and there's Jack Benny's program in the middle of the night!" (78). The mention of specific products—Coke and Jack Benny's program—emphasizes the dubious nature of the freedom offered by Howard's newest piece of technology, presenting Howard in the role of consumer in relation to both the soft drink companies and the entertainment industry that exists largely for the purpose of selling its products through advertising. But the less free Howard appears, the more does he convince himself that he can reconfigure the world to suit his desires, with technology at the very nexus of this contradiction.

By the end of the play, Willy and Biff have the confrontation that has been building through the entire action of the play—but their argument resembles two men attempting to escape from the same net rather than the clash of two fundamentally different ideas. Biff would reject Willy's money-centered mentality, even as he calls himself "one dollar an hour" and argues that he and his father are both "a dime a dozen," thus demonstrating his own inability to think of himself as other than commodity (132). Willy argues for an identity not lashed to the marketplace—"I am not a dime a dozen! I am Willy Loman and you are Biff Loman!" (132)—and then commits suicide in an attempt to turn himself into cash in Biff's pocket. In the "Requiem" that closes the play, Happy condemns Willy's suicide only on the grounds that "[t]here was no necessity for it," as if his suicide would be fine if it proved economically *useful* (137). And Charley—the man who once chillingly invited Willy to think of Biff as a broken bottle that will not return its nickel deposit (31)—rewrites the tragedy of Willy as a paean to the salesman: "A salesman is got to dream, boy; it comes with the territory" (101). In ironic contrast to Linda's repeated "We're free" at Willy's graveside, the characters of Miller's play seem as trapped as they ever were. They are trapped because the choices they would make—between talk and action, the present and the past, the country and the city, the natural and the technological world—are ultimately complicated by the dominance of money relations in American life.

Notes

1. The Depression loomed large in the imagination of Arthur Miller in a manner that is hard to overstate. A period that saw Miller's father's failure in business and the consequent rapid downward spiral of his immediate family, the Depression, Miller wrote, "was only incidentally a matter of money. Rather it was a moral catastrophe, a violent revelation of the hypocrisies behind the façade of American society" (*Timebends* 114).

2. Early in his autobiography, Miller gives us one such man in his description of his maternal grandfather. A formidable businessman rather obsessed with his physical appearance, Louis Barnett, according to Miller, never uttered "a word . . . that might have some attachment to a thought" or indeed "a sound that was not immediately useful or a mere greeting or a goodbye." He had, Miller tells us, "a tendency to direct action" evidenced both by his preference for physical violence over words when communicating with union organizers in his employ and by his belief that Franklin Roosevelt should not be allowed to run for President of the United States against Hoover "because Roosevelt had never run a business" (*Timebends* 5).

3. Here and throughout this paper (unless otherwise noted), italics appear in the original.

4. By 1951, just two years after *Salesman* opened in New York, C. Wright Mills saw increasingly little difference between most lawyers and other businessmen. He noted that while the popular image of lawyers has always been rather ambiguous, by the mid-twentieth century a shift occurs whereby "the public has become for the lawyer what the public has been for the lawyer's chief client [the large corporations]—an object of profit rather than of obligation" (122). This new lawyer emerging in the first half of the twentieth century is a "groomed personality" and "a businessman himself, a proprietor of high acumen, good training, many contacts, and sound judgement" (Mills 123). "The top men" in law firms are "chosen as are film stars, for their glamour" (124). Mills' portrait of the emerging twentieth-century lawyer has him as a kind of legally sanctioned confidence man, a paid persuader who wraps his morally questionable practices in the cloak of professionalism as he climbs the social and economic ladder. In Miller's play, "contacts" and image seem as important to the lawyer Bernard's suc-

cess as they would be to any salesman's: we are told he is to play tennis at the home of a friend who has his own courts (which both impresses Willy greatly and seems to imply that the football-playing Biff, rather than choosing the wrong values, merely chose the wrong sport), and his waiting with valise in hand for a train resembles in important respects a popular image of the salesman. He is even told by his father to "Knock 'em dead," one of Willy's favorite trite phrases to describe selling (95). This coupled with the contradictory and clichéd advice he offers Willy—"If at first you don't succeed. . . ." followed by "sometimes, Willy, it's better for a man just to walk away"—complicates Christopher Bigsby's reading of Bernard and Charley as evidence that "a full-hearted commitment to capitalism is not incompatible with humane values" (Miller 95, Bigsby 84). The characters demonstrate, rather, the disturbing ubiquity of salesmanship in twentieth-century America.

5. After tripping and nearly jabbing a prostrate Biff in the eye with the point of his umbrella, Ben admonishes Willy's son: "Never fight fair with a stranger, boy. You'll never get out of the jungle that way" (Miller 49).

6. Ben's first response to Willy's question is both less forthcoming and more indicative of Ben's use for "talk": "Oh, there's a story in that" (Miller 47).

7. Eisinger (mistakenly, in my view) sees *Salesman* as romanticizing the American agrarian myth.

8. Of the traveling salesman of the first quarter of the twentieth century, Spears writes: "Despite the claims to modernity that ran throughout the literature, the salesman remained only human, which is to say that no matter how scientific his rhetoric or approach appeared, he represented the continuity of face-to-face relationships in a world increasingly given to effacing them. Janus-faced, the twentieth-century traveling man was neither drummer nor scientific salesman, but frequently and sometimes tragically he was both."

Works Cited

Aristotle. *Politics*. Trans. Benjamin Jowett. New York: The Modern Library, 1943.

Austin, John L. *How to Do Things with Words*. 2d ed. Cambridge: Harvard University Press, 1975.

Barthes, Roland. *S/Z*. Trans. Richard Miller. New York: Hill and Wang, 1974.

Benn Michaels, Walter. *The Gold Standard and the Logic of Naturalism: American Literature at the Turn of the Century*. Berkeley: University of California Press, 1987.

Bigsby, C.W.E. *Modern American Drama: 1945–2000*. 2d ed. Cambridge, UK: Cambridge University Press, 2000.

Eisinger, Chester E. "Focus on *Death of a Salesman*." *American Dreams, American Nightmares*. Ed. David Madden. Carbondale: Southern Illinois University Press, 1970. 165–74.

Hofstadter, Richard. *Anti-intellectualism in American Life*. New York: Knopf, 1963.

Marx, Karl. *Capital: A Critique of Political Economy*. Ed. Frederick Engels. Trans. Samuel Moore and Edward Aveling from 3d German ed. 3 vols. New York: International Publishers, 1967.

___________. *Economic and Philosophic Manuscripts of 1844*. Ed. Dirk J. Struik. Trans. Martin Milligan. New York: International Publishers, 1964.

Miller, Arthur. *Death of a Salesman*. New York: Penguin, 1977.

___________. *Timebends: A Life*. New York: Grove, 1987.

Mills, C. Wright. *White Collar: The American Middle Classes*. New York: Oxford University Press, 1951.

Murphy, Brenda. "Willy Loman: Icon of Business Culture." *Michigan Quarterly Review* 37, no. 4 (Fall 1998): 755–766.

Murphy, Brenda, and Susan W. Abbotson. *Understanding Death of a Salesman: A Student Casebook to Issues, Sources, and Historical Documents*. "Literature in Context" series. Ed. Claudia Durst Johnson. Westport, CT: Greenwood Press, 1999.

Sheehan, Paul. "Marx, Money, and Monstrosity in *Great Expectations*." *Q/W/E/R/T/Y: Arts, Littératures & Civilisations du Monde Anglophone* 9 (1999): 97–104.

Shell, Marc. *Money, Language, and Thought: Literary and Philosophic Economies from the Medieval to the Modern Era*. Baltimore: Johns Hopkins University Press, 1982.

Shorris, Earl. *A Nation of Salesmen: The Tyranny of the Market and the Subversion of Culture*. New York: Norton, 1994.

Simmel, Georg. *The Philosophy of Money*. Trans. Tom Bottomore and David Frisby. London: Routledge & Kegan Paul, 1978.

Spears, Timothy. *100 Years on the Road: The Traveling Salesman in American Culture*. New Haven: Yale University Press, 1995.

Thompson, E. P. "Time, Work-Discipline, and Industrial Capitalism." *Past and Present*, no. 28 (December, 1967): 56-97.

Williams, Raymond. *The Country and the City*. New York: Oxford University Press, 1973.

___________. "Modern Tragic Literature: From Hero to Victim." *Willy Loman*. Ed. Harold Bloom. Major Literary Characters series. New York: Chelsea House, 1991.

Salesman and the 1930s Theatres of Social Protest

Joshua E. Polster

In 1949, Clifford Odets—the Clifford Odets white hope of the theatre of the 1930s—returned to the stage, after many years in Hollywood, with *The Big Knife*. In the same year, Arthur Miller premiered *Death of a Salesman*, which, according to theatre critic John Gassner, was a "consummation of virtually everything attempted by that part of the theatre which has specialized in awareness and criticism of social realities. It [was] a culmination of all efforts since the 1930s to observe the American scene and trace, as well as evaluate, its effects on character and personal life." Instead of Odets's new play, which Gassner considered a "failure of genius," it was Miller's drama that was seen as successfully resounding the voice of the 1930s social dramas and, at the same time, developing the art form: "Generally our 'social' playwrights' efforts . . . stressed the scene rather than the character even when they transcended special pleading or political agitation. Miller's achievement lies in successfully bridging the gulf between a social situation and human drama. The two elements in *Death of a Salesman* are, indeed, so well fused that the one is the other" (Weales 219–22). To Gassner, Miller was the rightful heir to the 1930s social dramas, and, in general, the new 'white hope' of political theatre.

In 1968, however, critic Eric Bentley did not see Miller as an effective social playwright or *Salesman*, in particular, as a good or "well fused" play. Instead, Bentley castigated Miller for confusing the social and psychological elements in *Salesman*.

> Mr. Miller says he is attempting a synthesis of the social and the psychological, and, though one may not see any synthesis, one certainly sees the thesis and the antithesis. In fact, one never knows what a Miller play is about: politics or sex. If *Death of a Salesman* is political, the key scene is

> the one with the tape recorder; it if is sexual, the key scene is the one in the Boston hotel.
>
> (250)

According to Bentley, the human tragedy destroyed the social play and the social play destroyed the human tragedy. Willy Loman could be a victim only of his flawed character or of society, but not of both. Such a position, however, ignores the relationship between the self and its sociopolitical context—the projection of psychological disruptions onto society and social disruptions onto the psyche. Nonetheless, Bentley's criticism, and many similar to it, created a decisive split in the reading of the play. Contemporary productions and readings of *Salesman*, for example, have largely preferred interpreting the play more as a family or psychological drama than as a social drama. *The New York Times* article "A Salesman Who Transcends Time," for instance, compared the original *Salesman* production to the more recent Broadway revivals (in 1984 and 1999). Arthur Miller and director Elia Kazan, the article recalled, gave the premier production of *Salesman* a political urgency: Truly great work, Miller declared, is "that work which will show at one and the same time the power and force of the human will working with and against the force of society upon it." The more recent Broadway revivals, however, were "more psychological than sociological."

> Yet in Robert Falls's darkly hued new staging from Chicago, *Death of a Salesman* seems less a social drama about what Harold Clurman called "the breakdown of the whole concept of salesmanship inherent in our society" than a fierce portrait of a father and son, caught in a fatal embrace of love and resentment and guilt. And Brian Dennehy's Willy Loman seems less a man, in Mr. Miller's words, who "embodies in himself some of the most terrible conflicts running through the streets of America today" than a perpetual adolescent caught in the dizzying gap between reality and his own expectations. This Willy Loman, like Dustin Hoffman's in 1984 on

> Broadway, [has] dilemmas [that] are more psychological than sociological, more existential than environmental.
>
> (Kakutani AR1)

In Ben Brantley's review of the 1999 *Salesman* Broadway revival, he too saw the absence of the social drama in the human drama:

> Robert Falls's powerhouse staging, first seen at the Goodman Theater in Chicago last fall, never looks [at Willy Loman] as a martyr to a success-driven country. Instead, it demands that you experience Willy's suffering without sociological distance, that you surrender to the sense of one man's pain and of the toll it takes on everyone around him.
>
> (Brantley 1999)

Such readings were not restricted to the critics alone. When director Robert Falls wanted insights into the character of Willy Loman, he did not consult Wall Streeters; instead, he sent Miller's script to psychiatrists. "They said," Falls recalled, "that Willy was manic-depressive, with hallucinatory aspects." The Loman character of Falls's production was not a suicidal victim of the capitalist machine but a poor man struggling with a psychological condition. The solution to Loman's problem, therefore, was not the destruction of American capitalism, but Prozac. Miller, who saw the Broadway production, argued, "Willy Loman is not a depressive. He is weighed down by life. There are social reasons for why he is where he is" (McKinley WK5). The playwright's argument, however, went largely unheard, and the Loman character continued to be seen in a psychological context. One audience member, for instance, wrote to the editor of *The New York Times*, "Willy Loman has Alzheimer's Disease. All of the signs. All of the symptoms. I wonder if Arthur Miller knows" (McDonald AR4).

In short, the further removed *Salesman* is from its initial production, the further removed it is from its connection to the 1930s social dramas. This article, therefore, will restructure *Salesman* back into its original sociopolitical context and suggest how *Salesman* is in constant dialogue with the social plays from the major theatres of social protest during the 1930s: the Theatre Union, the Group Theatre, and the Federal Theatre Project. This paper goes against the typical contemporary readings of *Death of a Salesman* to allow the play to resonate more deeply with its sociopolitical context.

> The outstanding new playwrights of the thirties were Lillian Hellman and Clifford Odets. . . . In the late forties Arthur Miller and Tennessee Williams emerged; men who kept alive—this is particularly true of Miller—some of the impassioned social conscience of the thirties.
>
> (Clurman, *Fervent Years* 302)

When Arthur Miller began playwriting in the late 1930s, the communist and socialist reaction in the United States against the Great Depression, capitalism, fascism, and isolationism was being played out in the three major left-wing theatres of the 1930s: the Theatre Union, the Group Theatre, and the Federal Theatre Project. Each of these theatres provided an alternative discursive space to the bourgeois space of Broadway, which primarily showed frivolous escapist productions such as musicals, bedroom farces, comedies, mystery melodramas, musical revues, and psychological plays. In *Drama Was a Weapon*, Morgan Himelstein recorded that, "Of the 1,500 presentations offered by the independent managers of Broadway from 1929 through 1941, only 743 treated primary themes of social, political, or economic significance. . . . The impresarios understood that people went to theatres to be entertained, not to be educated or converted to a political cause" (215).[1] The left-wing theatres were, therefore, created in response to a highly conscious and critical society's need for a great social debate about how best to run its government in a time of economic crisis, political instability, and impending war. In the leftist theatres, this conversation took the form of the social drama. For the purposes of this article, social drama will be understood as any didactic theatre space or play that illuminates and challenges social attitudes or institutions, and suggests changes that are either liberal-reformist or revolutionary, by personal or collective action. This definition borrows also from Victor Turner, who saw social drama as occurring when two cultures—a dominant and a dominated—come into conflict, and this conflict plays out in some form of social and political performance (9–12). By the end of the 1930s, each of these leftist theatre spaces—the Theatre Union, the Group Theatre, and the Federal Theatre—were able to uniquely challenge the social attitudes and institutions of the dominant capitalist society but ultimately were dominated by this society and were unable to survive in the political and economic structure. The pervading theatre scholarship documents how the economic forces of the 1930s motivated the development of the social drama, but during the postwar economic boom the social drama drastically declined or ceased to exist.[2] This, however, can be misleading.

The discourses of these political theatres did not die. It is difficult altogether to eliminate a presence or idea without leaving a trace. When ideas are unattractive to power and, as a result, become censored in their original form, instead of dying they can be transferred into a new, politically acceptable outlet. The left-wing discourses of the Theatre Union, the Group Theatre and the Federal Theatre Project were not completely suppressed and silenced but continued into the plays and productions of Arthur Miller and others. Though many of Miller's plays deal with the social drama, the 1949 production of *Death of a Salesman* was the performance of his major work on the professional stage that most closely carried out the discourses of the 1930s theatres of social protest.

When Miller began writing in the late 1930s, theatres and productions all over the country were in decline. According to Oscar Brockett, "By 1937 there were only forty-four theatres [in New York], and in 1939–40 the number of new productions had dwindled to eighty. The theatre outside of New York was even more adversely affected. . . . [B]y 1940 there probably were no more than two hundred [theatres] in the entire nation" (508–09). Gone, or on their way to being gone, were alternative theatres such as the "little theatres" of the early twentieth century and later organizations such as the American Laboratory Theatre, Theatre Union, Group Theatre, Federal Theatre, and the Communist-driven workers' theatres that viably challenged the bourgeois complacency of Broadway. Many of these alternative left-wing theatres could not survive the advent of radio and "talking films" or the disastrous effects of the Great Depression; or, as was the case with the workers' theatres, they declined along with Soviet disillusionment from the Spanish Civil War, the Soviet Purges, and the German-Russian Pact.

For emerging leftist playwrights in the 1940s, such as Miller, Broadway was the main venue, and if playwrights did not bow down to commercial theatre, their work, for the most part, was not produced.[3] The social drama, though, was not completely transformed into bourgeois theatre;[4] instead, a left-wing discursive space moved in and coexisted within the commercial space. These strange bedfellows managed to coexist in a period of economic and sociopolitical unrest without canceling each other out.[5] The discursive space of the social drama from the Theatre Union, the Group Theatre, and the Federal Theatre Project did not entirely expire but found its way into a new space—into the dramaturgy and the premier production of *Death of a Salesman*. *Death of a Salesman* opened at the Morosco Theatre in New York on February 10, 1949. Directed by Elia Kazan, Miller's play successfully ran for 742 performances.[6] On its opening night, men and women were remembered as being stunned into silence, openly weeping, and then remaining in the theatre long after the show to discuss the play and how well it resonated with their own lives. "They were weeping," Miller would later say in an interview, "because the central matrix of the play is . . . what most people are up against in their lives. . . . They were seeing themselves, not because Willy is a salesman, but the situation in which he stood and to which he was reacting, and which was reacting against him, was probably *the* central situation of contemporary civilization. It is that we are struggling with forces that are far greater than we can handle, with no equipment to make anything mean anything" (Griffin 35). These forces at work were the agents of capitalism—the ideological strategies of the dominant power structure—and their erosive affects on the public and private space. "It is," as Eleanor Clark recognized in *The Partisan Review*, "the capitalist system that has done Willy in; the scene in which he is brutally fired after some forty years with the firm comes straight from the party line literature of the thirties" (631–35).

The party line literature of the thirties was best seen at the Theatre Union (1933–37), one of the main theatres of the thirties that had a great influence on Miller; during his years at the University of Michigan, Miller was greatly influenced by the Theatre Union's proletarian plays like Clifford Odets's *Waiting for Lefty*. The Theatre Union was the first fully professional workers' theatre and the most important in the 1930s to carry out the critique of United States capitalism. Its aim was to produce overtly propagandistic plays about the working class, written from the perspective of the working class, for a working-class audience, financially supported by working-class organizations. It announced:

> We produce plays that deal boldly with the deep-going social conflicts, the economic and cultural problems that confront the majority of the people. Our plays speak directly to this majority, whose lives usually are caricatured or ignored on the stage. We do not expect that these plays will fall into the accepted social patterns. This is a new kind of professional theatre, based on the interests and hopes of the great mass of working people.
>
> (Bigsby, *Critical Introduction* 204–05)

When the Theatre Union was first established, it emphasized Marxist ideology over theatrical aesthetics, which was clearly demonstrated by its slogan, "Theatre is a weapon" (Reynolds 37). The Theatre Union was created out of the need for a new kind of working-class theatre that portrayed issues concerning economic and social problems but was not limited to the agitprop styles of earlier political theatres such as the German-speaking Prolet-Buhne (1925), the Workers' Drama League (1926), the New Playwrights (1927), and the Workers' Laboratory Theatre (1929).

The driving influences behind the Theatre Union and many of the political theatres in the 1930s were closely linked to the oscillating foreign policies of the Soviet government and their effects on American Communism. Communist policy dramatically changed Communist theatres in the United States in terms of style and content. For example, in 1935, there was a growing concern about fascism in Russia; as a result, a new policy termed the Popular Front was introduced at the Seventh Congress of the Communist International (Comintern).[7] This new policy set aside previous revolutionary objectives and advocated cooperation with the liberal bourgeoisie.[8] This drastic turn in policy changed the artistic direction of the workers' theatres as well.

In this stage of the Comintern policies, there was dissatisfaction with the schematic form of agitprop plays for the new nonrevolutionary audience. The Communist Party's Chief Cultural Administrator, therefore, said that all plays had to be in the style of socialist realism, so that the proletarian audience could more clearly understand the messages from the didactic plays. There was a new emphasis on the playwright—instead of nonliterary agitprop—and more easily recognizable and accessible characters and plots. *Workers' Theatre*, the journal of the League of Workers' Theatres, affirmed the new policy of the Popular Front: ". . . we must . . . examine the bourgeois theatre very closely, learn the methods it employs in its propaganda, and—as far as possible—adopt the technique it uses to make its propaganda effective" (Rabkin 48). The new reforms of the Popular Front caused conflict at the Theatre Union. It still intended to perform Marxist plays, but it also had to curb its communist agenda in order to appear as a Popular Front theatre.

The transition to social realism was difficult for many communist-influenced theatres, but it is in this artistic and sociopolitical context that the plays of the Theatre Union, the Group Theatre, and the Federal Theatre Project would—despite their political stance—go on to Broadway, after proving financial promise. These plays—such as *Marching Song*, *Mother*, *Waiting for Lefty*, *Golden Boy*, *Paradise Lost*, *Triple-A Plowed Under*, *Revolt of the Beavers*, *Power*, and *One-Third of a Nation*—managed to carve out a discursive space for their leftist ideology on Broadway, as *Death of a Salesman* would later.

The dramaturgy of *Salesman*, however, is more than socialist realism. In *Salesman*, Miller applied psychology to the structure and characters of the social drama that went beyond the works of the Theatre Union and those of earlier social dramatists such as Henrik Ibsen. In his article "On Social Plays," Miller wrote:

> [The generation of Ibsen, Anton Chekhov, and George Bernard Shaw,] and the left-wing playwrights of the thirties who amplified their findings and repeated their forms, were oriented either toward an arraignment of some of the symptoms of efficiency men or toward the ultimate cure by socialism. . . . The social drama in [these] generation[s] must do more than analyze and arraign the social network of relationships. It must delve into the nature of man as he exists to discover what his needs are, so that those needs may be amplified and exteriorized in terms of social concepts. Thus, the new social dramatist, if he is to do his work, must be an even deeper psychologist than those of the past, and he must be conscious at least of the futility of isolating the psychological life of man lest he fall always short of tragedy, and return, again and again and again, to the pathetic swampland where the waters are old tears and not the generative seas from which new kinds of life arise.
>
> (*Theater Essays* 61)

Applying psychoanalysis to the stage, Miller uses in *Salesman* a stream-of-consciousness and expressionistic dramatic technique to further portray the play's emotional and ideological content.[9] *Salesman* fluently moves from a somewhat realistic and objective depiction of the Loman family, to a literal and subjective presentation of Willy's memory, to imaginary and symbolic representations of his thought. *Salesman* clearly goes beyond a realistic portrait of the Loman family and gives, in addition, a complex presentation of dreams within dreams and symbols within symbols. In this way, *Salesman* is able to surpass the realistic limitations introduced by the Popular Front that had caused difficulty at the Theatre Union.

The Theatre Union eventually disbanded primarily because of its constant financial troubles. It had not created a sufficiently strong and lasting proletarian audience and financial base of support. The Theatre Union had to stay competitive with both Hollywood and Broadway and, at the same time, manage a low ticket price that a proletarian could afford. This left the theatre financially and artistically vulnerable and made it overly concerned with and dependent on Broadway critics. "[Its] continual inner struggle [was] between the desire to do plays which would be afraid of nothing and the knowledge that such productions would be lambasted by the critics and avoided by the moneyed patrons" (Rabkin 66). The final straw came when the Theatre Union lost liberal members who had found promise in the Roosevelt administration and could no longer compete with the government-subsidized Federal Theatre Project, which was able to offer free or greatly reduced ticket prices.

The Theatre Union had a lasting impact on Arthur Miller. For instance, the fever of the Theatre Union's political dogma, its sole purpose, can be compared to what Broadway producer Robert Whitehead called Miller's "rabbinical righteousness" (Berger 2). This was Miller's unwavering morality, his fearless crusade of personal and social responsibility in the face of injustice, which strongly reverberates throughout all of his plays. Miller, like the Theatre Union, helped agitate people, to move them toward critical awareness and action. He also saw his plays as "a kind of a weapon." Miller said that

> [. . . when my plays get] produced in some foreign country, especially in Latin America this has been true, it's either that a dictator is about to arise

> and take over, or he has just been over-thrown. I'm glad something of mine is useful as a kind of a weapon like that. It speaks for people against tyranny, and that's nothing to be ashamed of.
>
> (Martine 14)

On the opening night of *Salesman*, for example, Miller remembered how "a woman who shall not be named was outraged, calling it 'a time bomb under American capitalism'" (*Timebends* 184). Miller admittedly hoped this was true. With *Salesman*, the playwright—like the Theatre Union—attempted to illuminate the failure of a society that values only the driving self-interest of material success.

Before Miller embraced socialism, he was a self-proclaimed Marxist. The Marxist attack on the failure of capitalism and its corrosive effects on the individual, family, and society was a recurring theme in Miller's work. In addition to *Death of a Salesman*, it is seen in *The Crucible*, *Enemy of the People*,[10] *A Memory of Two Mondays*, *After the Fall*, *The Price*, and *The American Clock*. These plays were "drawn from life and informed by the Great Depression, the event that he believed had a more profound impact on the nation than any other in American history, except possibly the Civil War" (Berger 1). Miller's own family was hit hard by the Depression, when his father lost his prosperous coat-manufacturing business. Miller recalled, "Until 1929 I thought things were pretty solid and somebody was in charge, probably a businessman and a realistic, no-nonsense fellow. In 1929 he jumped out of the window" (Times Online 1). These political and personal elements from Miller's life would clearly appear in *Salesman*, an intimate portrait of the playwright and his family's struggles during the Great Depression.

In the Theatre Union's brief span of existence, it was able to produce some of the most important plays of the 1930s, such as *Peace on Earth*, *Stevedore*, *Marching Song*, *Mother*, and *Waiting for Lefty*. The lasting importance of the Theatre Union was its ability to create a professional discursive space for proletarians to engage in Marxist critiques of the social fabric of a capitalistic society. The Theatre Union, in addition, helped agitate and encourage milder leftist theatres, such as the Group Theatre, to take on a more active political voice. Harold Clurman, producer-director of the Group Theatre, recalled how the success of the Theatre Union affected his company:

> [The Group actors'] conscience was troubling them over the fact that we, the first to have spoken of a theatre with social significance, were making money with a play [*Men in White*] that to our more intimate critics was on the level of a *Saturday Evening Post* story, while downtown the Theatre Union had already put on *Peace on Earth*, an anti-war play, and were preparing *Stevedore*, a rousing play on the Negro problem.
>
> (*Fervent Years*, 129–30).

Despite the successful Group Theatre (1931–1941) productions of Odets's *Waiting for Lefty* and *Awake and Sing!*, it was not, overall, a revolutionary Marxist theatre that utilized its dramas as a weapon in the class struggle against capitalism. The aims of the Group Theatre—founded by Harold Clurman, Lee Strasberg and Cheryl Crawford—were more moral and aesthetic than politically dogmatic. The plays were a reflection of contemporary social issues, but they did not prescribe to a specific solution or attempt to cultivate a proletarian audience to rehearse for the communist revolution. At the core of the Group was its unfettered determination to produce quality art not for its own sake, but for a collective purpose.

The Group was an artist collective that reflected and responded to the larger, collective body of contemporary U.S. society and not to a specific group or ideology. Despite protests from the radicalized actors within the company who saw the Group's interest leaning away from plays that helped to create change in the world, the founders of the Group tried to remain outside the political theatres of social protest. In a forty-page paper responding to the actors' protests about how Melvin Levy's *Golden Eagle Guy* failed to illuminate the contemporary social issues, Clurman wrote that the aim of the Group Theatre "was not and never had been to become a political theatre" (*Fervent Years* 136). Despite the Group's unwillingness to subscribe to a specific political solution, the Group did predominantly sponsor leftist plays—such as *The Big Knife*, *The Gentle People*, *Retreat from Pleasure*, and *Night Music*—but only five plays specifically suggested Marxist solutions—such as Odets's first four plays and Erwin Piscator's *The Case of Clyde Griffiths* (Rabkin 78).

The Group Theatre did not completely separate itself from the Broadway theatres. It had a soft leftist stance that allowed it to attract both Broadway and radical theatre audiences. Its early leftist successes with Odets put the Group Theatre in favor with the Marxists, and the successes of Odets on Broadway let it keep company with the bourgeoisie. Despite its accessibility to different theatre audiences, the Group Theatre always remained sympathetic to the Left. It rejected the values of Broadway at the same time it staged its work there. Critics of the Group Theatre considered this double stance an example of the weak ideological purpose of the Group. Clurman, however, claimed that he did not have an interest in such political debates; his interests were more in the aesthetics of theatre, specifically in acting and production. Konstantin Stanislavsky, not Marx, was the patron saint of the company, and the works of Odets and other playwrights were admired by the founding members not for their politics, but for their dramatic qualities. The Group Theatre, however, did not reside in an isolated bubble during the political and cultural unrest of the 1930s. As Clurman wrote, "Every wind of doctrine was reflected in some corresponding ripple in the flow of our lives" (*Lies* 222). The plays of the Group Theatre responded to the plight of the proletariats, the corruption of capitalism, the threat of fascism, the absurdity of war and the Great Depression.

Miller's work—which is deeply moralistic, penetrative and critical of U.S. idealism and social culture—reflected the Group Theatre's interest in creating a more ethical and aesthetic theatrical approach to dealing with social questions, instead of creating a select audience united by a select political solution. Similarly, Miller's work is more moral than political, more dramatic craft than agitprop, and was written for the proletariat as well as the bourgeoisie. He believed that all people of all classes must govern themselves outside of the arbitrary political constructs of society—that one must listen to his or her own sense of personal and social responsibility. Miller was wary of any dogmatic ideology that could distance a person from his or her sense of self. In *Incident at Vichy*, for example, it is not the communist, the socialist, or even the liberal that escapes Nazi persecution, but the humanist, the one who follows his own moral compass.

The Group Theatre, of all the aforementioned theatres, had the greatest impact on Miller's playwriting career. For the next three decades after the collapse of the Group Theatre, members from the Group—Harold Clurman, Elia Kazan, Bobby Lewis, Boris Aronson—would collaborate with Miller on some of his most important plays: *All My Sons*, *After the Fall*, *Incident at Vichy*, and *The Price*. When Clurman, Kazan, and Lewis reassembled as the Lincoln Repertory Theatre, it was Miller's discursive work that they wanted as the voice for their new theatre space. It was *Death of a Salesman*, however, that most strongly signified The Group Theatre. Miller, himself, thought of *Salesman* as "the last gasp of the Group Theatre" (Gottfried 134).

In addition to Kazan, Group veteran Lee J. Cobb would play Willy Loman.[11] Other Group veterans included Arthur Kennedy as Biff and Anne Revere, who was Kazan's first choice for Linda Loman before Mildred Dunnock took over the role.[12] Kermit Bloomgarden, the producer of *Death of a Salesman*, had also been involved with the Group Theatre as the business manager.[13] Miller was pleased that so many of the Group were working for *Salesman*. "Oh God, I love those people," he said. The Group's combination of artistic and political commitment was similar to that of the playwright. "They weren't like anybody else," Miller thought. "They were desperate about themselves" (Gottfried 134). In his autobiography, Kazan described the Group Theatre and its close association with *Salesman*:

> [The Group Theatre] died in 1941 but there were people who had been influenced by the Group or its leaders . . . and that thing, that element in the theater of a kind of spiritual realism still existed. It was alive within the actors, and the people I got in this play were part of my family. . . . And they fitted Art's play perfectly.
>
> (Gottfried 134)

Death of a Salesman brought together not only those from the Group Theatre but many leftist theatre artists and professionals who had been scattered since the thirties, including press agent Jim Proctor and his assistant Merle Debuskey. Martin Gottfried writes:

> Proctor had a history of working with serious-minded producers, while Debuskey was fresh from the Provincetown Players and the plays of Eugene O'Neill. Both were devoted to the causes of the Left, the same as Kazan, Miller, Bloomgarden, Cobb, Kennedy and Chalmers.[14] This wasn't coincidental.
>
> (143)

When Proctor and Debuskey arranged interviews and feature stories, they gave a unique spin to Miller's play. "At that time in American Drama," Debuskey said, "a play had an antagonist and a protagonist and you knew they were individuals. In *Salesman*," he told the editors, "the antagonist is not an individual; the antagonist is society" (Gottfried 143–4).

Harold Clurman, who directed the touring production of *Salesman*, also observed how Miller's play resounded the voice of the earlier leftist plays of social protest, specifically Arthur Richman's *Ambush*, J. P. McEvoy's *The Potters* (1923), Elmer Rice's *The Adding Machine* (1923), George Kelly's *The Show-Off* (1924), and Clifford Odets's *Awake and Sing!* and *Paradise Lost* (1935). The co-founding director of the Group Theatre clearly saw the social drama within the play. "*Death of a Salesman* is a challenge to the American dream" (*Lies Like*

Truth 69). He recognized how *Salesman* continued the left-wing tradition, seen in the productions of the Group Theatre, of bringing to light the false promises of the American Dream.

In short, Miller's experience seeing Group Theatre productions in his youth had a profound and lasting effect on his dramaturgy. In addition to the dramatic quality of the Group's work, his experience seeing their plays helped plant the belief in him that the theatre served a larger community, that it had a social identity and purpose at the heart of its activities. "I had my brain branded by the beauty of the Group Theatre's productions. With my untamed tendency to idealize whatever challenged the system—including the conventions of the Broadway theatre—I was inspired. . . . [From] my fifty-five-cent balcony seat it was all a dream of utter integrity of aims and artistic means" (*Timebends* 230).

The Group Theatre did not last longer than a decade. Like Broadway theatres, the Group was dependent on subsidies and never managed to finance itself independently. Similar to the Theatre Union, "There was no group or combination of groups—private or civic, economic, artistic, social or political—interested enough, conscious enough, strong enough to give consistent support to organizations such as the Group Theatre" (*Fervent Years* 283). In the end, it more resembled Broadway than the financially and artistically independent theatre it originally set out to be (*Critical Introduction* 163). According to Clurman, "The Group Theatre was a failure because, as no individual can exist alone, *no group can exist alone*" (*Lies* 263). The Group Theatre, of course, was not a failure. It succeeded, as did the Theatre Union, in creating a discursive space for the social drama, and this discourse—the "fire" of the Group Theatre—did not die out. Clurman remembered when

> things looked bad for the Group's future. With the uncertain state of our organization and the collapse of the Theatre Union, it seemed pretty clear that our day in the theatre was definitely over. Certain commentators on the drama in New York wrote obituaries (under such titles as "Whither Revolt?") on the whole Left theatre movement, in which an I-told-you-so sat-

> isfaction was barely concealed. . . . Beneath their bluster, the chirping mourners did not see that some of the fire that appeared extinguished in organizations like the Group and the Theatre Union had gone into various elements of the Federal Theatre Project. . . .
>
> (*Lies* 199–200)

The Federal Theatre Project (1935–39) was the most ambitious and well-organized government-subsidized theatre project in the history of the United States. In the brief four seasons of its existence, the Federal Theatre produced more than 1,200 individual productions and employed more than 13,000 people in 35 states, in an impoverished country wracked by the Great Depression (Flanagan 377–436). The Federal Theatre—along with the other Federal Arts projects in art, music, and writing—was a part of the Works Progress Administration (WPA). The WPA, one of the many alphabet-soup relief programs that President Roosevelt created during his first hundred days in office, was formed to help eliminate unemployment by hiring 3.5 million workers in a number of projects financed by the federal government. Hallie Flanagan, the director of the Federal Theatre Project, saw the theatre as serving a dual purpose: to fulfill both economic and social needs in the country. She envisioned a theatre that would help create a more politically critical culture and that would be accessible to all classes, races, and cultures. Similar to the Group Theatre and dissimilar to the Theatre Union, the Federal Theatre was forbidden to propagandize a specific political ideology.

> . . . avoid all controversial issues—political angles of any degree—special appeals—racial or group appeals—or interferences in any of these directions since Federal Theatre is interested only in presenting good theatre, neither adopting nor assuming any viewpoint beyond presenting a new and vital drama of our times, emerging from the social and economic forces of the day.
>
> (121)

The Federal Theatre may not have prescribed a specific political solution to the social unrest, but there was a strong leftist sentiment in parts of the Federal Theatre Project. This resulted, no doubt, from the influence of Flanagan's ties to left-wing theatre previous to the Federal Theatre Project. After winning a Guggenheim Fellowship in 1926, she studied Theatre in Europe and the USSR. When she returned to the States, she was a contributing editor of *New Theatre* and wrote *Can You Hear Their Voice?*, an experimental theatre piece that utilized German and Soviet agitprop techniques to dramatize the plight of Arkansas farmers during the drought. The leftist parts of the Federal Theatre Project were only a small section of a much larger whole.

The Federal Theatre produced a wide variety of work, which included classical and modern dramas, children's dramas, dance dramas, foreign language dramas, Negro dramas, radio dramas, religious dramas, pageants and spectacles, puppet shows, vaudeville and circus acts, musicals, and Living Newspapers. Some of the many important productions to come out of the Federal Theatre Project were Orson Welles's "Voodoo" *Macbeth* (1936), *It Can't Happen Here* (1936), *Revolt of the Beavers* (1936), *Triple-A Plowed Under* (1936), *The Cradle Will Rock* (1937), *Power* (1937), and *Sing for Your Supper* (1939). In addition to these productions, the Federal Theatre created community drama and dramatic training workshops and published its own periodical the *Federal Theatre Magazine* (Flanagan 378–79). The various parts of the Federal Theatre Project demonstrated its efforts to reflect the sociopolitical diversity of its nation.

The Federal Theatre left an impression on Miller as a young playwright.[15] After Miller graduated from the University of Michigan, he turned down a high-paying job as a Hollywood scriptwriter in order to work for the Federal Theatre Project, which was already near its end.[16] Miller's modest but livable weekly income of $22.77 gave him the freedom and encouragement to write. While there, he was influenced by the Federal Theatre's aim to create a theatre with the social purpose of creating a more enlightened and critical society. Miller was also inspired by the Federal Theatre's left-wing social dramas, specifically the epic-style Living Newspapers.

The purpose of the Living Newspapers, originally under the direction of Elmer Rice, was to create works that provided social commentary and enlightenment in the format of the revolutionary theatres prior to the Popular Front. They utilized the techniques of agitprop, epic theatre, constructivist theatre, political cabaret, and popular film documentaries, such as *March of Time*, to dramatize the plight of the proletariats. In a later interview, Miller recognized the importance of the Living Newspaper and its influential commitment to political and social issues:

> [The Federal Theatre Project] created the Living Newspaper which was a journalistic theatre dealing with the big issues of the time: the question of medical care, the agriculture of the United States which was falling apart, we were slaughtering pigs to keep the price of pork up while people were starving in the city. They would tackle these big issues.
>
> (Bigsby, *Critical Study* 24)

Despite the aim of the Federal Theatre Project to produce plays of sociopolitical diversity, its major opponent, Congress, saw works like the Living Newspapers as proof of the government-funded projects' overall subversive and communist-sympathizing infrastructure.

By the end of the 1930s, the conservative Congress was gaining more power, which it used to disrupt the Roosevelt administration. Many powerful businessmen (including those on Broadway), Republicans, and conservative Democrats felt that the relief efforts of the Roosevelt administration—such as the National Industrial Recovery Act, the Wagner Act, and Works Progress Administration—were undermining the free-enterprise system, unionizing the country, and quickly taking it in the direction of socialism. There was a general fear in the 1930s that communist and fascist subversives would attempt to overthrow the U.S. democratic institutions. Roosevelt's programs, such as the Federal Theatre Project, were seen as dens of subversive activity that recruited and rehearsed the oncoming overthrow of the U.S. government. In addition, political profiteers attempted to link the Roosevelt administration to housing radicals in order to dethrone the president and advance their own careers. In 1938, Congress, led by Martin Dies, created the House Committee on Un-American Activities (HUAC) to investigate subversive activities in organizations. The Federal Theatre Project was one of its chief targets. J. Parnell Thomas, a Republican member of the committee, demanded "a thorough cleaning of the Federal Theatre Project . . . [which] has become part and parcel of the Communist Party, spreading its radical theories through its stage productions" (Houchin 146).

In December of 1938, Hallie Flanagan was called before HUAC. Despite her strong defense—which provided statistics on the diverse makeup of Federal Theatre audiences and the low costs of performances; plot synopses of each play; and a sworn statement that no policy-making administrator of the project was affiliated with the Communist Party and that the majority of employees were a part of the theatre union and not the Workers' Alliance—Flanagan was unable to convince the committee that the Federal Theatre Project was not affiliated with the Communist Party (Houchin 148).[17] The Living Newspapers received the harshest attacks. In response, Flanagan said, "the whole of Federal Theatre was greater than any of its parts just as it was greater than any personality connected with it" (205).

According to Flanagan, only ten percent of all the Federal Theatre plays dealt with political issues, such as housing, power, agriculture and labor (361). This, however, was enough to make certain members of the power structure nervous. Flanagan asked,

> Were they afraid? . . . I could see why certain powers would not want even 10 per cent of the Federal Theatre plays to be the sort to make people in our democracy think. Such forces might well be afraid of thinking people. And also were southern Congressmen and Senators afraid of Federal Theatre

> not because it stirred up class hatred, but because it made for a better understanding between classes and races?
>
> (Flanagan 361)

After the HUAC hearings on the Federal Theatre Project, the Federal Theatre received one last fatal blow. In January of 1939, the New Deal was in bad shape, but Congress refused to give Roosevelt the full amount of supplemental appropriations needed to continue his relief programs. As a result, Roosevelt was trapped into signing a bill that cut the Federal Theatre Project in order to salvage the WPA. Roosevelt bitterly told the House that "[This bill] singles out a special group of professional people for a denial of work in their profession. It is discrimination of the worst type" (Houchin 152). The passage of the 1940 Appropriations Bill denied federal funding and forever abolished the Federal Theatre Project, but its discourse continued in Miller's work.

In a review of *Death of a Salesman*, Harold Clurman wrote of how Miller combined elements of the Living Newspapers with his ethical and aesthetic theatrical approach:

> The truth of *Death of a Salesman* is conveyed with what might be compared to a Living Newspaper, documentary accuracy. With this there is a grave probity and a sensitivity that raise the whole beyond the level of what might otherwise have seemed to be only agitation and propaganda. Other playwrights may be more colorful, lyrical and rich with the fleshed nerves and substance of life; Miller holds us with a sense of his soundness. His play has an ascetic, slate-like hue, as if he were eschewing all exaggeration and extravagance; and with a sobriety that is not without humor, yet entirely free of frivolity, he issues the forthright commandment, "Thou shalt not be a damn fool!"
>
> (Weales 215)

The Theatre Union, the Group Theatre, and the Federal Theatre Project successfully carved out their own discursive narrative spaces within a dominating and oppressive capitalistic power structure. Each of these theatres was created from a societal need to illuminate, critique, and find solutions to the social, political, and economic problems of the 1930s. These theatres may not have survived, but their voice—the "fire that appeared extinguished"—was passed on in *Death of a Salesman*.

Notes

1. This figure does not include Broadway productions by the Playwrights' Company, Theatre Guild, the Group Theatre, Federal Theatre, and the Mercury Theatre.

2. See, for example, Oscar Brockett's *Century of Innovation: A History of European and American Theatre and Drama Since 1870*.

3. This assertion excludes the Off-Broadway movement that was developing throughout the country: venues such as the New York City Center (1943), American Repertory Company (1946), Living Theatre (1946), Theatre 47 (1947), Alley Theatre (1947), and Arena Stage (1949).

4. For an understanding of bourgeois theatre, please see Joshua E. Polster, "Rethinking Arthur Miller: Symbol and Structure." Diss. University of Washington, 2006.

5. As mentioned earlier, critics such as Eric Bentley disagree and state that playwrights, such as Miller, cancel social significance in the bourgeois drama.

6. *Salesman* would soon receive, among others, the Pulitzer Prize, the New York Drama Critics' Circle Award, the Antoinette Perry Award, the Donaldson Award, and the Theater Club Award.

7. The Popular Front was also called the "People's Front" or "United Front."

8. There were those within the American Communist Party who disagreed with the policies of the Popular Front and felt that they undermined the ultimate objective of overthrowing the capitalist society.

9. Miller originally considered the title "The Inside of His Head" and envisioned the set with "an enormous face the height of a proscenium arch that would appear and open up, [so] we would see the inside of a man's head. . . ." (*Collected Plays* 23).

10. In addition to the Theatre Union, the social dramas of Henrik Ibsen were largely influential on Miller's dramaturgy. Ibsen's plays—such as *Pillars of Society*, *A Doll's House*, *Ghosts*, and *An Enemy of the People* (which Miller adapted in 1950)—were well-constructed revolutionary attacks on "The State," which was responsible for the suffering and segregation of humanity. According to Ibsen, "The State is the curse of the individual. How has the national strength of Prussia been purchased? By the sinking of the individual in a political and geographical formula. . . . The State must go! That will be a revolution which will find me on its side. Undermine the idea of the State, set up in its place spontaneous action, and the idea that spiritual relationship is the only thing that makes for unity, and you will start the elements of a liberty which will be something worth possessing" (Goldman 5).

11. Cobb performed with Kazan in Odets's *Golden Boy*.

12. Anne Revere eventually turned town the opportunity to play Linda Loman for a role in a movie.

13. Bloomgarden, in fact, had given Kazan his first job as an office boy at the Group Theatre.

14. Thomas Chalmers played Uncle Ben.

15. The Federal Theatre Project, in fact, was responsible for Miller's first off-campus production. Seven months after the University of Michigan production of *They Too Arise*, the Detroit branch of the Federal Theatre picked up the play and extended its brief run for one performance.

16. Lee Strasberg, who was impressed by Miller's *The Grass Still Grows*, wrote a letter recommending Miller to the Federal Theatre and Writers Project.

17. Years later, when Miller was suspected of being a communist, it was his turn to stand before HUAC. During his defense, Miller had a similar voice—the same conviction, intelligence, and integrity—as Hallie Flanagan. Both individuals were unwilling to submit to injustice and, instead, fought for the survival of their sociopolitical discourse.

Works Consulted

Atkinson, Brooks. "Review of *Death of a Salesman*." *New York Times*. Sec. 2. 20 Feb. 1949.

Bentley, Eric. *What Is Theatre?* New York: Atheneum, 1968.

Berger, Marilyn. "Arthur Miller, Moral Voice of American Stage, Dies at 89." *New York Times*. 11 Feb. 2005.

Berkowitz, Gerald. *American Drama of the Twentieth Century*. London and New York: Longman, 1992.

Bigsby, Christopher. *Arthur Miller: A Critical Study*. Cambridge: Cambridge University Press, 2005.

___________. *Critical Introduction to Twentieth-Century American Drama*, Vol. 1. Cambridge: Cambridge University Press, 1982.

___________. *Critical Introduction to Twentieth-Century American Drama*, Vol. 2. Cambridge: Cambridge University Press, 1984.

___________. "The Early Plays." *The Cambridge Companion to Arthur Miller*. Cambridge: Cambridge University Press, 1997.

___________. *Modern American Drama, 1945–1990*. Cambridge: Cambridge University Press, 1992.

Brantley, Ben. "Attention Must Be Paid, Again." *New York Times*. 11 Feb. 1999. AI.

Brockett, Oscar, and Robert Findlay. *A History of European and American Theatre and Drama Since 1870*. Englewood Cliffs, NJ: Prentice-Hall, Inc., 1973.

Centola, Steven, ed. *Echoes Down the Corridor*. New York: Viking, 2000.

Clark, Eleanor. "Review of *Death of a Salesman*." *Partisan Review*. XVI. June, 1949.

Clurman, Harold. *The Fervent Years*. New York: Da Capo Press, 1983.

___________. *Lies Like Truth*. New York: The Macmillan Company, 1958.

Flanagan, Hallie. *Arena*. New York: Duell, Sloan and Pearce, 1940.
Goldman, Emma. *The Social Significance of Modern Drama*. New York: Applause Books, 1987.
Goldstein, Malcolm. *The Political Stage: American Drama and Theater of the Great Depression*. New York: Oxford University Press, 1974.
Gottfried, Martin. *Arthur Miller: His Life and Work*. Cambridge: Da Capo Press, 2003.
Griffin, Alice. *Understanding Arthur Miller*. Columbia: University of South Carolina, 1996.
Himelstein, Morgan. *Drama Was a Weapon*. New Brunswick, NJ: Rutgers University Press, 1963.
Houchin, John. *Censorship of the American Theatre in the Twentieth Century*. Cambridge: Cambridge University Press, 2003.
Kakutani, Michiko. "A Salesman Who Transcends Time." *New York Times*. 7 Feb. 1999.
Kazan, Elia. *A Life*. New York: Da Capo Press, 1997.
Levine, Ira. *Left-Wing Dramatic Theory in the American Theatre*. Ann Arbor: UMI Research Press, 1985.
McDonald, George. "Doctor's Diagnosis." *New York Times*. 28 Feb. 1999.
McKinley, Jesse. "If the Dramatic Tension Is All in His Head." *New York Times*. 28 Feb. 1999.
Martin, Robert, ed. *Arthur Miller: New Perspectives*. Englewood Cliffs, NJ: Prentice-Hall, 1982.
Martine, James, ed. *The Crucible: Politics, Property, and Pretense*. New York: Twayne Publishers, 1993.
Miller, Arthur. *Collected Plays, 1944–1961*. New York: Penguin Putnam, 2006.
___________. *Death of a Salesman*. New York: The Viking Press, 1958.
___________. "On Social Plays." In *A View from the Bridge*, pp. 1–18. New York: Viking, 1955.
___________. *The Theater Essays of Arthur Miller*. Ed. Robert Martin. New York: Da Capo Press, 1978.
___________. *Timebends*. New York: Grove Press, 1987.
Murphy, Brenda. *Miller: Death of a Salesman*. New York: Cambridge University Press, 1995.
Nathan, George Jean. "Review of *Death of a Salesman*." *The Theatre Book of the Year, 1948–1949*. New York: Alfred A. Knopf, Inc., 1949.
Odets, Clifford. *Waiting for Lefty and Other Plays*. New York: Grove Press, 1979.
Patterson, Michael. *Strategies of Political Theatre: Post-War British Playwrights*. Cambridge: Cambridge University Press, 2003.
Rabkin, Gerald. *Drama and Commitment*. Bloomington: Indiana University Press, 1964.
Reynolds, R. C. *Stage Left: The Development of the American Social Drama in the Thirties*. Troy, NY: The Whitston Publishing Company, 1986.
Rowe, Kenneth. "Shadows Cast Before." *The Theater Essays of Arthur Miller*. Ed. Robert Martin. New York: Da Capo Press, 1978.

Shapiro, David. *Social Realism: Art as a Weapon*. New York: Frederick Ungar Publishing Co., 1973.

Smiley, Sam. *The Drama of Attack: Didactic Plays of the American Depression*. Columbia: University of Missouri Press, 1972.

Times Online. *Arthur Miller*. 12 Feb. 2005. http://www.timesonline.co.uk/article/0,,60-1480417,00.html

Turner, Victor. *From Ritual to Theatre: The Human Seriousness of Play*. New York: Performing Arts Journal Publication, 1982.

Weales, Gerald, ed. *Death of a Salesman: Text and Criticism*. New York: The Viking Press, 1972.

King Lear, King Oedipus, and Willy Loman: Tragic Strategies in *Death of a Salesman*

Neil Heims

i.

The issue of whether *Death of a Salesman* is or is not a tragedy has pervaded discussions of the play ever since it opened at the Morosco Theatre on Broadway on February 10, 1949. Seventeen days after the opening, Miller himself broached the issue in a column for *The New York Times* called "Tragedy and the Common Man" (Miller, *Theater Essays* 3–7) and a month later printed a similar piece, "The Nature of Tragedy" (Miller, *Theater Essays* 8–11), in *The New York Herald-Tribune*. In those pieces he distinguished tragedy from pathos, which he called "the mode for the pessimist," and asserted that, as a genre, tragedy, in which "lies the belief . . . in the perfectibility of man" (qtd. in Miller, *Theater Essays* 7), "arises when we are in the presence of a man who has missed accomplishing his joy," and that it "is the most accurately balanced portrayal of the human being in his struggle for happiness" (qtd. in Miller, *Theater Essays* 11). In his pursuit of a democratized definition of tragedy, Miller distinguished between rank and stature. He argued that the tragic qualities of *hybris* and *hamartia* are not by definition limited to socially prominent or powerful individuals. (*Hybris* refers to a pride that stands up to undefeatable and unapproachable forces. *Hamartia* signifies a tragic flaw, something in the protagonist that, although an outgrowth and version of his very strength, also leads to his downfall. Paradoxically, it is just his flaw, his overstepping, that makes him a hero because of the struggle it forces upon him.) A salesman, Willy Loman, for example, although he does not carry the social rank of a king, may, indeed, be a king's equal in stature and, consequently, the worthy protagonist of a tragedy if his experience and his confrontation with that experience—if the situation he creates and endures inside an already given, even hostile, world—touch, express, struggle with something fundamental and universal to mankind.

Although in the "Introduction" to the 1957 edition of his *Collected Plays* (Miller, *Theater Essays* 113–170) Miller asserted "I set out not to 'write a tragedy' in [*Death of a Salesman*] but to show the truth as I saw it" (qtd. in Miller, *Theater Essays* 144), he did not say that in *Death of a Salesman* he did *not* write a tragedy. The sense of his argument is that it is fair to say that he did and in doing so, revised or expanded the genre. Indeed, he proceeded in his "Introduction" to discuss the ways Aristotle's apparent exclusion of "low" characters from the possibility of being protagonists of tragedy was historically determined by the Greek institution of human slavery and has been historically superseded, just as, Miller noted, Greek medicine and geometry have been (Miller, *Theater Essays* 145). Miller not only wrote *Death of a Salesman* but played a determining role in shaping the discourse about it.

As early as June 1949, *Death of a Salesman* was being seen not only as a tragedy but as a play with affinities to Shakespeare's *King Lear*. The uncredited critic in *The Guardian*, an English newspaper, on July 30, 1949, writing about the London opening of the play, said, "many people including this critic, who saw it in New York . . . found it something comparable to an American *King Lear*." Critics like R. H. Gardner, in "Tragedy of the Lowest Man" (Gardner 122–134), and Esther Merle Jackson, in "*Death of a Salesman*: Tragic Myth in the Modern Theater" (Jackson 27–38), not only focus on *Death of a Salesman* as a tragedy but also make specific comparisons between Willy Loman and Lear. Gardner rejects Willy as a common-man King Lear, calling him "dumb" and "one of the biggest bores in literature," asserting that Willy does not, like Lear, grow out of his delusion. Whether Willy does become enlightened or if he has ever been deluded are both arguable. Whether Willy's early flirtations with suicide are qualitatively different from his ultimate suicide is a question at the heart of the play. Certainly, Willy's insight into his conflict with Biff changes. He realizes, and that is what kills him, his own hand in Biff's downfall, finally making the connection between Biff's sudden decline and Biff's discovery of Willy's fraudulence. In Willy's last angry confrontation with Biff, he realizes, too, that the degree of Biff's alienation from and rage at him are the measures of his love for him. It is akin to Lear's realization that Cordelia's silence proclaims her love more truthfully and ardently than all her sisters' fancy and convoluted rhetoric.

Whether Willy's braggadocio and self-aggrandizement are the results of delusion is likewise unclear. Willy is, after all, a salesman, and a salesman, as his neighbor, Charley—who remains loyal to Willy the way Kent does to Lear, despite Willy's unrelenting insults—says over Willy's grave, a salesman lives "out there in the blue, riding on a smile and a shoeshine." It is equally a matter for discussion whether Lear dies enlightened or deluded. His early pride and sense of godlike omnipotence, after all, may not have been delusory even if they are mistaken or inappropriate attitudes about his own mortality and the truth of what it is to be a man. Overweening pride and a sense of godlike power are attributes that adhere to the office of the absolute majesty conferred by kingship. Whether Lear dies believing Cordelia still lives or that her breath is indeed stopped may not really matter very much, either. What is important about what Lear learns is not that he was deluded in believing that Cordelia did not love him. He learns by his tragic error a new way of understanding what love is, that love is a matter of moving towards the beloved rather than drawing the beloved towards himself. In the common, but no less true, understanding, love is an act of surrendering and giving rather than domineering and receiving. As such Lear's fall resembles the "fortunate fall" of Christianity, which sacrifices the vanity and chaos of the world for the beatitude of heaven. The fall of Eve and Adam prepares the way for Christ's ascension. In Lear's case Lear is purged of vanity through suffering and realizes bliss through renunciation of his original self. Whether in his prayer in the storm, "Poor naked wretches," or in his long sermon to Gloucester in Dover in act 4, scene 6, beginning at line 110 with the words, "When I do stare see how the subject quakes," Lear shows an understanding of the human condition that was not his when he banished Cordelia. That the evil machinations of such degenerate characters as Edmund and of

Lear's two elder daughters thwart Lear's newfound delight is another matter. Although both Lear and Willy Loman come to understand love as giving rather than getting, their tragedy is that that realization comes when they have nothing other to give than their lives for their love since the situation around them has become so tainted by their past errors that they are hapless despite their enlightenment. Willy, moreover, does not attain the lofty wisdom Lear approaches regarding humanity as a whole. But the audience at a performance of *Death of a Salesman* or a reader of the play, through observing and enduring Willy's plight, well may.

Jackson, unlike Gardner, asserts that *Death of a Salesman*, "like . . . *King Lear*, [is] a mythic apprehension of life" and speaks of Willy as a "traditional tragic protagonist." She also cites Miller's bare-bones sketch of *Death of a Salesman*, which he renders in conventional-mythic terms, in order to show that the play has a right to be considered a tragedy. The story, as Miller renders it schematically, sounds very much like *King Lear*.

> An aged king—a pious man—moves toward life's end. Instead of reaping the benefits of his piety, he finds himself caught in bewildering circumstances. Because of a mistake—an error in judgment—a tragic reversal has taken place in his life. Where he has been priest, knower of secrets, wielder of power, and symbol of life, he now finds himself adjudged defiler, usurper, destroyer, and necessary sacrifice. Like the traditional hero, Loman begins his long season of agony. In his descent, however, there is the familiar tragic paradox; for as he moves toward inevitable destruction, he acquires that knowledge, that sense of reconciliation, which allows him to conceive a redemptive plan for his house.
>
> (Bloom 29)

Rather than puzzling, however, over whether *Death of a Salesman* is or is not a tragedy, whether Miller's redefinition of tragedy is acceptable, or whether it is even possible to write a tragedy about ordinary people and about social issues, an examination of some similarities and differences regarding action, plot, character, and construction in *Death of a Salesman*, *King Lear*, and the first two of Sophocles' Theban plays, *King Oedipus* and *Oedipus at Colonus*, can help to show some tragic strategies Miller used in *Death of a Salesman* and illuminate the humanity of each of the plays, bringing a sense of presentness to the older plays despite their classic austerity or Elizabethan currents and of permanence or universality to the contemporary one despite its mid-twentieth-century trappings.

ii.

Death of a Salesman begins on a note of anxiety that begins as a response to one event but expands to influence the tone of the entire play. "Trepidation" is the word Miller uses in the stage direction. Hearing a noise, Linda calls out "Willy!" from inside the bedroom, and he enters and explains, "It's alright. I came back." But his assurance is hardly reassuring. "Why? What happened? Did something happen, Willy?" Linda asks. And his answer, "No, nothing happened," still does not calm her sense that something is wrong. She persists in digging. "You didn't smash the car, did you?" It is a question driven by fright, not by reproach. It is a question that indicates that she always is frightened, not *of* him, but *for* him.

As she lives continually on the edge of fear, he lives always on the verge of explosive irritation. "I said nothing happened," he says. "Didn't you hear me?" But hearing is not believing, and Linda tries again: "Don't you feel well?" This question does affect him sensibly and allows him to unload. The question is not a challenge that can shame his behavior or a calling into question of a decision he has made or an indication of her doubt about his sense of responsibility. It does not take him to the brink of something he will be unable to face or ashamed to admit, something like an acknowledgment that, in terms of his dreams for himself and his family, his life is a failure, something he will have to banish from his awareness with a grand fantasy and aggressive boastfulness—two characteristics of his that repeatedly emerge when he is under siege by the reality of his galling unimportance and declining fortune in the world. Linda's question allows him to collapse, to complain of a tormenting force beyond himself. It allows him to express pity for himself and, by that expression of what he feels to be deserved pity, to excuse himself for being unable to do what his image of himself requires he do in order for him to have a sense of pride in himself. "I'm tired to death," he says. "I couldn't make it. I just couldn't make it, Linda," he tells her.

Willy is telling Linda his version of his story. He presents himself as a beaten hero facing an obstacle beyond his already established power or his comprehension. This is the way, also, that he sees his son Biff. Biff appears to Willy as a hero who inexplicably has not achieved his heroism and who is, consequently, a source of grief and not joy. Willy refuses to know why, preferring bewilderment to an enlightenment that must be forced upon him by the mechanisms his faults have put in motion and which will reveal to him the full measure of his failure. As he complains to Linda, Willy is not puffing himself or blustering. He is not pretending to be what he is not. In fact, his exhaustion indicates how much of himself he actually has spent in dedication to supporting his family. He is overwhelmed, like Lear, with the sense of being "a man more sinned against than sinning," a man in need of pity, and unlike Lear, he does have a wife who does pity him but is unable to do anything for him and whose displays of love for him usually irritate rather than soothe him. To accept her kindness, after all, would be to admit his neediness, something his pride resists.

Like Lear's confusion at his sudden fall from what he was, Willy Loman's understanding of his plight is amorphous. He sees himself as insulted and injured, as washed up. But he also needs, for the sake of his proud self-image, to deny this insight or, at least, to attribute his condition not to any flaw in himself but to a changed and hostile world. He does not see why he is as besieged and beleaguered as he is beyond seeing the ingratitude of others who have no use for him anymore. Willy is old, worn out, and slowly being consigned to an industrial scrap heap by the laws of a callous capitalism, because he has no more economic usefulness. He has lost his surplus value. It is not so different from Lear's situation. Lear's value, after all, was a socially conferred value, a mark of his office. Once his official power is gone, just as once Willy's commercial power is gone, he is only, like Willy, a man who has wronged a beloved child whom he did not know how to love. But Lear quickly realizes that he wronged Cordelia in the first scene, and how. Willy keeps the knowledge of how he has wronged Biff buried until it breaks out of him in the climactic scene in the restaurant towards the end of the second act.

Willy's lack of productivity as a salesman and the way he is, in consequence, abandoned by the company he has given his life to do not constitute his tragedy. These are social facts that certainly Miller takes to be deplorable. (The tone of the play allows an audience to understand as much, and extra-literary elements—Miller's own political statements and acts—confirm it.) But tragedy is about an internal situation, not an external one, no matter how grim that outer one is. Willy's tragedy lies not only in his response to his rejection by the mercantile society but also in his earlier adaptation to the demands of commerce. These are facts about him, not about the conditions surrounding him.

The surrounding world's attitude towards Willy is only the practical and consequential manifestation of his trouble. Like Lear, Willy knows the pain of having exploitative and thankless children who cannot and do not succor him in his old age. In Lear's case, the audience has no idea what Lear has done in the past to make his elder daughters Goneril and Regan the abusive monsters that they are. At best, we can make up stories. In *Death of a Salesman*, it is clear what Willy has done throughout their lives to shape his sons' attitudes because of the seamlessly interpolated memory scenes. (Indeed, such a causative way of thinking regarding the psychology of behavior that underlies Miller's play may not even be applicable inside the epistemology of *King Lear*'s universe.) Like Lear, Willy is no longer valuable or viable inside a social order he once seemed able to negotiate. Like Lear, Willy is weary and longs for tenderness. Both Willy and Lear, however, because of themselves, not because of the admittedly oppressive circumstances of the world, are unable "to shake all cares and business from our age, / Conferring them on younger strengths, while we / Unburthened crawl toward death" (I.i.41). Lear cannot "set my rest / On [his youngest daughter Cordelia's] kind nursery" because he casts her out. That Lear feels thwarted by Cordelia when she refuses to compete in his unseemly and degrading ritual of proclaiming love and loyalty does not mean that *she* intends to thwart him. She tells him quite carefully, "You have begot me, bred me, loved me: I / Return those duties back as are right fit, / Obey you, love you, and most honor you." But she asserts her independence, too, which ought to make him see how much truer her love is than her sisters', but he does not. "That lord whose hand must take my plight shall carry," she tells her father, "Half my love with him, half my care and duty." Pride in his station and a selfish commitment to willful domination and having his way, characteristics Willy Loman completely shares with Lear, make Lear unable to see the correctness and virtue, as well as the devotion, in Cordelia's words. Her love will not be bullied. Rather than accepting Cordelia's devotion as she offers it, Lear fulminates against her and banishes her. Lear is not, however, really thwarted by Cordelia's response but by the response he must make to her response given who he is or, at least, who he believes he is.

Like Lear, but without the intensity of Shakespeare's language, which turns drama into poetry and poetry into human reality, Willy fulminates against his sons with an intensity that turns fact into mystery. Despite (because of) his intense desire for their love and for their success, especially Biff's—for his sons' triumphs feed his pride—Willy has isolated himself from them and crippled them. But he is blind to that because the idea of success through appearance that he instills in them is all he knows. For Willy maintaining a winning appearance is a major component for success in his work. For his sons, success is an image that can stand apart from the reality of made effort. By his effort to pull them towards him, really, to seduce them into being his worshippers, Willy pushes them away simply because he cannot maintain the godlike image he has wrought of himself and he gives them a skewed idea of how success is achieved. Lear pushes Cordelia away by the blindness of a furious pride. Willy cuts his bond with Biff far less deliberately. Having brought the boy to the point of worshipping him, he devastates him when Biff discovers Willy is not a god. If Willy is not authentic, then neither is Biff, for his authenticity depends completely on Willy's authorizing it. What Willy has been trying to form Biff into was a grander version of himself that he (Willy) might worship, narcissistically, in return.

The confrontation that alienates Biff from Willy, although it is a wellspring of the action of the play, is also the result of the situation that Miller is anatomizing in the play. Unlike Cordelia's devastating encounter with Lear, the scene between Willy and Biff in the hotel in Boston does not occur within moments after the play has opened. Consequently, it cannot and does not appear to be what is propelling the action in *Death of a Salesman* as far as the audience can know, from the start of the play, as the rift between Lear and Cordelia does. Willy's betrayal of Biff follows upon a lifetime of demands he has made on Biff, demands that the boy struggled to fulfill and succeeded in fulfilling by subverting and by ignoring himself, by defining himself by the standard of his father. When his father crashed before his eyes, so did Biff.

Willy's betrayal is revealed towards the end of the play. It is something Willy and Biff have both known throughout the play, and it is the thing they do not discuss, although it underlies their conflicts and is the effective cause of Biff's failure. When the scene in Boston finally is played in Willy's memory in the restaurant, the revelation of the reversal comes as an enlightenment for the audience more than for Willy or Biff. It gives the audience the tragic insight that the genre conventionally demands of its protagonist. Light shines for the spectators. Willy's insincerity, which is, in him, not a vice but a vocational skill that has penetrated to the depth of his character, is the *hybris* of Willy's salesmanship, the mark of his power in the world, and it is his tragic flaw. With regard to facing the power of paternal authority, Biff is the opposite of Cordelia, weak where she is strong, human where she is a force of nature. With love, she opposes her father's demands with her own actuality and never abandons him. Biff, at first, as he is growing up, succumbs to Willy's demands and then, with resentment when he sees Willy's integrity dissolve, he spites him, as Willy correctly reproaches him, by using the only weapons he has against his father, himself and his father's dreams for him. He subverts Willy by sabotaging himself. Consequently, unlike Cordelia, he is entirely unable to come to his father's rescue. When Willy begs his boss Howard not to let him go, saying, "But I gotta earn money, Howard. I'm in no position to—," Howard's response, "Where are your sons? Why don't your sons give you a hand?" burns. Willy cannot answer truly but retreats into his fantasy world. "They're working on a very big deal," he says (Miller, *Death of a Salesman* 83).

Willy does not stage one ritual test of his sons' love. He constantly has been demanding that love, that devotion—especially Biff's—throughout the time preceding the action of the play, and these demands are brought into the present, into the play, through memory. (Miller has integrated the psychology of his protagonist with the narrative problem of presenting the back story, the events preceding the events of the play. Past events, or at least Willy's version of past events, are not presented as flashbacks but as present memory events so that the play shuttles between external events and the interior events of memory and fantasy.) Willy has always demanded that his sons, especially Biff, conform to his idea of what they ought to be. What breaks the bond between Biff and Willy is not that Willy has made his demands or that Biff is incapable of meeting them. The break comes because Willy breaks Biff's heart and his spirit when he betrays the image of himself that he has been broadcasting to him, when Biff discovers that Willy is not the man he projected himself to be, that he is not the hero to please that Biff had been made to think he was, that he is a little man pursuing tawdry diversions with a vulgar mistress at his devoted and self-sacrificing wife's expense.

iii.

If in its content and conflicts *Death of a Salesman* resembles *King Lear*, formally, in terms of the structure of tragedy, the play is closer to Sophocles' *King Oedipus* than to *King Lear*. The genius of *King Oedipus* does not lie as much in its account of the myth that Sigmund Freud used to give life to his understanding of the eternal conflict between generations as it does in the way Sophocles turns an assortment of events into a complex plot by knitting the events together with causes and consequences, revelations and reversals. Both *Death of a Salesman* and *King Oedipus*, unlike *King Lear*, begin with a mystery: Why is Thebes cursed with a plague? Why are Willy's sons lost men? *Lear* begins on a note of confusion. "I thought," the Earl of Kent says to the Duke of Gloucester privately, a few moments before a state ceremony in which octogenarian Lear will hand over his power to his daughters and their husbands, "the king had more affected the Duke of Albany than of Gloucester." Gloucester shares the confusion. "It did always seem so to us," he replies, "but now, in the division of the kingdom, it appears not which of the dukes he values most." This inability to focus reflects the fundamental condition of Lear himself, who is unable to distinguish between flattery and sincerity and who cries out in anguish soon after he realizes he has surrendered his power to the two daughters who have contempt for him and banished the one who honored him, "Is there anyone who can tell me who I am?" The drama of *King Lear*, within the sections of the play devoted to Lear, is the drama of torment and developing insight. There is no mystery. The audience knows what Lear's flaw is, has seen him commit his proud and tragic error. The drama of the play is not psychological. It is metaphysical, an account of Lear's recognition of what a man is, a recognition that is brought about by the reversal of his fortune. Reversal, in *King Lear*, is not a climactic event, nor is it a single event either. Were Willy to cry out the same words as Lear, "Is there anyone who can tell me who I am?" it would be a question not about the very place of Man in the Cosmos but a question about his, Willy's, identity as a displaced and ruined man in society.

In both *Death of a Salesman* and *King Oedipus*, revelations about the protagonists and reversals of their fortunes, contingent upon those revelations, coming simultaneously, serve as the fulcrums for the dramatic action. As *King Oedipus* begins, a plague is wasting the city of Thebes, and the people of Thebes are seen supplicating their hero king, Oedipus, to come to their aid once more, as he previously did when he freed the city from the domination of the monster, the sphinx, who demanded yearly sacrifice of its youth, by answering its riddle. As Oedipus proceeds to search for the cause of the plague that is making barren the land and people of Thebes, he learns that he himself is the cause. In a roadside brawl far from the city, he has slain his father, not knowing that the man with whom he fought for the right-of-way on the road was his father and the king of Thebes. After having defeated the sphinx, Oedipus was married, as a reward, to Thebes' widowed queen and, thus, has lain with his mother. The revelation of these two facts signals the reversal of his fortune from honored king to disgraced pariah. Part of the genius of Sophocles as a storyteller is that he shows the pride, stubbornness, and anger that are at the core of Oedipus' personality as he dramatizes the king's encounters with several Thebans as he seeks to discover the crime that is the cause of the plague.

Like *King Oedipus*, *Death of a Salesman* begins with a sort of plague gripping the fortunes of Willy Loman's house. Not only is Willy barren, but his two sons also have seen their lives go to waste. Unlike Oedipus, Willy does not undertake a course of action to uncover the cause of the plague ravaging his household. He attempts to barrel through as if things were not as they are, but the repressed returns despite his efforts at denial. Unlike in *King Oedipus*, where the revelation and reversal occur inside the real time of the play and explain (and, consequently, begin to undo) the plight of Thebes, the revelation and reversal in *Death of a Salesman* have actually occurred before the beginning of the play and they are presented, through memory, in the restaurant scene towards the end of the play. Moreover, Willy is not the only tragic figure in *Death of a Salesman*. Just as Biff participates in Willy's dreams of glory, so he participates in Willy's tragedy. Willy, in fact, deep down, knows that he is untrue to his wife and something of a falsifier regarding his career, but Biff does not know that, just as Oedipus, although he has slain his father and lain with his mother, does not know it until it is revealed. For Biff, then, what happened in the hotel in Boston signaled a revelation about his father *and* about himself and the reversal of his, Biff's, fortune more than his father's. *King Oedipus* and *Death of a Salesman* are psychological dramas, inexorably rushing to reveal guilty, hidden family secrets and the effects of their excavation. *King Lear* is not. It is a meditation on the place of Man in the Cosmos and not just the causes but the uses of suffering. Formally, as a tragedy, despite its resemblance to *King Lear* and its divergence from *King Oedipus* in its plot, *Death of a Salesman* is nearer to Sophocles' *King Oedipus* than to *King Lear.*

Since the reversal of Lear's fortune and the revelation of his temperament precipitate the action of *King Lear, King Lear* is not a play of discovery and revelation the way *King Oedipus* and *Death of a Salesman* are. It is a play about what happens after the fall from illusionary heights occurs rather than discovering that one is, actually, fallen. It is about what transcendental illumination can occur after that first revelation of a flaw that brings about the reversal of fortune. In this regard, *King Lear* is more like *Oedipus at Colonus*, the second in Sophocles' Theban trilogy composed of *King Oedipus*, *Oedipus at Colonus*, and *Antigone*. *Oedipus at Colonus* begins with Oedipus in a situation similar to Lear's in act 5, scene 3. A chastened and tender Lear is imprisoned with his beloved Cordelia. A blind and bereft Oedipus is led, in exile, by his beloved daughter-sister, Antigone. "My daughter—my daughter," Oedipus cries out, ". . . Who will be kind to Oedipus this evening / And give alms to the wanderer? / Though he ask little and receive still less, / it is sufficient: / Suffering and time, / Vast time, have been instructors in contentment" (Greene and Lattimore 93). After his fall, Oedipus enters the terrible realm of the sacred, where he struggles against the forces of earthly power to install himself in a transcendental sphere. This is also what the trajectory of *King Lear* is. In terms of particulars, *Death of a Salesman* resembles *King Lear*; in terms of its construction, it resembles *King Oedipus*. *King Lear*, although its basic story resembles *Death of a Salesman*, thematically is closer to *Oedipus at Colonus*. Lear, like Oedipus at Colonus, becomes sacred, once exiled from his realm. Willy flounders and can only, once he realizes his error and the burden of its consequences, sacrifice himself, killing himself not as an act of self-pity but as an attempted expiation for a guilt that has become indelible, ineradicable, even identical with his character. His tragic triumph is also a mark of his unremitting pride.

Works Cited

Bloom, Harold, ed. *Arthur Miller*. New York: Chelsea House Publishers, 1987.

Gardner, R. H. "Tragedy of the Lowest Man." From *The Splintered Stage: The Decline of the American Theater*. New York: Macmillan, 1965. 122-34.

The Guardian. Review of *Death of a Salesman*, by Arthur Miller. 30 July 1949. http://www.guardian.co.uk/stage/1949/jul/30/theatre.artsfeatures.

Jackson, Esther Merle. "*Death of a Salesman*: Tragic Myth in the Modern Theater." From *Modern Critical Views: Death of a Salesman*. Ed. Harold Bloom. New York: Chelsea House Publishers, 1987.

Miller, Arthur. *Death of a Salesman*. From *The Portable Arthur Miller*. Ed. Christopher Bigsby. New York: Penguin Books, 1995. 19-131.

___________. *The Theater Essays of Arthur Miller*. Ed. Robert A. Martin. London: Methuen, 1994.

Shakespeare, William. *King Lear*. Ed. Russel Fraser. New York: Signet/New American Library, 1963.

Sophocles. *Oedipus at Colonus*. *Sophocles 1*. Trans. Robert Fitzgerald. Ed. David Greene and Richmond Lattimore. New York: The Modern Library, 1954.

Arthur Miller's *Death of a Salesman*: History of Criticism

Amy Sickels

Opening Night

One of America's most popular plays, Arthur Miller's *Death of a Salesman* has probably generated more debate than any other modern drama in America. The scholarship on Arthur Miller is extensive, spanning more than fifty years, and, out of all of Miller's plays, *Death of a Salesman* is by far the most discussed. Countless academic articles and books have been written about the play, and it is one of the most likely American plays to appear on high school and college reading lists. *Death of a Salesman* was not Miller's first play, but it was the one that began to attract the attention of theatre critics, and though he wrote many others, this would be the play that ultimately determined Miller's long-lasting fame and reputation. Selling 11 million copies, *Death of a Salesman* is considered by many to be the quintessential American drama.

When Arthur Miller wrote *Death of a Salesman*, which he did in about six weeks in 1948, he was responding to the new postwar American affluence. Despite the country's newly acquired wealth, Miller felt that the Depression (a major impetus for his work) was still looming and that Americans were living under the constant fear that at any time, everything would disappear. *Death of a Salesman* revolves around the last twenty-four hours in the life of Willy Loman, a sixty-three-year-old traveling salesman whose ideas of success conflict with the reality that he is living. Much of the play takes place inside of his mind, as he remembers significant events from his past. Deciding that he is worth more dead than alive, Willy commits suicide, hoping that the insurance money will support his family and give his son Biff a new start and a chance to succeed. While addressing the emotional conflicts within one family, the play critically examines the myth of the American Dream.

The original production opened on February 10, 1949, at the Morosco Theatre on Broadway. The highly respected Elia Kazan directed the production, and Lee J. Cobb starred as Willy. Everyone involved in the production felt nervous and tense on opening night, not knowing how the New York audience would react. When the curtain went down, there was a hushed moment, and then at once the audience exploded into wild applause. Both Kazan and Miller were caught off guard by how many men and women in the audience were openly sobbing. Miller's realistic, tragic portrayal of Willy Loman struck an emotional chord with American audiences, and many people, including Kazan, felt as if Miller had written about their own fathers.

The next morning, across the city, the newspaper reviews were enthusiastically positive. Glowing reviews appeared in *The New York Times*, the *Sun*, the *Daily News*, the *New York Post*, and the *Daily Mirror*, with reviewers describing the play as a powerful new tour de force. Critic Howard Barnes in the *New York Herald Tribune* called it "a great play of our day" (qtd. in Bigsby, *File on Miller* 22). The production ran for 742 performances to packed audiences. It received many accolades from the critics, winning the Antoinette Perry Award, the New York Drama Critics' Circle Award, and the Pulitzer Prize. Within a year of its Broadway premiere, it was playing in every major city in the United States, and despite its American themes, the play also appealed to international audiences: as early as 1951, it was shown in at least eleven countries abroad. With this single play, Miller secured his fame, and *Death of a Salesman* soon made both Arthur Miller and the character Willy Loman household names.

1950s Politics

After the initial praise from newspaper reviewers, the critical intelligentsia began to weigh in, and despite its popularity with audiences, *Death of a Salesman* did not receive universal praise from theatre critics and scholars. In the early years, critical reception toward Miller in the United States was mixed, and some critics developed an uneasy, even hostile, relationship with Miller. Throughout his career, Miller wrote extensive prefaces, introductions, and essays, and gave interviews and lectures, explaining, defending, and analyzing his own work. He often provoked critics, which probably began with an essay he wrote, in response to criticism about *Death of a Salesman*, for *The New York Times* in 1949 titled "Tragedy and the Common Man." Many considered the tone to be pompous, but it was Miller's controversial definition of classical tragedy that started a critical debate defining tragedy that continues today.

Death of a Salesman has received a wide variety of critical responses that often focus on the tragic, personal, or social message of the play. After its premiere, the play was often either wholeheartedly praised or criticized for its critique of American capitalistic society, with political ideals often coloring critical responses. One of the most scathing critiques came from Eleanor Clark, a writer for the *Partisan Review*. In an 1949 essay titled "Old Glamour, New Gloom," she described the play as "straight from the party line literature of the Thirties." She also called it "clumsy," "specious," "flat," and "a very dull business." Eric Bentley also criticized the play in his 1949 review in *Theatre Arts*, attacking everything from the lighting to what he considered the play's conflicting aims of tragedy and social drama. Yet Miller's play also achieved a good deal of praise within the scholarly circle. With critics providing interpretations and analyses, the play received much more scholarly attention than any of Miller's previous works, and *Death of a Salesman* years later, would continue to be his most talked about play.

Though audiences had flocked to *Death of a Salesman* during its premiere, public reception shifted in the 1950s when Miller's popularity began to wane and both critics and audiences grew more uneasy with his work. It was the height of McCarthyism in the United States, during which a rampant fear of Communism and anti-American values raged across the country. During the late 1940s and the 1950s, thousands of Americans were accused of being Communists or communist sympathizers. The most famous examples of McCarthyism were the Hollywood Blacklist and the investigations and hearings conducted by Senator Joseph McCarthy. The Hollywood Blacklist was a list of entertainment professionals who were denied employment in the field because of their political beliefs or associations, real or suspected. It damaged the careers of many actors and writers, and promoted ideological censorship across the industry.

During this time, conservatives viewed Miller's *Death of a Salesman* as a caustic attack on capitalism and on the American Dream of achieving wealth and success. As controversy began to surround Miller's leftist sympathies, Miller's audience began to edge away. In 1950 Miller adapted the 1881 social drama of Henrik Ibsen's *An Enemy of the People*, which addresses the greed and hypocrisy of the bourgeoisie, to reflect McCarthyism in the United States. The play closed after only thirty-six performances. Meanwhile, the film version of *Death of a Salesman*, directed by Stanley Kramer and set to be released in 1951, also suffered repercussions from the political climate. Fearing the House Committee on Un-American Activities (HUAC)—a committee of the United States Congress that investigated Communist influence in the arts—Hollywood attempted to steer clear of anything that may be considered "un-American." Consequently, Columbia, the film's production company, proposed to show a trailer along with *A Death of a Salesman*, supportive of American businesses: in the short film, business school professors explained how Loman did not represent a typical salesman. When Miller threatened to sue Columbia, the film was released on its own, but not to success. It was picketed by the American Legion and other groups in major cities in the United States. Audiences at the time were wary of watching anything that was critical of American values, and the fear of communism extended well beyond America. Overseas, in Dublin in 1951, *Death of a Salesman* was picketed by anti-Communist demonstrators, and though the audience seemed enthusiastic, political ideology set the tone for the Dublin press.

In 1952, Elia Kazan, who had directed *Death of a Salesman* on Broadway, appeared before HUAC, and under the fear of being blacklisted from Hollywood, he named eight people from the Group Theatre who had been fellow members of the Communist Party. After Kazan's testimony, Miller ended his friendship with him, and they did not speak for ten years. After the testimony, Miller traveled to Salem, Massachusetts, to research the witch trials, and in response to the growing anti-Communist hysteria, he wrote *The Crucible* as an allegorical play that compared HUAC to the Salem witch hunt. When the play opened on Broadway in 1953, it was considered widely unsuccessful but later became one of Miller's most frequently produced dramas. Not long after the play opened, HUAC denied Miller a passport to attend the play's opening in Brussels. In 1956, Miller was called to testify before HUAC, but he refused to name names. He was found guilty of contempt, but in 1958 his conviction was reversed by the U.S. Court of Appeals. Though critical and popular appeal waned for *Death of a Salesman* during this volatile period, eventually the play would make a popular and critical comeback.

The Debate Surrounding Tragedy

Much of the scholarly criticism, both past and current, focuses on whether or not *Death of a Salesman* functions as a "true" tragedy. Miller provided much of the impetus for this debate with his well-known essay "Tragedy and the Common Man," which upset many of the central assumptions about the genre that Aristotle had described some two thousand years before, and started off a heated debate among critics. Traditional classical tragedy, as in Greek theatre or Shakespeare, depicts a hero who is often upper-class and who challenges, because of some personal flaw in his nature, the moral values of his society; for example, *Oedipus* is considered a classic Greek tragedy. The hero suffers, while society and its sacred values remain unbreakable, and in the end, the hero experiences an epiphany or self-realization.

Willy Loman is not a typical tragic hero. He belongs to a lower economic class and is not particularly smart. Furthermore, the society in which he lives is an amoral, capitalistic big-business society. In "Tragedy and the Common Man," Miller argues, "the common man is as apt a subject for tragedy in its highest sense as kings were." He argues that tragic heroes are defined by their willingness to sacrifice everything in order to maintain their personal dignity. Loman is flawed in his skewed idea of what makes a person successful, but he refuses to give up that popular vision. Miller viewed Willy Loman as a believer in the American Dream, who in the end chooses not to suffer the loss of dignity. The essay was reprinted many times, and now is a popular reading assignment for high school and college students. When it appeared in *The New York Times*, some influential critics, including George Jean Nathan, Eleanor Clark, and Eric Bentley, saw the essay as a challenge, and it became a starting point for astute critical discussions about dramatic tragedy.

Miller continued to defend Willy Loman as a subject of tragedy in interviews and essays throughout his career, although in the later years he became less insistent on describing the play as classical tragedy. Still, the play attracts unending debates on the definition of tragedy. Following the publication of Miller's essay, and then again in the 1960s, critics evaluated *Death of a Salesman* with regard to the definition of tragedy. For example, in his essay "Confusion and Tragedy: The Failure of Miller's *Salesman*" (1961), Richard J. Foster strongly argued that *Death of a Salesman* is not a tragedy for various reasons, including that the hero, Willy, is "a childish and stupid human being, and his societal role of a salesman is of only very minor consequence" (82). On the other hand, Esther Merle Jackson in her 1963 article "*Death of a Salesman*: Tragic Myth in the Modern Theater," situates the play in the tradition of tragedy, arguing that the play is a myth, a "tragedy of consciousness," and that Willy Loman, as the common man, is also a hero. The debate also caused critics to ponder a larger argument—is tragedy even possible in American theatre, as exemplified in Remy G. Saisselin's essay "Is Tragic Drama Possible in the Twentieth Century" published in *Theater Annual* in 1960.

This debate on tragedy and *Death of a Salesman* continues. Critics have argued the play cannot be considered a tragedy for a variety of reasons, including the absence of divine order, a common hero who never attains self-knowledge or -realization, and language that is more banal than lofty. In 1991, scholar Harold Bloom wrote, "All that Loman actually shares with Lear and Oedipus is aging; there is no other likeness whatsoever. Miller has little understanding of Classical or Shakespearean tragedy; he stems entirely from Ibsen" (1). Some critics have agreed that there is a tragic element or nature in the play, but stop short of declaring it a conventional tragedy. In *The Temptation of Innocence in the Dramas of Arthur Miller*, Terry Otten writes, "Although not 'high tragedy' in Aristotelian terms, *Death of a Salesman* is something more than melodrama or 'low tragedy' in its relation of tragic vision, choice, awareness and consequence" (59).

Social Drama

Miller credited not only classical tragedy as the dominating influence on his work, but also the plays of the Norwegian playwright, Henrik Ibsen, the father of modern drama. Ibsen's social plays, such as *Pillars of Society*, *Ghosts*, and *An Enemy of the People*—in which he articulated the conflict between individual desire and social responsibility—were strong influences on Miller. Many consider Miller to be one of America's great social dramatists and *Death of a Salesman* to be one of the great social dramas of the 20th century. Early critics examined the play as an example of social determinism, focusing on capitalism and the myth of the American Dream as societal forces that shape Willy Loman. In the late 60s and the 1970s particularly, critics addressed social concerns in the plays, in such as Louis Gordon's "*Death of a Salesman*: An Appreciation," which was published in Warren French's *The Forties: Fiction, Poetry, Drama* (1969). In "Family Dreams in *Death of a Salesman*" (1974), Irving Jacobson focuses on the characters' need to transform the impersonal social world into a place of familial warmth.

But is the play a tragedy, a social drama, or a personal story, or all three? Critics still debate these questions. Harold Bloom praises many aspects of the play, but considers Miller to be confused as to his intentions or at least their execution: "A tragedy of familiar love is not primarily a social drama, one concerned with the illusions of society, and Ibsen was careful to keep the two modes unconfused. Miller is richly confused, and never more so than in his depiction of Loman" (1). The genre of *Death of a Salesman* provokes debate, as it defies simple categorization or easy description.

Expressionism and Realism

Death of a Salesman also introduced theatregoers to what Brian Parker in his 1966 essay "Point of View in Arthur Miller's *Death of a Salesman*" describes as a "successful mingling of realism and nonrealism." The set, designed by Jo Mielziner, accentuates the symbolism of the play, and aided the depiction of the movement of time, memory, and Willy's inner thoughts. These expressionistic techniques evoke the emotion of the play, and yet the play is also grounded in realism. Critic Brenda Murphy terms Miller's technique "subjective realism"—a blending of realistic and expressionistic devices to create the impression of what was actually going on inside the protagonist's head. Thus, the audience witnesses both the present and the past as they occur simultaneously—the viewer sees what happens to Willy Loman objectively but also how he subjectively views the events.

By using what he termed "time bends" Miller broke the conventional restraints of time and place in theatre. As Willy Loman becomes more absorbed in the past, the action takes place in his mind, so that the play shifts in setting and time. This expressionistic style was appreciated by many early critics, who often compared him to another popular playwright of his time, the well-known Tennessee Williams. In an article in 1963, "*Death of a Salesman*: Tragic Myth in the Modern Theater," scholar Esther Merle Jackson described the lyricism and emotion of the play, calling the structure "the instrumentation of vision, a complex theater symbol: a union of gesture, word, and music; light, color, and pattern; rhythm and movement." Over time, this style would become typical of theatre and would no longer seem original or experimental, but at the time, audiences were surprised, and many of the early critics focused on the play's set design, movement, and style.

The Characters

The play's protagonist Willy Loman has been the subject of many articles and books, provoking debate and analysis ever since Miller introduced him to American audiences. Willy is self-deluded, believing wholeheartedly in the American Dream of success and wealth. When he fails to achieve this, he commits suicide—yet until the end he never stopped believing in this American Dream. Many early articles in the 1950s, an era when psychoanalysis was a dominant force in American academic psychiatry, viewed Willy through a psychoanalytical lens. For example, the psychoanalyst Daniel E. Schneider analyzed Willy's flashbacks and focused on what he considered a variation of the Oedipus complex in *The Psychoanalyst and the Artist* (1950). Thirty years later, Leonard Moss in *Arthur Miller* (1980) examined the psychological dimensions of Willy Loman and the other characters, and critic Neil Carson also explored Willy's inner life as a psychological drama in *Arthur Miller* (1982). Other critics viewed the play's characters through the lens of social determinism and regarded Willy as the American Everyman. Critic Thomas Porter, for example, views Willy as representative of American salesman in the lower class who has been shaped by forces in society, in *Myth and Modern American Drama* (1969). Willy Loman has been examined as a hero, a symbol, and a sellout. A complex character, open to many interpretations, Willy Loman is the subject of Harold Bloom's book *Willy Loman: Major Lit-*

erary Characters (1990). Though Willy Loman has inspired the majority of criticism and analyses, critics, especially recently, have also focused on Linda, Biff, and, to a lesser degree, Happy. Willy and his son Happy both delude themselves, but Biff, whom Willy sees as an underachiever, refuses to be self-deceived; early on, his father and the dream of success were shattered for Biff. Much of the play's drama revolves around the complicated relationship between Biff and Willy, generating much critical attention. Willy's wife, Linda, also believes in the American Dream, but she is more grounded than her husband. A tough, realistic, complex character, she tries to hold the family together and represents the emotional core.

Revivals

According to critic Brenda Murphy, during 1951–75, to maintain control over the play, Miller did not allow any professional productions to be mounted within one hundred miles of Broadway, and then he authorized a production by the Philadelphia Drama Guild in 1974, directed by George C. Scott. After escalating tension, Scott left the production and Miller took over. Reviews of the play were mixed, many attributing problems in the production to the change of directors and also to the Jo Mielziner–inspired set, which now seemed dated.

Despite Miller's attempt to maintain control, there were many university, community, and professional theatres throughout the country, and amateur productions in the New York area, that produced *Salesman*. According to Brenda Murphy, "Since its premiere, there has never been a time when *Death of a Salesman* was not being performed somewhere in the world" (Murphy, *Miller* 70). Many of these productions have been unique and provocative. For example, in 1951, there was a Yiddish version, which provoked debate about the play's language and its relationship to Jewish-American culture. Years later, in 1972, the first professional production cast with all African Americans brought race and ethnicity to the forefront of critical discussions.

Miller published plays, fiction, and screenplays throughout the 1960s and 1970s, but nothing he wrote ever matched the fame of *Death of a Salesman*. For the most part, during this period, his popularity diminished. Yet, from the time of its premiere, *Death of a Salesman* never stopped being written about and discussed, and revivals always elicited more books, articles, and reviews. In 1975, with George C. Scott as Willy, *Death of a Salesman* opened at the Circle in the Square Theatre and ran for seventy-one performances to mixed reviews, but in the 1980s the play experienced a major revival, both at home and abroad.

The 1979 production of *Death of a Salesman* in London started this major revival. The London show, a spectacular success, helped to secure Miller's reputation. According to Murphy, "Not since *Salesman*'s extraordinary first-night reviews in 1948 had the play or Miller received such universal and such enthusiastic praise" (Murphy, *Miller* 93). Then, in 1983, Miller directed *Death of a Salesman* in Beijing, the People's Republic of China. Many critics were skeptical, claiming that such a quintessentially American play could never be successfully staged in a Communist country, yet the play, making its Chinese-language debut, was a tremendous success, moving its audience to tears. Though the Chinese could not relate to the salesman occupation or to a capitalistic society, the story of Willy's family, his despair, and broken dreams drew them in. Thus, Miller's view of humanity proved to be universal, and the play impressed Chinese audiences the same way it had American audiences.

A year after the Beijing production, in 1984, a revival on Broadway starring Dustin Hoffman as Willy Loman generated more popularity and praise for the play. The production ran for seventy-nine performances at the Broadhurst Theatre, and then reopened in September and ran for another eighty-eight performances. Hoffman created a Willy Loman who was much different from Lee J. Cobb's but was just as memorable. The production won the Tony Award for Best Reproduction. Hoffman also played the lead in the 1985 CBS TV production, which was broadcast to an audience of more than 25 million viewers. The revival was the source of many more articles and reviews, securing the popularity of Miller and the play.

Feminism in the 1980s

In the 1980s, feminist critics began to examine the play. The character of Linda, Willy's wife, had already provoked a variety of critical interpretation since the premiere, and now feminist critics began to focus on her, arguing that Miller denies her a significant role by depicting her as a reflection of a male perspective. Scholar Kay Stanton suggests that women in the play are subjected and exploited in her 1989 article, "Women and the American Dream of *Death of a Salesman*," and Gayle Austin argues in "The Exchange of Women and Male Homosocial Desire in Miller's *Death of a Salesman* and Hellman's *Another Part of the Forest*" (1989), that the play eliminates women as active subjects, restricting them or rendering them absent. Other critics, such as Jan Balakian, who suggests that Miller is accurately depicting postwar America, a culture that subordinated women, have challenged these attacks. Critic Brenda Murphy argues that many critics seem "trapped in the critical cliché that Arthur Miller cannot write about women" ("1999 Revival" 39), and explains that Miller never envisioned Linda as a weak or submissive character.

1999 Broadway Revival

The play's major Broadway revival in 1999 coincided with the celebration of its fiftieth anniversary, inspiring critics to examine it in both familiar and new ways. The 1999 revival, directed by Robert Falls, starred Brian Dennehy as Willy Loman and Elizabeth Franz as Linda, and opened at the Eugene O'Neill Theatre on February 10, 1999. It ran for 274 performances and won the Tony Award for Best Revival of a Play, Best Actor, Best Actress, and Best Direction. This highly praised production sparked a new interest in *Salesman*, presenting new interpretations of the play for a new generation.

Newspaper reviews were overwhelmingly positive, with reviewers praising the acting, especially pointing out Franz's depiction of Linda as a strong, fiery character, instead of the weepy woman often portrayed in productions. Other differences, from previous productions, included a focus on Biff's story as a major crux of the drama, and a concentration on family dynamics instead of social forces. In "The 1999 Revival of *Death of a Salesman*: A Critical Commentary" Brenda Murphy discusses the new issues arising from the revival and analyzes the deemphasizing of Miller's critique of capitalism. She also points out that many reviewers missed the subtleties and felt more comfortable evaluating the play in terms of the familial tensions, "downplaying if not ignoring its sociopolitical meaning" (30). Directors' various interpretations, critics' diverse critical responses, and audience responses reveal the many layers and complexity of *Death of a Salesman*.

Multitude of Viewpoints

Many scholarly books also appeared around or right after the time of the 1999 revival, and overall, the tone toward Miller and *Death of a Salesman* was overwhelmingly positive. Throughout the 1990s and later, critics have examined the play through various lenses, such as feminist, social, and Marxist, and continue to explore and defend the play's relevancy to twenty-first-century America. Matthew Roudané points out the varied popular and intellectual responses to the play reveal it to be "a play to which all—social deconstructionists, Jungians, Marxists, poststructuralists, and so on—react" (24).

The critical interpretations of *Death of a Salesman* are varied and complex, to be sure. For example, John S. Shockley in "*Death of a Salesman* and American Leadership: Life Imitates Art," published in 1994, describes Loman as the "Reagan prototype," arguing that both men were salesmen selling the American Dream of materialistic wealth.

In his book *Communists, Cowboys, and Queers: The Politics of Masculinity in the World of Arthur Miller and Tennessee Williams* (1992), David Savran explores the construction of Cold War masculinity in the male characters of the play. Other critics, such as Normann Helge Nilsen in a 1994 article "From Honors at Dawn to *Death of a Salesman*: Marxism and the Early Plays of Arthur Miller," analyze the influence of Marxism on the play. Heather Cook Callow looks at the masculine and feminist characteristics of the characters in "Masculine and Feminine in *Death of a Salesman*." Other recent critics have focused on Willy's Jewish ethnicity, his midwestern roots, and the complexity of the father-son relationships.

Critics have also focused on the international appeal of Miller, as Enoch Brater reveals in *Arthur Miller's Global Theatre* (2007). Since the premiere of *Death of a Salesman*, the play has been produced all over the world, including in South Africa, Israel, Taiwan, and Korea. Though each production faces challenges in terms of translation and cultural differences, audiences all over the globe have been moved by the play and seem to understand or identify with the plight of Willy Loman.

Lasting Reputation

In the last decade of his life, Miller's reputation solidified as one of America's most important dramatists. He was presented with many awards to recognize the contributions he made to the American stage, including the International Spanish Award, Premio Príncipe de Asturias de las Letras in 2002 and the Jerusalem Prize in 2003. When he died in 2005 at age eighty-nine, friends, critics, fans, mourned him. Many newspaper articles and scholarly articles appeared around this time.

Death of a Salesman was the play that built Miller's reputation, despite his numerous other works, and it has survived fifty years of criticism. Critics have called it sexist, flawed, and sentimental. They have argued that the protagonist is unworthy as a subject of tragedy, criticized the language, and disagreed with Miller's political themes. But critics have also praised its depth and emotional power. Christopher Bigsby suggests that "those who saw this play at the time, and in the over fifty years since that first production, have connected to it less through its comments on a culture wedded to a myth than through characters whose hopes and illusions seem instantly recognisable and archetypal" (Bigsby, *Arthur Miller* 101), and Harold Bloom admits, "I myself resist the drama each time I reread it, because it seems that its language will not hold me, and then I see it on the stage . . . and I yield to it. Miller has caught an American kind of suffering that is also a universal mode of pain" (3). *Death of a Salesman* continues to be well loved by audiences, and provides critics with endless material. More than just an American drama, *Death of a Salesman* is a critique of the universal human situation and continues to hold up as a powerful play, drawing audiences and critics from around the world.

Works Cited

Austin, Gayle. "The Exchange of Women and Male Homosocial Desire in Arthur Miller's *Death of a Salesman* and Lillian Hellman's *Another Part of the Forest*." *Feminist Rereadings of Modern American Drama*. June Schlueter, ed. Rutherford, NJ: Fairleigh Dickinson University Press, 1989.

Balakian, Jan. "Beyond the Male Locker Room: *Death of a Salesman* from a Feminist Perspective." *Approaches to Teaching Miller's Death of a Salesman*. Matthew C. Roudané, ed. New York: MLA, 1995.

Bigsby, Christopher. *Arthur Miller: A Critical Study*. Cambridge: Cambridge University Press, 2005.

____________, ed. *File on Miller*. London: Methuen, 1987.

Bloom, Harold, ed. *Willy Loman: Major Literary Characters*. New York: Chelsea House Press, 1990.

Brater, Enoch. *Arthur Miller's Global Theatre*. Ann Arbor: University of Michigan Press, 2007.

Callow, Heather Cook. "Masculine and Feminine in *Death of a Salesman*." From *"The Salesman Has a Birthday."* Stephen A. Marino, ed. Lanham, MD: University Press of America, 2000: 65–77.

Clark, Eleanor. "Old Glamour, New Gloom." *Partisan Review* 16 (1949): 631–36.

Foster, Richard J. "Confusion and Tragedy: The Failure of Miller's *Salesman*." From *Two Modern American Tragedies: Reviews and Criticism of Death of a*

Salesman and A Streetcar Named Desire. John D. Hurrell, ed. New York: Scribner's, 1961: 82–88.
Jackson, Esther Merle. "*Death of a Salesman*: Tragic Myth in the Modern Theater." *College Language Association Journal* 7 (September 1963): 63–76.
Murphy, Brenda. *Miller: Death of a Salesman*. Cambridge: Cambridge University Press, 1995.
___________. "The 1999 Revival of *Death of a Salesman*." From *"The Salesman Has a Birthday": Essays Celebrating the Fiftieth Anniversary of Arthur Miller's Death of a Salesman*. Stephen A. Marino, ed. Lanham, MD: University Press of America, 2000.
Nilsen, Normann Helge. "From *Honors at Dawn* to *Death of a Salesman*: Marxism and the Early Plays of Arthur Miller." *English Studies: A Journal of English Language and Literature* 75, no. 2 (March 1994): 146–156.
Otten, Terry. *The Temptation of Innocence in the Dramas of Arthur Miller*. Columbia: University of Missouri Press, 2002.
Parker, Brian. "Point of View in Arthur Miller's *Death of a Salesman*." *The University of Toronto Quarterly* 35, no. 2 (January 1966).
Porter, Thomas E. *Myth and Modern American Drama*. Detroit: Wayne State University Press, 1969.
Roudané, Matthew C. "*Death of a Salesman* and the Poetics of Arthur Miller." From *The Cambridge Companion to Arthur Miller*. C.W.E. Bigsby, ed. New York: Cambridge University Press, 1997: 60–85.
Savran, David. *Communists, Cowboys, and Queers: The Politics of Masculinity in the World of Arthur Miller and Tennessee Williams*. Minneapolis: University of Minnesota Press, 1992.
Shockley, John S. "*Death of a Salesman* and American Leadership: Life Imitates Art." *Journal of American Culture* 17, no. 2 (Summer 1994): 49-56.
Stanton, Kay. "Women and the American Dream of *Death of a Salesman*." From *Feminist Rereadings of Modern American Drama*. June Schlueter, ed. Madison, NJ: Fairleigh Dickinson University Press, 1989: 67-102.

CRITICAL READINGS

Focus on Arthur Miller's *Death of a Salesman*: The Wrong Dreams

Chester E. Eisinger

The structural principle of Arthur Miller's *Death of a Salesman* (1949) is the antithesis between dream and reality, and the play concerns competing dreams and the identity crisis. One dream schema is the urban dream of business success. The other is the rural-agrarian dream of open space, a right relation to nature worked out in terms of the garden concept. In the play, dream is also self-delusion, or the serious entertainment of aspirations impossible of fulfillment because they are based on false conceptions of one's talents and capacities. In such a case, reality shatters dream. And out of such misapprehensions of one's potential for achievement, of possibilities and opportunities, arises the identity crisis. Reality falls short of the dream in part because man chooses the wrong dream. And man chooses the wrong dream because he does not know himself. Willy Loman is lost because he does not know who he is. His son Biff is lost through most of the play, but he finds himself; he achieves a sense of personal dignity and comes to understand his rightful place in society.

The stage directions at the beginning of the play tell us that *Death of a Salesman* is about dreams. An air of the dream clings to Willy's house. Willy is a man of massive dreams and turbulent longings. What are the dreams Miller calls upon in the play? They are conceptions as old as America. The business-urban-success dream begins with the Puritans' doctrine of the calling, which was a codification of the Protestant ethic, designed for an essentially mobile middle-class people whose primary interest was in the economics of trade and production. Franklin's secularization of the Protestant ethic made it available to every business-industrial community in the country. And Franklin fulfilled in his own life the middle-class dream of the shopkeeper whose shop came to keep him; he rose in wealth and eminence through the application of the middle-class virtues of thrift, industry, and prudence which had passed to Poor Richard by way of Puritan treatises like Cotton Mather's *Essays to Do Good* and Defoe's *Essay upon Projects*. The apotheosis of worldly success through business and industry accords with the Hamiltonian view of the national destiny and reached its highest pinnacle after the Civil War under the sanction of individualism. The businessman, living in accordance with Franklin's worldly ethic, was a viable American hero until the collapse of the economy in 1929.

The rural-agrarian dream begins with the freehold tenure policies of the Puritans who made land freely available to settlers from the Old World, with all the economic and moral implications inherent in the state of yeomanry. In the eighteenth century, Jefferson was the great spokesman for the agrarian dream and Crèvecoeur its poet. Between them they held forth a vision of a nation of independent yeoman farmers who, in the Lockean tradition, had a natural right to the land. The bright idea of property meant that the farmer, owning his land, could guarantee his own economic well-being, and indeed in fertile America achieve that cornucopia-like abundance that underlies the serenity of such versions of rural well-being as "Snow-Bound" (1866). Beholden to no man, the farmer was the mainstay of democracy, enjoying a state of independence that the factory worker, dependent for his job and his bread upon an employer, could not afford. Farmers were the chosen people of God because they worked under His benevolent gaze, out in the open where they could establish a right relationship with His natural world. Their occupation guaranteed their moral, spiritual, and physical health. Closely associated with this vision is the ideal of craftsmanship, the notion that a man must be able to work with his hands and that such work is not only real but superior to the nonproductive work of thinking or selling. This dream survived in the slogan that the farmer was the backbone of the nation, and it accounts for the often frenzied but futile effort today to save the family-size farm as though it were a national asset. It accounts in part for the disproportionate political power wielded by rural areas in state and national governments up until very recent years. It survived in literature in fiction like Willa Cather's "Neighbor Rosicky" (1932) and John Steinbeck's *The Grapes of Wrath* (1939) and in a cultural movement like Southern agrarianism, which set forth its principles in *I'll Take My Stand* (1930).

In *Death of a Salesman* Miller gives us various versions of the urban-business-success dream. Dave Singleton and Charley represent its ideal form. In Willy's sentimentalized view, Singleton was the eighty-four-year-old drummer who in twenty or thirty different cities used to go to his hotel room, put on his green velvet slippers, and sell his line simply by telephoning buyers. He was a model for Willy, because he showed that a salesman could be remembered, loved, and helped in many different places in the country. Success, esteem, and affection are all embodied in Dave, and these are goals that Willy wanted to achieve. Charley is, apparently, a successful businessman who is giving Willy enough money to live on, who offers Willy a job in an effort to shore up Willy's self-respect, and who has in the past counseled maturity and sanity in Willy's life. Nothing is ideal about this character, except that without dreaming he has achieved the terms of the business dream, a good man who has found a stable way of life and financial security and whose son, a source of pride to him, has grown up to practice law before the United States Supreme Court. Although Willy has been jealous of Charley and irrationally impatient of him, Charley has remained Willy's friend and professes to understand what he was. He explains Willy to Biff at the end of the play, after Biff has said that Willy never knew who he was: "Nobody dast blame this man. You don't understand: Willy was a salesman. And for a salesman, there is no rock bottom to the life. He don't put a bolt to a nut, he don't tell you the law or give you medicine. He's a man way out there in the blue, riding on a smile and a shoeshine. And when they start not smiling back—that's an earthquake. And then you get yourself a couple of spots on your hat, and you're finished. Nobody dast blame this man. A salesman is got to dream, boy. It comes with the territory." This is an incongruous speech for a practical man like Charley to make, summoning up, as it does, the ineffable and intangible mystique of salesmanship. It serves well enough as an epitaph, but it carries little conviction, so obviously is it a romanticized conception of the salesman.

Willy Loman himself gives us the corrupted version of the urban-business-success dream, for which Uncle Ben and Howard, Willy's boss, are the hard and compelling symbols. At the heart of this dream in Willy's factitious rendering of it is the cult of personality. It is necessary to make a good appearance and to be well-liked. Appearance is a key concept, for a salesman must appear to be more than he is: better liked, more successful, more optimistic, more necessary to the life of his firm. Then the police will protect his car when it is parked on the streets of any New England town, and the doors to the buyers' offices will swing open when he appears. Techniques of personality and human manipulation replace substantive contributions, and the salesman wins friends and influences people after the pattern that Dale Carnegie has formulated, and he exercises charm in the manner of some model drawn from the films. The mythic version of the success dream is Uncle Ben's: "When I was seventeen I walked into the jungle, and when I was twenty-one I walked out. And by God I was rich." The air of exoticism and terror that clings to Ben's achievement rests on the same sense of mystery that Conrad (more effectively) evokes in *Heart of Darkness* (1899). Mystery surrounds the getting of money, a secret is involved which Ben can explain only cryptically and Willy cannot guess. Violence and trickery are necessary, as Ben shows when he spars playfully with Biff. Suddenly he is standing over the boy with the point of his umbrella at Biff's eye: "Never fight fair with a stranger, boy," he says. "You'll never get out of the jungle that way." Finally, Howard gives us the dehumanized version of the dream, for he shows us the heartlessness of the business ethic. When Willy can no longer make money for the firm, Howard fires him, despite his long years of service, because "everybody's gotta pull his own weight" and "you gotta admit, business is business."

Development of the rural-agrarian dream begins in the first paragraph of the stage directions; Miller tells us that a melody is heard played on a flute, "telling of grass and trees and the horizon." Music of the flute opens and closes the play; it is Willy's music and it attaches him at once to growing things and to the out-of-doors. Willy owns a single-dwelling house in the city. The house itself is marginally attached to the rural-agrarian dream, affording the family a place of its own and a sense of belonging, of social status and pride. Willy's hope had been for a home shaded by magnificent elm trees, graced by a lawn and a garden. This ambience for his house is what really attaches Willy to the out-of-doors. It is Willy's effort to create a fruitful relationship with the world of nature by which he would satisfy aesthetic and spiritual needs; the garden will serve the primitive urge to grow his own food. So deeply powerful is Willy's impulse to buy seeds and plant a garden that he follows it, almost without volition, at the most desperate hour of his need—when he has been fired from his job and when his sons have deserted him. Or it might be said that he has recourse to sowing his garden, this ancient ritual by which man sustains himself, when all else has failed him. Miller gives us that painful scene in which Willy wanders out in his yard at night, trying to plant by flashlight.

Further, Willy is a self-reliant man who can work with his hands. He can build his own concrete porch or put up his own ceiling. He believes that a man who cannot handle tools is not a man. This notion of masculinity is perhaps related to the Loman family tradition of westering—Willy's father took him as far west as South Dakota, at least, and Ben had gone to Alaska. This western orientation has encouraged the freedom and individualism of Willy's life style, a style that leads him to resist the confining demands of the city. He has inherited from his father that large optimism characteristic of the frontier. These details suggest rather than constitute a pattern of rural-agrarian aspiration both in their positive identification with elements of this dream and in their anti-urbanism.

The predictable difficulty is that the city and business blight the fulfillment of Willy's rural-agrarian dream. Ironically, he comes fully to own the little house, which is like the homestead, only on the day he is buried, when the last payment on the mortgage is finally made. It was not his, and more, it is alien in the city, surrounded and intimidated by the huge structures around it. These shut off air and light, so that no grass, not even carrots, will grow. Builders have chopped down the elm trees. The fragrance of peonies and daffodils, once so intoxicating in the spring, is now only a memory. The independence and virility of life beyond the horizon becomes, in the city, a "measly manner of existence," as Biff says: "To get on that subway on the hot morning in summer. To devote your whole life to keeping stock, or making phone calls, or selling or buying. To suffer fifty weeks of the year for the sake of a two-week vacation, when all you really desire is to be outdoors, with your shirt off. And always to have to get ahead of the next fella." The city and the pursuit of success enforce a way of life that is essentially corrupting, distorting the human personality. All the Loman men have been the victims of such distortion.

Under the pressure to succeed in business, the appearance of things is always more important than the reality, and the truth about one's accomplishments is never impressive enough; it is, consequently, necessary to delude everyone, even oneself, so often that lying becomes the habitual mode of discourse and hypocrisy the accepted moral stance. Or so Willy thinks. In the perverted and desperate affirmation of his optimism, he assures himself and Linda, his wife, that he is vital to his firm in New England. He exaggerates the volume of his sales; actually, he is not selling enough to justify his continued employment; he had always teetered on the thin edge of failure. He lies to himself and others about Biff's business accomplishments, also. The value scheme induced by this pressure pervades Willy's life. He sanctions Biff's thefts and his cheating at school, because these are the prerogatives of the popular schoolboy athlete and leader. He denigrates the need for learning in the name of a higher good, personality.

Willy carries on a sordid adultery, a painfully conventional affair between the traveling salesman and the other woman. He is driven into this relationship because of his own inadequacies and insecurities. He is lonely on the road, and his loneliness is intensified by his fear of business failure. When he fails to measure up to the model which he believes society to have constructed and which he accepts—the American businessman as rugged, independent, and successful—then he seeks comfort in his sordid little sin and wrecks his sentimental hope for familial bliss.

The erosion of Willy's character under the pressure to succeed eats away the moral center of the Loman family. In their home the two sons breathe in the easy morality of their father. The air there is polluted by the empty optimism and the phony maxims of the business ethic that Willy mindlessly repeats. This kind of home training makes Biff a thief and drives Happy to a refuge in easy sensualism and self-aggrandizing lies. The boys hold menial jobs but tell others and believe themselves that they are persons of consequence in the business world. So thoroughly has Willy indoctrinated them with dreams of success that they are victims of illusions. They work up totally impossible schemes for making money: an escape to the great West where they will become ranchers or the selling of sporting goods through the formation of rival athletic teams that will play each other throughout the country. These schemes are infantile; Willy's corruption prevents his sons from achieving a mature manhood.

Biff is aware of the corruption wrought in him by the impact of the business-success dream on the family. That corruption inhibits his quest for adulthood, which is related to his quest for identity. In the course of the play, he succeeds in stripping himself of illusion and self-deception, in coming to a knowledge of who he is and of coming to terms with that person. When he recognizes the total compulsion to evaluate himself, an act Miller speaks of in commenting on his own play, he provides the contrapuntal release to life that we must set over against Willy's defeat in suicide.

The crucial event that leads to Biff's self-knowledge is his visit to his former employer, Bill Oliver, to borrow money. The scheme is childish; Biff had been a shipping clerk in Oliver's business and had stolen a carton of basketballs from the firm, hardly the basis on which to ask for a ten thousand dollar loan. Oliver refuses Biff, and the latter then takes a pen from Oliver's desk. In one sense the theft is the act of a frustrated and humiliated man. In another it is simply further evidence of Biff's tendency toward habitual stealing. But why does he take a pen? A third way of regarding this act is to see the pen as a phallic symbol and Biff's theft of it his unconscious effort to become a man. Oliver's pen may be regarded as Oliver's surrogate penis. To possess the pen is to have at one's command the potency of Oliver, a successful man. Biff hopes in this theft to revive a version of himself as the man he once was: football hero, idol and lover of high school girls, leader of the neighborhood gang. He hopes to become the man his father wished him to be: a man in a man's world, a business success, a man with status. Because he is lost and impotent, Biff needs to re-man himself, and he tries now to do it in the image that his father and his own past have made available to him. His athletic glory has been gone for a long time; Biff is thirty-four when he commits this theft. He has lost his confidence in the pursuit of women. He has no recognizable place in the economic world. He is not only a failure, alienated from the conventional world of business; he is also a boy because he has no part in this world. He regards himself this way, and on separate occasions his father and his mother say he is like a boy. He seizes the pen, the phallus of a successful man, to throw off boyhood and assert manhood.

If Biff's effort had been successful, he would have become the man his sensual brother and his misguided father would have admired. But he fails. As he runs down the stairs of the office building with the pen, he realizes that he cannot claim his manhood in any synthetic way. The revelation comes to him that he can be a man only under the open sky, working with his hands. He cannot and need not rely on a mere symbol of manhood. This conviction transcends the phallic value of the pen and sustains Biff in his honest self-knowledge at the end of the play.

Nothing saves Willy. To the end he is guided by the ethics of opportunism that mark the corrupt pursuit of business success. He has been contemplating suicide throughout the play. When his affairs reach their apparent nadir, he seems to hear the voice of Ben counseling him to kill himself in such a way that his insurance money will go to Biff. He believes that he is sacrificing himself so that Biff may have twenty thousand dollars to begin his career. He goes to his death confident in Biff's love, but still believing in Biff's capacity to succeed in business. He misjudges his son as surely as he misjudges himself. Biff passes judgment on him at the grave: "He had the wrong dreams. All, all, wrong."

The culture, as we have seen, presented Willy with two dreams, and it thereby imposed upon him the burden of choice. A wise man might have selected the kind of life and promising fulfillment of his needs and aspirations appropriate to his capacities. But Willy is a confused and inadequate man. He never achieves a sense of personal dignity and of his rightful place in society because, not knowing who he is, he cannot make the right choices. The theme of the play, then, seems to be that every man must come to know himself or he is lost. Biff succeeds in the quest for self-knowledge but Willy fails.

Yet this statement of the meaning of the play may be too simple, for it rests on the assumption that if Willy, out of an acute understanding of his character, had chosen the rural-agrarian dream, he would have fulfilled himself and achieved the ideals of family and home that he wanted. This assumption must derive from Miller's uncritical acceptance of the myth of the garden. The culture has a strong emotional, really sentimental, attachment to this myth, an attraction which is in part a product of our nostalgia for primitivistic innocence. And we have, complementarily, a long history of anti-urbanism, as *The Intellectual Versus the City* by Morton and Lucia White demonstrates. But contemporary American culture does not honor the two dreams equally as viable alternatives. Our genius is technological and industrial. The processes that flow from these characteristics have transformed the farm and rendered the rural-agrarian dream obsolete.

Even in the play, there are intimations to be drawn from Biff's career that the satisfactions of the rural life may be limited. Miller has revealed the presence of two dreams in American culture, but it is not at all clear that he has given Willy a genuine choice. Instead he seems to be saying that the dichotomy in the culture in which the business-success dream is corrupt or corrupting and the rural-agrarian dream pure and life-giving is pregnant with paradox, because it is only the corrupt dream that we are expected to follow seriously. It is Willy as salesman whom Charley honors at the graveside and whom Linda accepts. Nothing is wrong with Willy as salesman except that he fails, and much that is wrong with Willy stems from the fact that he does fail. In the liberal tradition we are predisposed to regard Willy as the victim of business—this is the case, I suspect, with reader and author alike. Yet Miller is not uniformly hostile to business: Charley is a decent and patient man who has succeeded in business. To be sure, Willy is victimized by Howard, a gadget-minded and heartless businessman who is immune to appeals based on loyalty and long service, which constitute the refuge of a man who dares not make a case based on merit. But Howard is no more typical or symbolic than Charley.

The play, then, romanticizes the rural-agrarian dream but does not make it genuinely available to Willy. Miller seems to use this dream merely to give himself an opportunity for sentimentality. The play is ambiguous in its attitude toward the business-success dream, but does not certainly condemn it. It is legitimate to ask where Miller is going. And the answer is that he has written a confused play because he has been unwilling or unable to commit himself to a firm position with respect to American culture. Miller prepares us for a stock response—relief in escape to the West and the farm; firm satisfaction in the condemnation of the tawdry business ethic—and then denies us the fulfillment of our expectations. The play, makes, finally, no judgment on America, although Miller seems always on the verge of one, of telling us that America is a nightmare, a cause of and a home for tragedy. But Willy is not a tragic hero; he is a foolish and ineffectual man for whom we feel pity. We cannot equate his failure with America's.

From *American Dreams, American Nightmares*, ed. David Madden (Carbondale, IL: Southern Illinois University Press, 1970): 165-174. Copyright © 1970 by David Madden. Reprinted by permission of David Madden.

Family Dreams in *Death of a Salesman*

Irving Jacobson

One critic, perhaps facetiously, has called *Death of a Salesman*[1] a "tragedy for extroverts."[2] This differentiates Willy Loman from a dramatic tradition of introspective figures who, like Shakespeare's Hamlet or Milton's Samson, confront their situations in a profound social and metaphysical solitude. By contrast, a protagonist who cannot be alone, who cannot summon the intelligence and strength to scrutinize his condition and come to some understanding of it—whatever agony it may cost him—seems disqualified for the tragic stature literature can bestow. With reference to Aristotelian standards, Sheila Huftel has remarked that Loman fell only from "an imagined height."[3] Indeed, to an extent his drama represents merely the collapse of a Philistine. Yet if one does not look upon Loman with a scowl of condemnation for his adherence to values he barely understands, for his anti-intellectualism, his contradictions, his insensitivities and petty cruelties, he does not because the fall from a height only imagined is nevertheless a fall. Loman is not, as critics have too facilely stated, a modern Everyman but an anomaly, a bourgeois romantic, an odd synthesis of Joe and Chris Keller, or of Everyman and Faust. He moves one not with his mediocrity and failure but with the frustrated energies of his outreach beyond mediocrity and failure toward a relationship to society constantly denied him.

Loman wants success, but the meaning of that need extends beyond the accumulation of wealth, security, goods, and status. As Arthur Miller said in an interview, "The trouble with Willy Loman is that he has tremendously powerful ideas."[4] But he yearns toward them more than he lives by them. What Loman wants, and what success means in *Death of a Salesman*, is intimately related to his own, and the playwright's, sense of the family. Family dreams extend backward in time to interpret the past, reach forward in time to project images of the future, and pressure reality in the present to conform to memory and imagination. These "ideals," these dreams, can be examined in terms of four variables: transformation, prominence, synthesis, and unity.

I

Robert Hogan has noted that much of Miller's work developed from the image of man "struggling to be at one with society."[5] Miller elucidates the nature of this struggle in "The Family in Modern Drama," where he finds all great drama to be concerned with some aspect of a single problem: "How may a man make of the outside world a home?" What does he need to do, to change within himself or in the external world, if he is to find "the safety, the surroundings of love, the ease of soul, the sense of identity and honor which, evidently, all men have connected in their memories with the idea of family?"[6] This concern remains a constant in Miller's work. He is quoted in *Psychology and Arthur Miller* by Richard I. Evans as observing that his own sense of drama resides in the emotional tension within a person drawn to the past in order to orient himself to the present. His characters feel displaced from what they should be, even from what they "really" are.[7] Although Miller does not make explicit reference here to childhood and the family, the sense of radical loss and the passionate need to reattain some previous and necessary state seem fundamentally the same as in "The Family in Modern Drama."

With the success of *All My Sons*, wrote Miller, "It suddenly seemed that the audience was a mass of blood relations and I sensed a warmth in the world that was not there before."[8] He attributed success to the power to transform a relatively impersonal social world into a home that offered familial warmth. His next play, probably the most stunning portrayal of failure in the American theatre, dramatized a man's inability to achieve this transformation. Nothing Loman says or does can evoke that "warmth in the world." Instead, society responds to him with an indifference that can only seem cruel in juxtaposition to the hopes he carries with him even to the point of death.

Loman articulates his need in appealing to his employer with an image of the past, a Golden Age: "In those days there was personality in it, Howard. There was respect, and comradeship, and gratitude in it. Today it's all cut and dried, and there's no chance for bringing friendship to bear—or personality" (pp. 180–181). Earlier Miller characters found these values outside the business world: Gus in the Merchant Marine, in *The Story of Gus*;[9] Chris Keller in the Army, in *All My Sons*.[10] Loman once found them in having coffee with the mayor of Providence, in being recognized in places like Slattery's, Filene's, and the Hub, and by enjoying such good standing with New England policemen that he could park his car anywhere he liked without getting a ticket. His sense of self-value, then, depended upon the response of others. Such gestures of recognition provided signals that society, for a period in his life, was a home for him, one where he might hope to make his sons as happily at ease as he.

Prominence, whether gained through wealth, business associations, or public esteem, appeared to be the major catalyst in turning the world's indifference into warmth and admiration. Loman expressed awe at the prominence of Thomas Edison, B. F. Goodrich, and Frank Wagner, but the most compelling images of success were Ben, Dave Singleman, and Biff. The entrepreneur, the renowned salesman, and the star high school athlete represented possibilities in life to which Loman could not attain. They were surrounded men. At school, Biff was surrounded by admiring classmates and, at the Ebbets Field game, by cheering crowds and brilliant sunlight. At the peak of his career and at the end of his life, Singleman was surrounded by the affection of customers and fellow salesmen.

Ben, however, was surrounded by the mystery and power of his enterprising audacity. He represented a way of being at home in the world that differed from Miller's statement about the public response to *All My Sons* and from the attainments of other successful characters in *Death of a Salesman*. The world was a home for Ben not by the affection he won from it but by the command of his wealth, power, and mobility. In the world of finance he was as much a pioneer, a "great and wild-hearted man," as his father. His imagination and life extended as easily to Alaska, South Dakota, and Africa as to New York. Apparently indifferent to social relationships, he needed neither the human warmth of the family nor society's positive response. His sphere of action related to things and quantities rather than people; even his seven sons seemed more like commodities than members of a family. Thereby the play implies, not without irony, Ben was more capable of becoming at ease in the world than Willy Loman, whose refusal to join with his brother, a choice rooted in an ethic oriented to the family and to society, signaled his financial, social and family failures.

The world became a home for Dave Singleman in an opposite fashion. Like Ben, he enjoyed wealth, power and mobility; but these were more entirely enmeshed within social relationships. The nature and extent of his prominence was succinctly illustrated in his ability to sit in a hotel room and make his living by phone, comfortably attired in the luxury of green velvet slippers. This image has had a decisive power in Loman's life:

> And when I saw that, I realized that selling was the greatest career a man could want. 'Cause what could be more satisfying than to be able to go, at the age of eighty-four, into twenty or thirty different cities, and pick up a phone, and be remembered and loved and helped by so many different people?
>
> (p. 180)

Unlike Ben, Singleman achieved a success that presented him with a world of loyalty, aid, and love. His scope of action was spatially more limited in being national rather than international; but response to him was more personal. For Loman, the surest indication of public love for Singleman is that when he died the "death of a salesman" in the smoking car of a train on the way to Boston, people travelled from all over the country to attend his funeral. In juxtaposition to Loman's funeral in the "Requiem" of the play, this reveals the extent to which Singleman's prominence granted him a home in society that Loman cannot achieve. Singleman mastered his society not through the demonic qualities one perceives in Ben but through a synthesis of man's social and economic impulses.

The world became a home for Biff Loman when, as an athlete, he evoked affection and admiration from the people around him. His life seemed full of promise, with a choice of three college scholarships to signify the abundance of future success life can offer the already successful. When he became captain of the football team, a crowd of girls surrounded him after classes, and girls paid for him on dates. His friends waited for him after school, not knowing how to occupy themselves until he arrived to organize them into sweeping out the furnace and hanging up his mother's laundry. As contrasted with his friend Bernard, who was only "liked," Biff was "well-liked," which seemed to grant him, in Loman's view, certain allowances that could not be bestowed upon those who received less fervent popular esteem. At the all-star Ebbets Field game he was the tallest player, dressed in gold with the sun all around him while the crowd shouted "Loman, Loman, Loman!" (p. 171), so that his father sensed him raised beyond the level of the merely human by the extent of his prominence among others.

Prominence for Ben, Singleman, and Biff has an impersonal quality that contradicts Loman's repeated insistence upon the value of personality and what he calls "personal attractiveness." His heroes tend to stand among yet above other people. He remarks that at the Ebbets Field game Biff seemed like "Hercules—something like that" (p. 171), and his accounts of Ben's being "success incarnate" have more the tone of hagiography than family anecdote. For Loman these figures exist less as individuals with actual characters, talents, and problems than as mythological projections of his own needs and his society's values. This has two kinds of consequences for his life. For one, the means for achieving success remain a mystery to him. Although he perceives Ben as a sign that "The greatest things can happen!" he can never discover how those things happen. When he asks Ben how to succeed he receives not an answer but an incantatory formula: "When I was seventeen I walked into the jungle, and when I was twenty-one I walked out. And by God I was rich" (p. 157). Ben proves willing to use violence when it is necessary or useful, and he boasts of his mnemonic powers; but these cannot lead Loman to understand how Ben became wealthy, much less how anyone else might. Another consequence of Loman's mythological projection is that characters without strikingly luminous qualities, such as Charley or Linda, cannot move Loman deeply enough to help him. Charley's aid and friendship represent the only instance where someone in society does form something like a family tie with him. Yet Charley can offer only help, not promise; realistic advice, not transformation. He has succeeded in business, but no aura of magic power surrounds him or his advice.

The consequences of failing to attain prominence and to transform society into a home are loneliness, frustration, and ultimately despair. Because Loman needs gratification to take a social form, his life is crushed by indifference, criticism, rejection, and abandonment. In his scene with Howard Wagner he appeals to quasi-familial ties in the past—"I was with the firm when your father used to carry you in here in his arms" (p. 179)—but the reality that "business is business" and not a family makes his appeal irrelevant. At the same time that Wagner's act corresponds, figuratively, to rejection by a son, it also records a final loss of hope that family ties can exist on a social level. But, still unable to accept failure in his struggle to be at one with society, Loman prefers death with the illusion of transformation to life without it.

II

The assumption that prominence brings affection and privilege frequently has led the Lomans to boast or lie about themselves. Signs of prominence, what Loman and Happy refer to as "the old humor, the old confidence" (p. 137), can be used as a facade. Loman returns from a business trip exclaiming, "I'm tellin' you, I was sellin' thousands and thousands, but I had to come home" (p. 147). His fabrications create so extreme a polarization with his incapacities that an acceptance of failure—his own or Biff's—becomes impossible. Happy proves more calculating in the scene at Frank's Chop House, where he presents himself and his brother with false, glossy images for the sake of seducing women.

Happy's need to command attention comprises a persistent if minor note throughout the play. He admires and envies the merchandise manager—"when he walks into the store the waves part in front of him. That's fifty-two thousand dollars a year coming through the revolving door. . . ." (p. 140). The distorted reference to the Moses myth signifies the extent to which monetary values have absorbed religious emotions. When he asserts that he can become "number one man," Happy has the merchandise manager in mind; and this represents a decayed ideal, one of mere wealth and power, with neither Ben's daring nor Singleman's social prominence. Happy's need to be "number one" has another significance also, for he has never been the sole focus of his father's attention, always a poor second to Biff. He seems always to be merely present in the Loman household, an adjunct. At several points he makes an open bid for his father's attention, asking whether Loman has noticed how much weight he has lost; but his father never answers. As an adult, Happy envies the positions of those above him while achieving an underhanded sort of prominence by taking bribes and seducing "gorgeous creatures," including the fiancees of company executives. Although he describes himself as having "an overdeveloped sense of competition," he cannot compete on an appropriate level but instead does so sexually, or takes refuge in an athletic past, claiming he can outbox anyone in the office. He claims not really to want these forms of pseudo-prominence; but as much as his brother, though in a different form, Happy becomes a thief, stealing women for transient pleasure and stealing the illusion of prominence with lies.

Unlike his father and brother, Biff does not emulate the images of prominent men but rejects the years he has spent riding subways, keeping stock, buying and selling, feeling it ridiculous to spend a year in suffering for the sake of a two-week vacation. He surrenders his opportunities for a prominent adulthood by refusing to repeat a mathematics course after he has found his father with a woman in a Boston hotel room. Yet his need for the illusion of prominence continues with his repeated acts of petty theft—repetitions, in essence, of behavior his father once applauded as "initiative." As an adult he has the same problem as the young David Frieber in *The Man Who Had All the Luck*:[11] "I don't know what the future is. I don't know—what I'm supposed to want" (p. 138). However gratifying his life of simple physicality on ranches in the West, he has thought himself less than mature—"I'm like a boy" (p. 139)—and has found himself periodically returning home with a sense of incompletion and waste. Only the intense pressure applied by his father, and his experience of failure and theft in Bill Oliver's office, reconciles him in a final sense to his life of simple work, food, and leisure without expectations of prominence.

Insisting that it is not a matter of what you do but "who you know and the smile on your face!" Loman optimistically locates the secret of success in "contacts" and "personal attractiveness," expectant that "a man can end with diamonds here on the basis of being liked!" (p. 184). Yet even the means of becoming "liked" evade him, as in his contradictory advice to Biff:

> Be quiet, fine, and serious. Everybody likes a kidder, but nobody lends him money.
>
> (p. 168)

> Walk in with a big laugh. Don't look worried. Start off with a couple of your good stories to liven things up.
>
> (p. 169)

The inconspicuous diligence of a youth like Bernard is dismissed as "anemic." Instead of reconciling himself to failure in business skills,

Loman blames the responses of others: people do not "take" to him, they pass him by, find him too fat, poorly dressed, foolish, a "walrus" (p. 149). Under stress, his needs demand vicarious gratification through the success of his sons. This becomes evident in his response to an insult from his brother:

> BEN: Great inventor, Father. With one gadget he made more in a week than a man like you could make in a lifetime.
>
> WILLY: That's just the way I'm bringing them up, Ben—rugged, well-liked, all around.
>
> (p. 157)

Because he habitually deflects consciousness of his own failure by focusing attention on his sons, Loman cannot accept Biff's way of life in the West on its own terms but tries to reabsorb him into a business-oriented culture. Unable to accomplish this, he perceives his life as an empty, infertile waste. "Nothing's planted. I don't have a thing in the ground" (p. 209).

III

Blurring distinctions, Loman tends to view prominence and transformation as identical, and this habit of mind prevents him from enjoying the skills he has and appreciating the supportive elements within his own family. Loman neglects the distinctions between different people, values and methods, attempting through sheer force of hope to reconcile the disparate. His decision not to join Ben in business is rooted in his assertion that the values of Ben can be synthesized with those of Dave Singleman, and this ignores the contrast Ben points out between social gestures and tangible commodities. He also ignores the differences between criminality and initiative, encouraging his sons to steal, so that the front stoop of the Loman house, which Biff claims to contain “more of him” than his career as a salesman, is built with stolen materials.

Happy and Biff formulate schemes to synthesize values, hoping to attain prominence and to reunite as brothers. Their short-lived dream of a Loman ranch in the West attempts to synthesize sports and commercialism, the pastoral and the urban, playfulness and seriousness, youth and adulthood. They imagine that their partnership will regain them the public attention they enjoyed in high school. Biff’s pastoral values reflect his father, who bewails the loss of open air and space, the overcrowded conditions of city life, and the absence of flowers almost as often as he condemns his son for becoming a farmhand. On a Loman ranch, Biff could not only do the kind of work he liked but also “be something.” Yet a brief but revealing bit of dialogue exposes the rapid death of this dream:

> BIFF: Hap, the trouble is we weren’t brought up to grub for money. I don’t know how to do it.
>
> HAPPY: Neither can I!
>
> BIFF: Then let’s go!
>
> HAPPY: The only thing is—what can you make out there?
>
> (p. 140)

The synthesis they try to create collapses under the weight of a single question. Happy’s later plan for a Loman line of sporting goods would also give them an opportunity to work together. “And the beauty of it is, Biff, it wouldn’t be like a business,” Happy exclaims, “We’d be out playin’ ball again” (p. 168). But this dream of synthesis, like that of a Loman ranch, founders upon the need for money.

The ultimate attempt at synthesis in the play is Loman’s suicide. Leonard Moss has noted that he chooses death “not simply as an escape from shame but as a last attempt to re-establish his own self-confidence and his family’s integrity.”[12] The insurance money makes it seem possible to synthesize the values of Ben and Singleman. For by entering the dark, unknown "jungle" of death Loman might bring out tangible wealth, "like diamonds," thus becoming as much an adventurer as Ben but within the skyscraper world of New York. He imagines himself then having a funeral as massive as Singleman's, one that would leave Biff "thunderstruck." Thus in a single act Loman hopes to achieve transformation, prominence, synthesis, and his lost unity with Biff.

IV

Scattered images of family unity in *Death of a Salesman* evoke the sense of loss: "All I remember is a man with a big beard, and I was in Mama's lap, sitting around a fire, and some kind of high music" (p. 157). Loman's very early family life remains the vaguest of memories, symbolized by the high-pitched sound of the flute which, as Edward Murray has noted, acts as an "auditory binder" in the play.[13] It juxtaposes Loman's pastoral longings for the past with the overbearing actualities of the city towering around him. Also, Loman's image contrasts the quiet repose of the past with the restlessness that characterizes the rest of his life. Another passage evoking an image of lost family unity captures his relationship with the young Biff, when life was "so full of light, and comradeship" (p. 213).

Loman wants to feel a unity of generations linking his father and Ben with him and his sons. He appeals to Ben: "You're just what I need, Ben, because I—I have a fine position here, but I—well, Dad left when I was such a baby, and I never had a chance to talk to him and I still feel—kind of temporary about myself" (p. 159). Yet the need for family unity is juxtaposed against the reality of family disintegration. Loman's father abandons his family, and Ben leaves soon afterward. Loman violates the unity of his family with the woman in Boston, not only by sexual infidelity but by giving her the stockings that should go to Linda. Biff leaves home because of his discovery, and Happy leaves to set up his own apartment and enjoy his women. Sex proves a powerfully divisive force among the Lomans, separating parents from each other and parents from sons. Happy abandons his father in another way, by merely sending him away to Florida when Loman's emotional breakdown becomes embarrassingly visible. He cannot respond sympathetically to his father's problems. "No, that's not my father," he dismissively remarks in the restaurant scene, "He's just a guy" (p. 205).

Linda remained loyal, but her constancy cannot help Loman. She can play no significant role in her husband's dreams; and although she proves occasionally capable of dramatic outbursts, she lacks the imagination and strength to hold her family together or to help Loman define a new life without grandiose hopes for Biff. Critics have attacked her as "profoundly unsatisfactory" as a character,[14] "not in the least sexually interesting,"[15] and a symbol of the "cash-payment fixation."[16] But given Loman's inability to accept disagreement from his sons or Charley, it is hard to suppose that he would tolerate a less acquiescent wife. He calls her "my foundation and my support," but her stability cannot prevent his collapse.

In "The Family as a Psychosocial Organization," Robert D. Hess and Gerald Handel have noted that "The family's life together is an endless process of movement in and around consensual understanding, from attachment to conflict and withdrawal—and over again. Separateness and connectedness are the underlying conditions of a family's life, and its common task is to give form to both."[17] In *Death of a Salesman*, beginning the process "over again" becomes impossible. The present action of the play forces an explosive reunion, bringing members of the family together in order to make their separateness explicit and irrevocable. This pattern typifies Arthur Miller's work; it occurs in *All My Sons*; it characterizes *After the Fall*,[18] and it encompasses most of *The Price*.[19] Attempts to recreate family unity—like Ben's offer of partnership, Biff's return home, or the brothers' schemes to go into business together—have the dual effect of illuminating areas of conflict and forever sealing family members off from one another. The peripatetic big dinner scene toward the end of the play, then, presents a cacophony of dissonant motives; and the centripetal forces of their separate lives prove stronger than the need for unity that brought the Lomans together. Torn between Happy's callous ability to let him continue living in illusion and Biff's cruel but necessary demand for honesty, Loman yields to a hope forged in despair: that Biff might finally recant and become "magnificent" with the insurance money. But his death changes nothing; it implies instead that a man's frenetic attempt to make the world a home can defeat the viability of his private home, even cost him his life.

From *American Literature* 47, no. 2 (May 1975): pp. 247-258. Copyright © 1975 by Duke University Press. Reprinted by permission of Duke University Press.

Notes

1. Arthur Miller, *Death of a Salesman: Certain Private Conversations in Two Acts and a Requiem*, in *Arthur Miller's Collected Plays* (New York, 1957), pp. 130–222. Further references to this edition will be noted in the text by page number.

2. Richard Watts, "A Matter of Hopelessness in *Death of a Salesman*," *Tulane Drama Review*, II (May, 1958), 64.

3. Sheila Huftel, *Arthur Miller: The Burning Glass* (New York, 1965), p. 114.

4. Arthur Miller, "Morality and Modern Drama: Interview with Phillip Gelb," *Educational Theatre Journal*, X (Oct., 1958), rpt. in *Arthur Miller, Death of a Salesman: Text and Criticism*, ed. Gerald Weales (New York, 1967), p. 175.

5. Robert Hogan, *Arthur Miller* (Minneapolis, 1964), p. 8.

6. Arthur Miller, "The Family in Modern Drama," *Atlantic Monthly*, CXCVII (April, 1956), 36–37.

7. Richard I. Evans, *Psychology and Arthur Miller* (New York, 1969), p. 56.

8. Arthur Miller, "Introduction to the Collected Plays," p. 22.

9. Arthur Miller, *The Story of Gus*, in *Radio's Best Plays*, ed. Joseph Liss (New York, 1947), pp. 307–319.

10. Arthur Miller, *All My Sons*, in *Arthur Miller's Collected Plays*, pp. 58–127.

11. Arthur Miller, *The Man Who Had All the Luck*, in *Cross-Section: A Collection of New American Writing*, ed. Edwin Seaver (New York, 1944), pp. 486–552.

12. Leonard Moss, *Arthur Miller* (New Haven, 1967), p. 45.

13. Edward Murray, *Arthur Miller, Dramatist* (New York, 1967), p. 34.

14. C.W.E. Bigsby, *Confrontation and Commitment: A Study of Contemporary American Drama 1959–66* (London, 1967) p. 35.

15. Henry Popkin, "Arthur Miller: The Strange Encounter," *Sewanee Review*, LXVII (Winter, 1960), 56.

16. G. Bliquez, "Linda's Role in *Death of a Salesman*," *Modern Drama*, X (Feb., 1968), 383.

17. Robert D. Hess and Gerald Handel, "The Family as a Psychosocial Organization," in *The Psychosocial Interior of the Family*, ed. Gerald Handel (Chicago, 1967), p. 10.

18. Arthur Miller, *After the Fall* (New York, 1964).

19. Arthur Miller, *The Price* (New York, 1969).

Women and the American Dream of *Death of a Salesman*

Kay Stanton

Arthur Miller's stated intention for *Death of a Salesman* was to create a "tragedy of the common man."[1] Although commentators argue over the meaning of "tragedy" in this phrase,[2] the word "man" has been taken as sexually specific rather than as generic in most responses to the play. Undoubtedly, the play is heavily masculine. Willy Loman is the tragic protagonist, and the effects of his tragic flaws are clearly engraved upon his sons. The roots of Willy's tragedy seem to be in his lack of attention from his father and his perceived inadequacy to his brother, Ben. All conflicts seem to be male-male—Willy versus Biff, Willy versus Howard, Willy versus Charley—so it has been easy for productions, audiences, and commentators to overlook, patronize, or devalue the significance of women in the play.[3] The tragedy of Willy Loman, however, is also the tragedy of American society's pursuit of the American Dream, which the play both defines and criticizes. Careful analysis reveals that the American Dream as presented in *Death of a Salesman* is male-oriented, but it requires unacknowledged dependence upon women as well as women's subjugation and exploitation.

The masculine mythos of the American Dream as personified in Willy Loman has three competing dimensions: the Green World, the Business World, and the Home. All three have ascendant male figure heads and submerged female presences. The Green World is the "outdoors" realm of trees, animals, handcrafting, planting, and hunting, and it takes both pastoral and savage forms. The pastoral aspect is associated with ancestral flute music and Willy's yearnings for his father and, in the next generation, with Biff's enjoyment of farm and ranch work, that which provokes Happy to call Biff "a poet," "an idealist."[4] The savage element is seen in Willy's beliefs about Ben.[5] Whereas Father Loman was a creative figure, moving in harmony with nature by making and disseminating music, Ben is an exploiter and despoiler of nature. In both pastoral and savage aspects, the Green World represents freedom and self-reliance and is a place to test and demonstrate one's masculinity. To Willy, "A man who can't handle tools is not a man" (44), and Biff tells Happy that "Men built like we are should be working out in the open" (23). As Ben is said to have walked into the jungle when he was seventeen and walked out when he was twenty-one, rich, the Green World was the means through which he entered manhood. What is submerged in both aspects is the femininity of nature and the dependence of the masculine on it. Biff states, "There's nothing more inspiring or—beautiful than the sight of a mare and a new colt" (22), and the jungle of Ben is a feminine symbol ("One must go in to fetch a diamond out" [134]), but the feminine is the raw material upon which the male asserts himself. Biff tells Happy that they should "Raise cattle, use our muscles" (23), and the jungle must yield its riches to Ben's mastery. Ben's superior masculinity is also proved by his having seven sons, but his wife is only mentioned as the communicant of the news of his death. Yet she is both producer—sustainer and survivor of life. Thus the female is the necessary element in the production of masculinity, but her role must be severely circumscribed.

The Loman family history can be pieced together through Willy's flashback conversation with Ben[6] (partly conflated with his conversation with Charley) and his present conversation with Howard. Apparently, Father Loman was a travelling maker and seller of flutes who went off to seek adventure in Alaska and deserted Mother, leaving her with two boys to raise alone. Then Ben ran off when he was seventeen and Willy was not quite four years old. Thus Willy and Mother were left alone together. The desertion by his father left Willy feeling "kind of temporary" (51) about himself and provoked Ben to imitate and surpass what his father had done. Both sons mythologize the father: to Willy he was "an adventurous man" with "quite a little streak of self-reliance" (81); to Ben he was "a very great and a very wild-hearted man" who with "one gadget" (the flute) supposedly "made more in a week" than a man like Willy "could make in a lifetime" (49). Both trivialize the role of their mother. Ben calls her a "Fine specimen of a lady" and the "old girl" (46) and assumes she would be living with lesser son Willy. But she is the woman who bore and raised Ben, whom he deserted and made no attempt to contact, not even knowing that she had "died a long time ago" (46). Willy's only other stated information about Mother Loman is his memory of being "in Mamma's lap" listening to "some kind of high music" coming from "a man with a big beard" (48). The mother thus provided the position of comfort from which to attend to the father. Mother is never mentioned again, although hers would be an interesting story. How did she support and raise the four-year-old Willy? Willy seems to have had no further communication from his father, which implies that Father Loman never sent money.[7] Mother must have had "quite a little streak of self-reliance" also.

Willy entreats Ben to tell his boys about their grandfather, so they can learn "the kind of stock they spring from" (48).[8] Mother Loman and her stock and Linda and hers seem to have had no bearing on the production of the boys. An Edenic birth myth is implied, with all Loman men springing directly from their father's side, with no commingling with a female.

In both Ben and Willy, the first desire of manhood is reunion with the father. When Ben ran off, it was "to find father in Alaska." Willy's questions about whether Ben found him and where he is are not answered directly. Ben states that he had had a "very faulty view of geography"; discovering that he was headed due south, he ended up in Africa rather than Alaska. Thus Ben avoids saying whether he knows anything about Father by returning attention to himself. But what he does reveal inadvertently is that, in trying to run toward his father, he actually ran further away in the opposite direction. He discovered his mistake "after a few days" (48), so he could have changed direction but did not. Instead of joining his father, he obviously decided to beat him.

Whereas Ben follows his father's path by running off for adventure, Willy follows it by becoming a travelling salesman. When Willy was "eighteen, nineteen," only slightly older than Ben had been at his departure, he was "already on the road" as a salesman. Yet, unsure "whether selling had a future" for him, Willy at that age "had a yearning to go to Alaska," to "settle in the North with the old man" (80–81) and to be with his older brother. Mother was most likely still alive at this point, and Willy felt that he must break from her to establish his manhood, as he believes his father and brother had done. But, less independent than they were, Willy wishes for a family connection that includes only the three male members, a rebuilding of the family without Mother. Willy continually attempts to find or build an all-male realm of patriarchal-fraternal community.[9] This yearning provides the basis for his refrain of the "liked" and "well liked," which are set apart from the "loved." Willy probably had decided that Ben, as first son, had been "well liked" by their father, and he was only "liked," if regarded with affection at all. Willy would have been loved by his mother, but because that love had not been earned or seized but given freely, it did not have the same value as being "well liked" by his father. Linda, as Willy's wife, seems to have picked up where Mother left off, replacing her. Linda sings Willy to sleep with lullabies and "mothers" him in countless ways—and she is made to seem responsible for Willy's rejection of Ben's proposition to go with him to Alaska.[10] But Linda is obviously being made the scapegoat in this episode. Ben's offer is not for the two brothers to work together: Ben merely proposes a job in Alaska, where he had "bought timberland" and needs "a man to look after things" for him because he is heading back to Africa. Even without Ben, Willy finds the offer tempting in terms of pastoral male community: "God, timberland! Me and my boys in those grand outdoors!" (85). Ben interprets it more aggressively: "Screw on your fists and you can fight for a fortune up there."[11] Linda's strongest objection is "why must everybody conquer the world?" (85)—she sees no value in cut-throat competition—but her supporting points are Willy's own statements about his career fed back to him. Willy refuses the offer after Linda makes reference to Dave Singleman.

When the adolescent Willy had "almost decided to go" to find his father in Alaska, he met Dave Singleman, an eighty-four-year-old salesman who had "drummed merchandise in thirty-one states" and who could now simply go into his hotel room, call the buyers, and make his living in his green velvet slippers. Willy saw that and "realized that selling was the greatest career a man could want" (81). Obviously, Willy found in Dave Singleman a substitute father figure. Singleman had explored and imposed his will (through selling) upon a vast territory, as Father Loman had, but Dave Singleman had managed it in a civilized and comfortable way: in a train rather than a wagon, a hotel room rather than around a fire, and with the Green World transformed into the ease of the green velvet slippers, which he wore even in his death in the smoker of a train. The myth of Dave Singleman is equally as strong for Willy as the myth of his father, imaging as it does for him the perfect life and death, as Dave Singleman died the "death of a salesman," with "hundreds of salesmen and buyers" at his funeral and sadness "on a lotta trains for months after that" (81). Singleman's name implies his lack of dependence on women, and he demonstrates to Willy that a life of material comfort without pioneer ruggedness can still be manly. The realm of comfort had probably been associated in Willy's mind with his mother. Through Dave Singleman's model, Willy realizes that it is possible to establish himself as "well liked" in an all-male community outside of and larger than the male immediate family. This community is the Business World, which provides more stability and comfort and more variety of and competition among consumer goods than those handcrafted in the vast outdoors. In the face of both temptations to choose the Green World, Willy chooses the Business World, the realm of his surrogate father, Dave Singleman.

The Business World has the potential to swallow up the achievements of the Green World: Willy tells Ben that "The whole wealth of Alaska passes over the lunch table at the Commodore Hotel, and that's the wonder, the wonder of this country, that a man can end with diamonds here on the basis of being liked!" (86). The myth of the American Business World provides Willy with the fantasy means of beating his father and his brother. But the complexity of the Business World also defeats the simplicity of the Green World. Ben proudly claims to have had many enterprises and never kept books, but such practices are impossible in the Business World. Decision-making and increased competition take the place of handcrafting and manual exploitation of resources. Yet women are the submerged element in this realm, too. As the male realm moves indoors, it brings in the female to attend to the details of daily maintenance considered too trivial for male attention—typing letters, keeping records, collecting evidence, and, perhaps the most important function, screening out lesser men. Instead of testing himself directly on feminine nature, a man in the Business World must test himself by making an important impression on the female secretary-receptionist before meeting with the male decision-maker. Thus the female provides access to the patriarchal male authority. This element is seen clearly in Biff's attempt to make a date with Bill Oliver's secretary to gain access to him, after waiting five hours unsuccessfully, and in The Woman's statement that Willy has "ruined" her because, after their sexual liaison, she now sends him directly to the buyers, without waiting at her desk. Woman as trivialized Earth Mother in the Green World becomes Woman as trivialized Bitch-Goddess Success in the Business World.

Women in the Business World are marked as whores simply because they are there, perhaps because of their function as access givers, although the reconstitution of the submerged shows them to be otherwise. As Willy, deeply and loudly involved in one of his flashbacks, approaches Charley's office to borrow money, Jenny, Charley's secretary, tells Bernard that Willy is arguing with nobody and that she has a lot of typing to do and cannot deal with Willy any more. She is an insightful, kind, put-upon, hard-working woman. When Willy sees her, he says, "How're ya? Workin'? Or still honest?", implying that her income is made through prostitution. To her polite reply, "Fine. How've you been feeling?", Willy again turns to sexual innuendo: "Not much any more, Jenny. Ha, ha!" (90–91).

Assertion of success for Biff, and especially for Happy, is also bound up with sexual exploitation of women. In their first appearance, they alternate between discussing their father and their own past and current lives, always coming to an association with women. When they recall their "dreams and plans" of the past, an immediate connection is made with "About five hundred women" who "would like to know what was said in this room." They hark back crudely to Happy's "first time," with "big Betsy something," a woman "on Bushwick Avenue," "With the collie dog!": "there was a pig!"[12] Happy states that he "got less bashful" with women and Biff "got more so"; when he questions what happened to Biff's "old confidence" (20–21), Biff returns the discussion to their father. Biff's self-confidence rests on sexual confidence; its diminishment is tied to his father.[13] For Happy, success is measured using women as markers, as he moves up from the initial "pig" with a dog to "gorgeous creatures" that he can get "any time I want" (24–25)—but to him they are still "creatures," not human beings like himself. Although Biff and Happy agree that they each should marry, find "a girl—steady, somebody with substance," "Somebody . . . with resistance! Like Mom" (25), Happy delights in turning other men's "Lindas" into his private objects of sport. He attributes his "overdeveloped sense of competition" (25) to his habit of "ruining," deflowering, the fiancées of the executives at the store where he works, then attending their weddings to savor his secret triumph publicly. Because he cannot accept his low status in the Business World, he must take what he interprets to be the possessions of his superiors—their women—robbing them of their supposed only value, the gold of their virtue and jewels of their chastity, and delivering the damaged goods for his superiors to pay for over a lifetime of financial support.

Happy uses women as Ben used the jungle and timberlands, and he carves out this territory for himself as Ben had. Just as Ben sought adventure like his father but found it in another direction, Happy sought the self-confidence of the older brother Biff and found sexual confidence, and it is now where he has superiority over his brother. Although they both hope to have a fraternal life together—male bonding with limited, sex-defined participation of women—they have competing versions. Biff, more attracted to the Green World, wants to buy a ranch that they both can work, and Happy plans for them to go into business together, share an apartment, and for himself to oversee Biff's having "any babe you want" (26). Later, in the restaurant, when Biff tries to tell Happy about his attempted meeting with Bill Oliver, to put forth Happy's own plan for going into business together, Happy turns Biff's attention to the "strudel" he has been attempting to pick up,[14] insisting that Biff demonstrate his "old confidence" (21) before he speaks of the Oliver meeting. Happy wishes to establish a safety net of sexual confidence to protect them against news of failure that he may anticipate and fear, and he perhaps wants unconsciously to show off his "success" to contrast Biff's probable failure. Magnanimous Happy will give this choice female morsel to Biff if he will only say he wants her—assuming in advance that she has no choice but to acquiesce.

During his assault on the "strudel," the "Girl" in the restaurant (later named Miss Forsythe), Happy quickly defines himself as a salesman and asks, "You don't happen to sell, do you?", with a double entendre on prostitution. Her answer is "No, I don't sell"; she is a model whose picture has been on several magazine covers. But Happy continues to insist to Biff that "She's on call" (101–2). At Happy's entreaty, she rounds up a friend, Letta, who is not a prostitute either.[15] Letta is to begin jury duty the next day, so we may assume that she is a responsible citizen without an arrest record, one qualified to hear evidence and evaluate testimony. When she asks whether Biff or Happy has ever been on a jury, Biff answers, "No, but I have been in front of them!" (114). This is supposedly a joke, but it later proves to be true when we learn that Biff had served three months in jail for theft. Woman as nurturer and care-giver was the submerged element in the Green World; Woman as judge and determiner of truth and value is the submerged element in the Business World.

Yet men in the Business World both need and despise the presence and participation of women, who are continually regarded as whores. Stanley, the waiter in the restaurant, calls the two women, whom he had never seen before, "chippies," presumably because they left with Biff and Happy. The double standard in full force, women are allowed no sexual adventurism: one real or supposed sexual experience and they are "ruined" forever by male standards.[16] Happy makes women like Miss Forsythe and Letta the scapegoats for his inability to marry: it is a "shame" that "a beautiful girl like that" (Miss Forsythe) can be "had" by him. He cannot marry because "There's not a good woman in a thousand" (103). This slander covers Happy's submerged fear that if he tries to marry a woman, another man might do as he does and "ruin" her. He cannot invest himself in one woman because he fears competing men who might rob him of his woman's supposed only value, the chastity of virginity and sexual fidelity.

In his initial conversation with Biff in the play, Happy himself makes a connection between his taking of women and taking of money: "Manufacturers offer me a hundred-dollar bill now and then to throw an order their way. You know how honest I am, but it's like this girl, see. I hate myself for it. Because I don't want the girl, and, still, I take it and—I love it!" (25). It is Happy, not any woman in the play, who is a prostitute. He is not only more sexually promiscuous than any of the women, but he also takes money under unsavory circumstances. Thus he projects his own whorishness onto women in the play's clearest character depiction of male-female Business World dealings. As Woman is present in the public world of business, her ultimate function is to absorb the projection of what the men cannot acknowledge in themselves.

Just as the Green World overlaps with and is transformed into the Business World, so the Business World overlaps with and transforms the Home, which also maintains remnants of the Green World. The Home is the only realm where Willy can be the father, the patriarchal authority, so he invests it with sanctity.[17] Much is made of the physical details of the Loman home in the opening stage directions. The home is "*small, fragile seeming*," against a "*solid vault of apartment houses*."

The house is symbolic of Willy, the apartment houses representative of the big uncaring society that has "boxed in" the little man. An "*air of the dream*" is said to cling to the Loman home, "*a dream arising out of reality.*" We are given a few particulars of the reality: "*The kitchen at center seems actual enough*," with its table, chairs, and the refrigerator, the palpability of which is underlined later through discussion of its repair needs. Other "real" elements are the brass bedstead and straight bedroom chair and "*a silver athletic trophy*" (11). The set reflects Willy's mind, and these elements are most real in life to him. The kitchen and bedroom are the traditional areas of Woman and Linda, and the trophy is the one tangible piece of evidence of Willy's son Biff's "success."

The house evidently also represents the myth of the man's Home being his castle—or here, castle in the air, the "*air of the dream*" (11) clinging to the Home. Willy's failure to get love from his father and brother in the Green World and his failures in the Business World can be obfuscated in the Home, where he is what he defines himself to be. In his interaction with his wife, Linda, Willy habitually patronizes, demeans, and expresses irritation at her; anything he says, no matter how trivial or self-contradictory, is made to seem more important than anything she says. Yet in one of his very few compliments to her, he says, "You're my foundation and my support, Linda" (18). His praise of her is not only placed wholly in the context of himself, but it also partakes of architectural imagery, defining Linda's place in the Home. She is the foundation and support of the Home, the "real" element that Willy can extrapolate from and return to as he constructs his fantasy life.[18]

The Loman men are all less than they hold themselves to be, but Linda is more than she is credited to be.[19] She is indeed the foundation that has allowed the Loman men to build themselves up, if only in dreams, and she is the support that enables them to continue despite their failures. Linda is the one element holding the façade of the family together. Yet even Miller, her creator, seems not to have fully understood her character.[20] Linda is described in the opening stage directions as follows: "*Most often jovial, she has developed an iron repression of her exceptions to Willy's behavior—she more than loves him, she admires him, as though his mercurial nature, his temper, his massive dreams and little cruelties, served her only as sharp reminders of the turbulent longings . . . which she shares but lacks the temperament to utter and follow to their end*" (12). She thus seems inferior to Willy; yet she demonstrates a level of education superior to his in terms of grammatical and mathematical ability, and she is definitely more gifted in diplomatic and psychological acumen. In her management of Willy, she embodies the American Dream ideal of the model post-World War II wife, infinitely supportive of her man. She makes no mistakes, has no flaws in wifely perfection. But the perfect American wife is not enough for American Dreamers like Willy. He has been unfaithful to her, and he rudely interrupts and silences her, even when she is merely expressing support for him. She can be the foundation of the house; he must rebuild the façade.

If the Loman house represents the Loman family, with Linda as the steady foundation and support, the façade is constructed with stolen goods. The enemy apartment buildings that so anger Willy have provided the materials that he and his sons used in such projects as rebuilding the front stoop. Linda knows that they need not have been "boxed in" by the apartment buildings; she says, "We should've bought the land next door" (17). Possibly she had suggested the idea at the appropriate time but was ignored. But Willy prefers to transfer the blame for the diminishment of his Green World: "They should've had a law against apartment houses. Remember those two beautiful elm trees out there? . . . They should've arrested the builder for cutting those down" (17). Of course, there is a law against stealing property, which Willy thought nothing of disobeying when he encouraged the boys to steal from the construction site, calling them "fearless characters" (50). Laws are for lesser men to follow, not the Loman men. In the realm of the Home, Willy and his sons are associated with rebuilding through theft, and Linda is associated with cleaning, mending, and repair.

In Willy's flashback sequences, Linda habitually appears with the laundry, suggesting that it is her responsibility to clean up the males' dirtiness, on all levels. In both past and present, she is shown mending, not only her own stockings but also Willy's jacket. Often when Linda speaks, she discusses repairs, which she oversees; she must mend the male machinery. Willy is "sold" by other salesmen or advertisements on the quality of products and fails to recognize that even the "best" breaks down from daily wear and tear—including Willy himself. Although Linda's functions of cleaning, mending, and overseeing repairs are traditionally "feminine," they are significant because they are the ones maintained when other traditionally "feminine" elements are appropriated by Willy. It is not Linda but Willy who asserts the importance of physical attractiveness, who prefers a fantasy life of glamour to the reality of daily toil, who suffers from the "empty nest syndrome," and who insists on having the most significant role in child-rearing.

Willy works hard at preventing Linda from having any substantive impact on shaping the boys' characters; he tries continually to make them his alone, just as he had implied that they had sprung from his "stock" alone. After thanking God for Adonis-like looks in his sons, Willy confesses to Linda that he himself is "not noticed," "fat," "foolish to look at," and had been called a "walrus" (37).[21] Evidently, the physical attractiveness, strength, and resilience of the boys derive from Linda rather than Willy, but "God," not she, is given credit. Although Linda is the continual presence in the boys' lives at home, as Mother Loman had been for Willy, Willy undermines Linda's authority when he returns from the road. In a flashback sequence, Linda disapproves of various manifestations of Biff's bad behavior and runs from the scene almost in tears after Willy refuses to support her. She represents human dignity and values: cooperative, moral, humane behavior as opposed to lawless assertion of self over all others through assumed superiority. Just as Woman was unacknowledged creator-sustainer of life in the Green World and determiner of value in the Business World, in the

Home, Woman, through Linda as submerged element, is the measure of human dignity and the accountant of worth.

Linda is the foundation and support not only of the Loman Home and Willy himself but also of the plea for sympathy for Willy of the play itself. She is used to establish Willy's significance as a human being to the boys and to the audience. In her most famous speech, she asserts that, although not a "great man," not rich or famous, and "not the finest character that ever lived," Willy is "a human being, and a terrible thing is happening to him. So attention must be paid. . . . Attention, attention must be finally paid to such a person" (56). Linda thus articulates his value and notes the real worth beneath the sham presentation. But the boys have been taught too well by Willy to disregard her message. When she reveals that the company had taken Willy's salary away five weeks before, and Biff calls those responsible "ungrateful bastards" (57), she states that they are no worse than his sons. The male world is ungrateful, unappreciative of such contributions as Willy made; only Linda understands and values them. Whenever she attempts to bring Biff and Happy to consideration for their father, they habitually shift blame away from themselves, pretend there is no problem, and/or change the subject and start bickering between themselves on their competing ideas and ideals. Just as Willy leaves the repair of household appliances to Linda, the boys leave the repair of their broken-down father to her.

The Loman men do see Linda as a validator of value, but they objectify virtue in her and assume that, if they have a woman like her, they will possess virtue and not need to develop it on their own. Both Biff and Happy wish to marry a girl just like the girl who married dear old Dad, and they believe such possession will immediately transform their lives and bring them to maturity. They, like their father, want to subtract value from a woman to add to their own; none of the Loman men is able to keep an accurate account of himself. In the Loman Home, only Linda understands what has value, what things cost, and how much must be paid to maintain and repair the Home life. Her other function, therefore, is computing the family finances, doing the family math. She must tactfully bring Willy to face the truth of his commissions from his inflated exaggerations of success to maximize such resources as there are, and Willy resents her for returning him to the foundation of himself as lesser money-earner from his dreams of wealth. As representative and accountant of worth, she must be trivialized and devalued, as must math.

As noted above, besides Linda and her spheres, the only other real element to Willy in the Loman Home is Biff's athletic trophy. Linda's significance in the Home is suppressed largely through the elevation of sports. The Loman men's idolatry of aggressive male-male competition relegates women into being the devalued objects and instruments of sports. Happy states that the "only trouble" with his promiscuity with women is that "it gets like bowling or something. I just keep knockin' them over and it doesn't mean anything" (25). Similarly, The Woman in the Boston hotel room, disabused of the idea that she means anything to Willy, interprets herself as his football. As instruments of sports, women are the means for starting the competitive game, the object they fight over, and the possession that marks the winners and assures them of being "well liked."

The worst mistake that Willy makes with his sons is in his foisting upon them the notion that sports success guarantees financial success. The adult Happy feels superior because he can "outbox, outrun, and outlift anybody in that store," so he cannot bear to "take orders from those common, petty sons-of-bitches" (24). He believes that the strength of his masculinity should overcome all competitors, although selling merchandise has little to do with displays of physical prowess. The adult Biff also finds holding a job difficult because of his self-image of athletic superiority. This is the "spirit" that Willy successfully manages to "imbue them with" (52), the spirit that he associates with Ben. Not only does Ben assert that making a fortune depends on screwing on one's fists, but he also provides a demonstration by challenging Biff, tripping him, and aiming an umbrella's point at his eyes in phallic threat, saying "Never fight fair with a stranger, boy. You'll never get out of the jungle that way" (49). Biff and Ben are family members, not "strangers," but Ben's aura is partly maintained by establishing distance between himself and other men: no man is allowed to seem his peer or comrade. This "overdeveloped sense of competition" that Willy cultivates in his boys, which can only be satisfied by being "number-one man," puts the boys in competition with each other (seen most clearly in their dream of selling sporting goods by heading competing teams) and ultimately in competition with their father.

Sports in the play partakes of Green World elements by providing an arena in which to test and demonstrate masculinity in its most elemental form. When Charley appears in his golf pants in one of Willy's flashbacks of Ben, Willy says, "Great athlete! Between him and his son Bernard they can't hammer a nail!" (51). Charley had been "man enough" to father Bernard, so he can still be a sports participant; similarly, the adult Bernard, father of two boys, is shown with tennis rackets. But golf and tennis are genteel, civilized sports; real men shine in boxing (shown in Willy's gift to the boys of a punching bag) and, especially, football. Because football is played outdoors on a green field and involves seizing territory in pursuit and manipulation of a valued object, it recaptures the savage Green World of Ben in the jungle with the diamonds. Because football is a male team sport that provides opportunity for an individual to "make an impression," "create personal interest," and be "well liked" (33), it epitomizes the Business World. The football star, Biff in high school, brings to the Home a trophy as validation of value, and feminine support comes in having "a crowd of girls behind him" (32) and in having "the girls pay for you" (28). For Willy, therefore, football becomes the ideal means of synthesizing the realms of Green World, Business World, and Home into his desired male community. As such a synthesis, football assumes mythic proportions; on the day of the Ebbets Field game, Biff appears "Like a young god. Hercules—something like that. . . . A star like that, magnificent, can never really fade away!" (68).

This fantasy synthesis, however, does not pass the test of reality. The values of sports fail to overcome the combined challenge of the feminine and math. Just as the Loman house is partly constructed with stolen materials, so Biff's success in high school is partly established through theft of knowledge, especially of math, from Bernard. Like Linda and the suppressed feminine elements of the Green World and Business World, Bernard in the sports synthesis is a demeaned and exploited presence. Because he "loves" Biff, without feeling a need to compete with him, Bernard is "anemic" (32), emasculated, made feminine by the hypermasculine standards of sports.

Through their belief in the justified predominance of male-male competition over feminine measurement of value, the Loman men can rationalize, even sanctify, theft. Willy steals from Linda the respect of parenting and steals through The Woman a higher place in the Business World than he deserves. Happy steals the women of his superiors to avoid competition in the prescribed arena and to inflate his sense of self-worth. Thus both younger sons, Willy and Happy, compete primarily through Woman as object, but older son Biff, like older son Ben, competes more directly with the male, making defeated men like women through emasculation.

Biff's theft of answers from Bernard, who loves him, is of a piece with his theft of a football from the locker room (indirectly from the coach) and the carton of basketballs and gold fountain pen from Bill Oliver. All involve theft of masculinity from a trusting and approving male authority figure. The confused Loman male sense of mathematics is such that one can only be something if everyone else is nothing. One must add to himself by seizing from others and never subtract from himself through giving to others; giving is what women and lesser men must do. Therefore, one becomes the most valuable by taking that which signifies value from all others, male and female. Female value in this system is relegated to support and sexual functions, and male value resides in the phallus. But one cannot have all and be number-one man unless one ultimately castrates the father. Each of

Biff's thefts is a preparation for and rehearsal of the theft of his father's phallus.[22]

Sports, then, only seems to be the perfect synthesis of the three realms and thus of the patriarchal-fraternal community that Willy seeks continually. Pushed to its inevitable conclusion, the sports mythos demonstrates that a paternal-fraternal community cannot exist in its forum. Willy wants to celebrate an ideal of brotherhood for lesser men (who are actually like himself) to follow, while he would be the patriarchal authority, idolized by all, especially Biff. Yet when Willy is rational, he believes that although Biff has the potential to be number-one man he himself does not. Biff cannot be both more than Willy and less than Willy: there is a glaring contradiction in logic—it does not add up. In fulfilling his expected potential, Biff would have to grow up, to surpass Willy, to recognize that his father is less than himself. For the "young god" to become an adult god, he would have to dethrone, "castrate," the "fake" god, Willy.

Even before the Boston incident, Willy was dangerously close to being "found out" as less than his stolen, self-constructed image in the boys' eyes.[23] He had promised to take the boys on a business trip; if he had done so, they would have seen that he was a "fake," that the waves did not part for him. If he had not taken them, he would have been a "liar." If Biff had not learned of The Woman, Willy would have had to confront the math teacher and probably fail to get the extra points for Biff. But these crises of faith in the father are forestalled because Biff witnesses him with The Woman.

When Willy and Biff meet in Boston, both have failed: Biff has failed math, and Willy has failed marital fidelity. These failures are accompanied by masculine dream-value system failures: Willy has failed to uphold the family as the sacred cornerstone of success, and Biff has failed to be universally well liked by lesser men. In present time, each blames the other for his failure, but The Woman is made the foundation of the failed relationship between father and son.[24] Although the Loman men contrast Linda as "somebody with resistance" with the women of the Business World, who can be "had,"[25] The Woman epitomizes those women, and she overlaps with and parallels Linda.

Willy continually links Linda and The Woman unconsciously. Linda's attempted ego-inflating praise of Willy in a flashback as the "handsomest man in the world" (37) to her (after he had confessed feeling foolish to look at) brings on a flashback within a flashback in the laughter and then the first appearance of The Woman. Although in context the laughter signifies The Woman's enjoyment of Willy's company, the dramatic effect is that she is laughing at him rather than with him. As he comes out of the flashback within flashback to the flashback, Linda's laughter blends with that of The Woman. The Woman's laugh returns when evidence of Biff's bad behavior, provided by Linda and Bernard, haunts Willy's flashback, testifying that Willy raised Biff by the wrong standards—his rather than Linda's.

The Woman is not even dignified by a name in the list of characters and speech headings, although her name may be Miss Francis. By being simply The Woman, she figures as a temptress, a femme fatale, and this impression is reinforced by her laughter, the music accompanying her appearances, and her appearance in a black slip. Yet her description in the stage directions is at odds with this impression. She is "*quite proper-looking Willy's age*" (38). Furthermore, she is far from being a prostitute—she is a business contact of Willy's, someone (probably a secretary-receptionist) with the power to choose whom the buyers will see—and she lives with her sisters. Her payment for sex with Willy is silk stockings. She needs silk stockings to wear to work and can probably ill afford them on her salary. Yet the stockings also become an important symbol. When she mentions the promised stockings, Biff understands his father's relationship with her, and when Linda mends her own stockings, it reminds Willy of his guilt. Thus Linda and The Woman are bound together by the stockings, which reinforce their other connections: they are good-humored women of about the same age who both genuinely like Willy.[26] The essential difference between them is that one has chosen to marry and work inside the Home, and the other has chosen not to marry and to work in the Business World. Linda herself is like a mended stocking, torn and tattered by Willy but still serviceable through the strengthening of her own moral fiber. The Woman is a "new" silk stocking, new territory on which Willy can test himself. Both are made to be objects, but both also witness the failures of masculine values.

Contrary to surface appearance, then, there are not two kinds of women in the play, good and bad. All of the women are conflated in the idea of Woman: all share more similarities than differences, particularly in their knowing, and having the potential to reveal, masculine inadequacy, although generally they have been socialized not to insult a man by revealing their knowledge to his face. The Loman men all agree that the truth of masculine inadequacy or failure must be kept from women, because if women do not know, men can maintain their pretenses among other men and to themselves. What most upsets Biff about his father's flashback ravings is that "Mom's hearing that!" (27), and Happy habitually lies about himself and other men to women. When Willy borrows money from Charley, it is to pretend to Linda that it is his salary—but Linda knows about the loans. Willy tries to force Biff into a fabricated version of the meeting with Bill Oliver, supposedly so he can have good news to bring to Linda—but it is he, not Linda, who craves good news from Biff. Linda also knows and tells her sons that Willy has been trying to commit suicide. Like Letta, she is associated with collection and evaluation of evidence. Not only does Linda find the rubber gas hose (during her repairs), but she knows of other suicide attempts that Willy has made with the car. As she begins to tell the story of the witness, she says, "It seems there's a woman," and Biff quickly responds, "What woman?" (58–59), obviously assuming that Linda means The Woman in Boston. Linda not only overlaps the function of Mother Loman, but she and the insurance company's woman witness are alike in knowing about Willy's suicide attempts; the woman witness is linked to The Woman in Biff's mind; Willy treats Jenny as he probably had treated The Woman; and, in the restaurant, Miss Forsythe and Letta provoke Willy's memory of The Woman, as had Linda. The synthesis that Willy seeks among the Green World, Business World, and Home is achieved not by male community but collectively through the women, who independently rise from their positions as submerged elements to join in a circle of femininity and summation of value that closes in, without acknowledgment, on the truth of the Loman men.

The emergence of suppressed Woman occurs in the midst of an intended paternal-fraternal celebration of triumph in the restaurant.[27] Linda was not invited; the savoring of success was for the men only. Willy was to have wrested a New York job for himself from his symbolic "son" Howard, and Biff was to have convinced his symbolic "father" Bill Oliver to invest in Happy's idea of the Loman Brothers sporting goods teams. But the dreams of success for the day failed to become realized. Howard, delighting in being a "father" himself (evidenced by his pride over his son's performance on the wire recorder)[28] is not impressed by Willy's assertion of fatherhood (his supposed fraternal relationship with Howard's father and his exaggerated claims to have "named" Howard) and in fact fires Willy for failing to "pull his own weight" (80). Biff fails also, not even making an impression on the secretary, let alone Bill Oliver, who sees him only momentarily and does not remember him. Enraged at being treated like a lesser man, Biff re-enters Oliver's office and steals his gold fountain pen, completing the castration of the symbolic father from whom he had stolen basketballs years before. Thus, once again, as in Boston, Willy has failed as father and Biff has failed as son. The restaurant scene recapitulates as well as calls forth the Boston scene as the double failures unfold, but now a transfer of phallic power takes place. Willy seems unable to face his failure to his family until he sees his sons grow into the same action. As Willy "betrayed" the family with The Woman, so Biff and Happy "betray" him by deserting him in the restaurant and leaving with Miss Forsythe and Letta.

In an early line in Willy's culminating flashback—"Willy, Willy, are you going to get up, get up, get up, get up?" (114)—The Woman's iteration of "get up" implies not only getting up to answer the knocking at the door but also getting up the ladder of success and, perhaps, erection. Sexual performance is one realm where a man cannot be a fake—the woman knows if he fails. Woman is the means not only of phallic inflation but also of phallic deflation, both by satisfying his need of her and by her potential for intimidation to impotence. Yet The Woman, like Linda and the women in the restaurant, complies by providing the man with what he desires, the necessary boost in self-confidence. Although her baby-talk manner of speech is meant to make her seem otherwise, The Woman has a sense of responsibility about her job and the intelligence to sense masculine feelings of inadequacy and say the "proper" things to dispel them, even if her own humiliation results. But she also grants herself the freedom of taking sexual initiative: "You didn't make me, Willy. I picked you" (38). And she unabashedly enjoys sex: "Come on inside, drummer boy. It's silly to be dressing in the middle of the night" (116). This implies that she has not yet been satisfied by Willy, and perhaps the laughter so often associated with her also represents his fear that she will laugh at his inadequacy/impotence, which he must overcome by diminishing her.

The Woman insists that Willy acknowledge the knocking, which literally is Biff knocking at the door and symbolically is Willy's own conscience knocking, which he tries to deny. Before Willy opens the hotel room door, he hides The Woman in the bathroom, associating her with "plumbing" and bodily functions. But The Woman becomes the means of destroying the masculine mythos by coming out of the bathroom.

When Willy lets Biff into the room, Biff confesses his math failure. Willy is shocked and tries to displace blame onto Bernard. But Bernard has not failed in loving submission to Biff—although he "stole" from Bernard, Biff only "got a sixty-one" (118). The numbers, so denigrated before, are extremely important now, and Biff needs Willy to get him the extra four points. If they had left then, Willy's failure would have remained secret, but his authority would have to be tested against that of another patriarchal figure. Biff, however, goes on to rationalize his failure. This unimportant math class comes right before all-important sports, so he "didn't go enough" (118), avoiding submission to its alternative value system. Then, too, he is not "well liked" by the teacher; Mr. Birnbaum "hates" Biff for doing a comical imitation of him in front of the class. Biff steals the teacher's self-esteem by imitating him and showing him as a lesser man. Thus, although Biff failed, he succeeds in displacing another male authority figure. Biff increases his own esteem of his classmates by decreasing their esteem for the teacher, and he repeats his imitation for his father's approval. Willy pauses to savor Biff's triumph over male authority and to share male communion by laughing at a supposed lesser man who holds Biff's fate in his hands. But just as Mr. Birnbaum had walked into the midst of Biff's ridicule, so does The Woman intrude into its repetition by joining in their laughter and coming out of the bathroom.

Undoubtedly, most readers and audience members feel tension as Biff and Willy talk, knowing that The Woman is hidden in the bathroom, and they are upset when she makes her presence known. The scene is set up in such a way as to protect the males and to put the blame entirely on her. If only she had kept her mouth shut! If only she had stayed in the bathroom where she belonged! But she does not; she insists on being part of the fun, of sharing in the male-defined game. When she enters, she not only laughs, but she also lisps her lines, imitating Biff's imitation of Mr. Birnbaum—but a woman must not be allowed to share in male camaraderie or to ridicule a lesser man.

To dispel Biff's shock at her presence, Willy begins his "*striving for the ordinary.*" He names her, probably giving her real name, but promoting her: "This is Miss Francis, Biff, she's a buyer" (119). Her promotion is in a sense true—she has been a buyer of what Willy is selling—himself as a likeable commodity.[29] She had also bought into the idea that she was a human being to him. But when she sees herself treated as an embarrassment, merchandise no longer desired, she insists at least on the material terms of agreement. Willy tries to force her out into the hall without her clothes, but she demands her promised stockings. Willy tries to deny, but she is armed with numbers: "You had two boxes of size nine sheers for me, and I want them!" (119). And Willy finally produces them for her.

What seems to make "Miss Francis" a "bad" woman is that she refuses to be walked on the way Linda is, that she dares to insist on being recognized and dealt with according to the terms of the contract, and that she understands and resents being humiliated. After she identifies herself as the football that has been kicked around in the male game, she takes her clothes and leaves. The Woman literally has been undressed and Willy literally has been dressed, but Biff has symbolically witnessed Willy defrocked of the patriarchal mantle and has encountered the deflated phallic reality of his father. Through the stockings, Biff has seen the sanctity of family life reduced to an exchangeable commodity: "You—you gave her Mama's stockings!" (121), he says, as he bursts into tears and gives up on his life in terms of Business World success. For once he seems to identify with Linda; if she as wife-mother can be reduced to an object of exchange by his father, so can he as son. Biff accuses his father of being a "liar" and a "fake" (121) and departs.

The projection of the undressed state onto The Woman, however, has left the resolution of the phallic conflict between father and son unresolved until the double masculine failures repeat themselves. In real time, Biff is now armed with two stolen phalluses: Bill Oliver's gold pen, representing the symbolic paternal power of the Business World, and the rubber gas hose, Willy's self-destructive phallus in the Home. Without either of them consciously recognizing it, Willy is "emasculated," put into the position of The Woman, as Biff deserts Willy, leaving his father "babbling in a toilet."[30]

Just as The Woman was the scapegoat for Willy's desertion and failure of the family, so Miss Forsythe and Letta are the scapegoats for his sons' desertion and failure of him. But as masculine failure had been the means of bringing The Woman out of the bathroom of the Business

World, so it brings Linda out of her limited position of foundation and support in the Home. Significantly, Linda is at her most assertive and ominous after the incident with The Woman. She flings down the boys' proffered bribe of flowers, presented by Happy as he displaced blame onto women for his and Biff's desertion of their father. But in her wrath, Linda is a superior match for both boys. They cannot cover up or smooth over the truth in her presence, although they sheepishly continue to try. Linda can be threatening not in her own right, but for Willy. Her reaction in this scene is perhaps what could be expected from a woman whose husband had been unfaithful. Yet her devotion to Willy is such that we believe she would not have come at him that way. Although Linda has bought into the system enough to condemn the women as "lousy rotten whores!" (124), she blames her sons more for going to them. She attempts to throw the boys out of the house and stops herself from picking up the scattered flowers, ordering them, for once: "Pick up this stuff, I'm not your maid any more." Linda finally declares her independence from her role, recognizing that she is better than they are.[31] For both Linda and The Woman, male failures have provoked female sense of injustice and realization of victimization. Happy turns his back on Linda's order, refusing to acquiesce to feminine dominance, but Biff gets on his knees and picks up the flowers, as he understands that he is a failure as a man. Willy has been put into the position of the humiliated and abandoned one, like The Woman, the football kicked around in the competition. Linda achieves this position through empathy with him but rises above it into female control, short-lived as it is: women can take charge when the men are defeated by one another. When Linda accuses Biff, "You! You didn't even go in to see if he was all right!" (124), she is condemning him partly for shunning all of her influence, the nurturing and tending, the human compassion. But Biff insists on seeing Willy now, over Linda's objections. Because he has become as bad as Willy in betraying Linda, he and Willy can understand each other.

Recognition of his own and Biff's failures in both the Business

World and Home makes Willy revert to the Green World as he attempts to reclaim his lost masculinity after the disaster in the restaurant. "The woods are burning!" (107), as he has previously noted, so he must buy some seeds, because "Nothing's planted. I don't have a thing in the ground" (122). His action will be futile in his yard, the remnant of the Green World remaining in the Home realm, because, as Linda knows, "not enough sun gets back there. Nothing'll grow any more" (72). The Green World has become a sunless/sonless void through male depletion of it, but Willy must continue to assert his masculinity on it, imposing the hoe, as Green World phallic symbol, on Mother Earth. In planting his seed, he attempts to renew Biff's conception—his own of Biff and Biff's of him, to start over as new father and new son on a pastoral basis.

The three realms of Green World, Business World, and Home, however, cannot be separated in Willy's mind, and, as he plants, he considers with a hallucinated Ben his suicide plan—he is actually digging his own grave. His previous suicide plans recapitulate his past and have submerged feminine elements. In the first attempt, femininely witnessed, he was driving down the road, went off track into a little bridge, and was saved only by "the shallowness of the water" (59). The road is symbolically connected with being "on the road" of the Business World, the bridge is perhaps sex as a connection out of his loneliness that he got off track into, and the shallowness of water the prescribed shallow but supportive function of Woman that "saved him." The second plan, associated with the Home, involves the phallic rubber hose, but the success of that attempt rests on the "new little nipple" (59), a feminine symbol, on the gas pipe. The third plan is formulated in "pastoral" aspect and approved of in "savage" aspect in the Green World, and it uses elements of the Business World and Home realms as well, thus becoming a replacement for the failed synthesis of the three realms in the sports forum. The suicide will be feminine in being a return to the womb, the pre-competitive sanctum. But as such, it will be another scapegoat for masculine failure.

The suicide plan provides Willy with the fantasy means of re-establishing a fraternal relationship with Ben. Although he had "missed the boat" of Ben's success, Willy can catch the "boat" of death to join the recently dead Ben and, through him, their dead father. In this proposed paternal-fraternal community, Woman is again made the foundation. Willy asserts to the hallucination of Ben that the proposition is "terrific" because "the woman has suffered" (126). But what his understanding of Linda's (and through his ambiguous phrasing, The Woman's) suffering is is not revealed. Apparently she has suffered because he has failed to live up to his own standard, not that he has ever seriously considered hers: "A man can't go out the way he came in, Ben, a man has got to add up to something" (125). Thus, the suicide synthesis, like the sports synthesis, involves a confused fantasy appropriation of math. Rather than continuing to live while "ringing up a zero" (126), Willy wants to turn himself into money through death as he perceives Ben had. His plan is a "twenty-thousand-dollar proposition" that is "Guaranteed, gilt-edged" (126). The money, which he will try to steal from the insurance company by making his death seem accidental, will be Willy's gold. Gold had been the value symbol associated with Business World success through Bill Oliver's gold fountain pen and with sports success as Biff in the legendary Ebbets Field game had appeared "in gold." But the death is also imaged as a "diamond, shining in the dark, hard and rough, that I can pick up and touch with my hand" (126). While he puts his seed into the earth, he wants to get something out, the diamonds that his brother found but that he had missed, the value to be appropriated from the Green World as he simultaneously adds and subtracts. A diamond is "Not like—like an appointment!" (126) that is soft in contrast to the manly hardness of the diamond. The death would be tangible in the money, but Willy quickly jumps to another appointment: the funeral, which he envisions will be "massive," attended by "all the old-timers" from four states, because, as Biff never realized in thinking him "nothing," "I am known!" (126). The suicide plan thus becomes the perfect merging of Green World, Business World, and

Home, as he, like Ben, will go into the dark jungle of the unknown and come out rich; will, like Dave Singleman, have the death of a salesman in a grand funeral and secure the hero-worship of Biff in the legacy of controlling Biff's future. In forming this synthesis, Woman is exploited once more. Although the plan had begun in relation to Linda, because "the woman has suffered," she has been left out of the grand male scheme again because the money will go to Biff, not her, so that Willy can "amount to something" by masculine standards by regaining the phallus and looking "big" in Biff's eyes.

Although the gold of the gilt-edged insurance policy and the diamond of suicide are presented in masculine terms, they too have submerged feminine significance, because gold and diamond are the elements of a wedding ring. Rather than interpreting gold and diamond as objects to be stolen, Willy could recognize that he already has them in Linda, could understand that value can be achieved rather than objectified and seized, if he submits himself to Linda's system of worth. In her system, big or little, inflated or deflated, are irrelevant to having compassion and dignity and sharing love. But Ben is the primary rival to that vision; he and the suicide plan ultimately represent infidelity to a true marriage with Linda.

Willy is preparing himself to enter the dark, yet he really wants to "get back to all the great times" that "Used to be so full of light and comradeship" (127). One of his main problems is that he yearns for the boys' adolescence that provided him with his own, out of which he and the boys have never quite grown. But the joy of their fraternal adolescence died in their struggle for phallic patriarchal power, and now Biff enters to take the hoe, the last remaining phallic symbol, away from Willy and to assert paternal authority by demanding that Willy return to the Home to "tell Mom" of their failures as father and son. As Willy has been trying to re-establish roots in a pastoral Green World, Biff has determined to uproot himself by leaving permanently for his pastoral Green World.

The confrontation scene between Willy and Biff begins in the Green

World remnant, the yard, but it must be played out in the Home, in front of Happy as lesser man, and especially Linda. When they enter, Linda withdraws into her support function for both of them, gently asking Willy, "Did you plant, dear?" (128), and allowing Biff the "public" credit for her idea, in fact demand, that Biff leave the Home forever. But Biff cannot leave without wanting Willy to shake his hand, thereby acknowledging his defeat and Biff as the winner. Neither Biff nor Willy is ready for it to be over until one has asserted authority over the other, so they begin a contest of competing reasons for Biff's failure: blaming it on Willy or attributing it to Biff's spite. Willy repeatedly turns to Linda to ratify his version, spite. Yet what Willy wants here is for Biff to maintain the masculine system of conspiracy, which involves protecting Woman (and themselves) from the truth of male failure. If he can make Biff submit to this version, Willy will both triumph over Biff and be safe in Linda's eyes. Although Biff repeatedly denies attributing blame to his father, Willy is too agitated to hear Biff's response. Instead, he accuses Biff of "trying to put a knife in me" (130)—using phallic weaponry against him. Then Biff rises to the challenge, not with a knife but with the rubber hose.

Just before he shows the hose, Biff says, "All right, phony! Then let's lay it on the line." The implication, especially through the word "phony," is that Biff will reveal Willy's infidelity in front of Linda and Happy, conflating infidelity with the suicide attempts. But both Linda and Happy already know about the hose and try to prevent Biff from disclosing that they know. It is like presenting the naked phallus in public: indecent exposure. Willy pretends not to recognize the hose, but it is the revelation of Willy's rising ("What is this supposed to do, make a hero out of you?") and falling ("This is supposed to make me sorry for you?") phallus. But even this is not enough; Biff perseveres that Willy is "going to hear the truth—what you are and what I am!" When Happy interrupts, Biff begins with him: "You big blow, are you the assistant buyer?", asserting that Happy is "full of it! We all are! And I'm through with it" (130–31). This affirmation, along with Biff's statement a few lines earlier that "We never told the truth for ten minutes in this house!" (131), implies that Linda is included, but not if we remember that she has never been given the status of being one of them. She alone has told the truth of what Willy is, what the boys are, and of Willy's suicide plans (albeit to the boys but not Willy). Again she is discounted, but with her value appropriated yet unacknowledged.

Now that Willy's phallic flaws have been made public, Biff must confess his own: "I stole myself out of every good job since high school!"—and he had spent time in jail for theft. Although Biff had earlier absolved Willy from blame, he places it now: Biff "never got anywhere" because Willy "blew me so full of hot air I could never stand taking orders from anybody! That's whose fault it is!" The tumescent image here connects with his calling Happy a "big blow" (131), and both reveal Biff's recognition of the artificially inflated phalluses of all the Loman men; he tries to make himself and them face their own deflated condition.[32] Willy's response is "Then hang yourself! For spite, hang yourself!" Thus Biff's confession of failure leads Willy unconsciously to the same conclusion as his own of suicide. But Biff answers that "Nobody's hanging himself" (131–32). He has finally learned that acknowledging limitations does not lead necessarily to self-annihilation but to choosing alternate paths—for him, acceptance of the pastoral Green World and rejection of the Business World.

Biff's castration of the Business World in his theft of the gold pen has resulted in his recognizing the pointlessness of stealing other men's phallic power to "become what I don't want to be" (132)[33] and his accepting the Green World as the appropriate realm for his truest inclinations. But because the Green World also involves asserting manhood, Biff still cannot be free to enter that realm until he completes his "castration" of Willy by imposing his new-found truth. He now turns, significantly, to the "real math" of value computation to do so, asserting to Willy that "I'm a dime a dozen, and so are you!", that Willy is only a "hard-working drummer" and Biff himself, on any turf, is "one dollar an hour." Furthermore, Biff is "not bringing home any prizes any more" (132), and Willy is not to expect them. Once he has defined himself as "nothing," Biff can and does cry. We have only seen him cry once before, in the hotel room, and these tears connect these two incidents. They culminate in the conclusion of the conflict, which had been delayed by sustaining the masculine myth between them. But this resolution has taken place on the grounds of relating represented by Linda: the emotional, compassionate way of interaction. Willy turns to Linda for an explanation of Biff's tears, recognizing that she can understand better. Biff has finally learned to love himself and Willy for what they are, pretensions stripped away—what Linda has been advocating and has demonstrated throughout, without recognition.

Biff asks to be let go, for Willy to "take that phony dream and burn it before something happens" (133). But he cannot carry through and reestablish a relationship on compassionate terms; he can only escape: "I'll go in the morning." And once again, Linda is made to do the difficult part: "Put him—put him to bed" (133).

At first it seems strange that Willy, who has gotten what he wanted—the return of Biff's love—still intends to commit suicide. He is enraptured because Biff has become a boy again; they have gone back to the day when Biff confronted him in the hotel room, and it has been "made right," with Biff acknowledging Willy as the one in control and with the power to "take and burn that phony dream." But neither Biff nor Willy follows through. Neither can handle a relationship that is based on "feminine" compassion and mutual self-recognition. Yet Willy is pleased because he now believes that Biff will accept the money; perhaps he has an idea that his suicide will burn away the phoniness from the dream but leave the dream intact.

Linda alone feels the danger and asks Willy to come to bed. But Willy must seize and make the most of this moment of glory, take the ball and run with it, listening to Ben again. Willy makes the same mistake that he has always made: not appreciating real moments of value as they happen because they have always got to be topped with bigger dreams for the future. That prevented his full enjoyment of the boys' youth, and that prevents him from living on. He can only think to top this moment by leaving Biff twenty thousand dollars. If Biff has done a great thing in crying to Willy, sacrificing his self-image to his father, Willy must sacrifice his life for Biff, still competing with him. Happy appropriately asks for recognition now, behaving as if he had been the source of the trouble, maintaining that he is going to be the perfect son, replacing Biff, staying and living out the dream. But Willy cannot even acknowledge his younger son as he pays increasing attention to his older brother. Therefore, Linda must give Happy the comfort he needs.

As Biff and Happy go to bed, only Linda remains as a living interactive presence for Willy. In his last moments on stage, he alternates between attending to the real voice of Linda and the fantasized voice of Ben. Linda continually entreats him to follow her, and she is put into direct competition with his desire to follow Ben. Willy cannot acknowledge the superiority of the feminine value system to his own, so he must choose Ben. Ben's way is presented erotically—"One must go in to fetch a diamond out" (134)—one must enter sexually, impose the phallus, to get a diamond—son—out. Linda's "I want you upstairs" (134) is both a command and, perhaps, a sexual invitation, to counter the sexuality of Ben's offer. But Willy cannot satisfy Linda on her terms. When Linda says, "I think this is the only way, Willy," meaning that Biff should leave, Willy conflates it with the suicide plan: "Sure, it's the best thing." And Ben agrees: "Best thing!" (134). Here is the only point where all three agree, but two are agreeing to a plan between them, to a dream in which Woman is left out, not to the basis of the real experience just past.

Willy is finally left alone with Ben, as he wishes. The male-male connection can now be savored only by males, with no female commentary. He shares with Ben his wonder that Biff loves him and always has. But instead of being content with love, Willy must inflate it to worship which he seeks to provoke in Biff by his suicide that Ben now urges him toward, promising, "It's dark there, but full of diamonds." When Linda calls, his reply, "Coming!" (135), answers Ben more than her.

Before following Ben, Willy "elegiacally" relives the preparation for the Ebbets Field game, the day of Biff's stardom, when Willy was the authority figure. After much advice, he says, "There's all kinds of important people in the stands" (135) and suddenly recognizes his aloneness in the male-defined game. Willy starts asking for Ben, but instead Linda calls again. She has repeatedly offered acceptance on the terms of love for being what he is, average, and Biff has just offered the same, but Willy must make one more grandstand play. Yet it is obvious that accepting love, the feminine way, frightens him. Responding to Linda's call, he tries to quiet her, but his "sh!" unleashes "*sounds, faces, voices*" (136) that swarm in upon him, and he tries to "sh" them too. They are probably the voices of truth represented by Woman, the contradictions and failures in his world view. In the midst of his "sh"-ing, the ancestral flute music of his father stops him, rising in intensity "*to an unbearable scream*" (136). The music of male harmonic blending is now the only thing he hears, although Linda, and even Biff following her lead, calls out again. But the music draws Willy to the car, another symbol of masculine unity in the play, and Willy, the car, and the music all crash, "*in a frenzy of sound*, which becomes the soft pulsation of a single cello string," which further develops into "*a dead march*" (136). Willy has crashed the car and killed himself, driven to the beat of the male song.

The scene dissolves into a dumb show of preparation for the funeral, with the "*leaves of day*" appearing "*over everything*" (136), suggesting Willy's final rest in the pastoral dream that was just as much death for him as were the other dreams. But as the Requiem begins, Charley notes that "It's getting dark, Linda" (137). Willy is finally put to rest in the darkness that he had sought, the void that the competing realms made of Woman, and he exists now only in the competing summations of his value presented by Linda, Charley, Biff, and Happy.

Critics have often been puzzled at Linda's speech of incomprehension at the grave, because she knew Willy was trying to kill himself.[34] But what she cannot understand is why. The reason is partly that Willy could not accept no longer being a boy or having a hope of boyhood in his sons—that the dreams could not be realized. Linda is always patronized for not understanding Willy's "massive dreams," but she comprehended the dreams well enough. Willy Loman's "massive dreams" were little more than adolescent male dreams of *being massive*. What Linda cannot understand is why those dreams of inflated masculinity are more important than family love, compassion, and respect—why real virtues are seen to have no honor and the "little man" cannot accept his dignity.

As the male characters present their competing versions of who Willy was and what he represents, it becomes evident that they understand him less than Linda does. Each identifies himself with Willy, making a male synthesis to contrast and outdo Linda. Biff relates to the camaraderie and construction, the "nice days" such as "Sundays, making the stoop." Forgetting that the stoop was constructed from stolen materials, Biff muses fondly, "there's more of him in that front stoop than in all the sales he ever made." Linda's reply may be meant as a punning sexual tribute: "He was so wonderful with his hands."[35] But then Biff says his famous lines, "He had the wrong dreams. All, all, wrong." Happy responds angrily, but Biff continues, "He never knew who he was," speaking as much about himself as Willy. Charley begins his "Nobody dast blame this man" speech partly to break up a pending fight between the boys. Oddly, in saying what a salesman is, Charley has to specify what he is not, including "He don't put a bolt to a nut"—which Willy actually did, albeit not as a salesman. Charley also is talking partly about himself: he has been the one unaccustomed to using the tools of reconstruction. Furthermore, it is Charley, the unsentimental, non-dreaming realist, who now says, "A salesman is got to dream, boy. It comes with the territory," thus combining his reality with acceptance of Willy's dream. This speech does little to reconcile Biff and Happy, who ignore it and continue their rivalry. Once again, Biff suggests his fraternal dream—that Happy go with him—but Happy says, "I'm not licked that easily" and refers once more to his fraternal dream, "The Loman Brothers!" Happy reaffirms the part of Willy that he identifies with: "the only dream you can have—to come out number-one man" (138–39). He plans to show Biff and everybody else that Willy Loman did not die in vain.

What Willy did die for if not in vain is not clear in any of the characters' minds, particularly not in Happy's, because not much earlier he had denied that Willy had any "right" to kill himself. Happy's speech is meant to be received by the audience as pathetic, and it is. For one, it defines the only dream possible as coming out "number-one man," women excluded, other men trampled beneath. Biff has now rejected it and turns to his mother. But Linda sends the men on their way, so that she, the only one who truly loved Willy, can be alone with him, and the flute music plays through her speech.

Alone at his grave, Linda asks Willy to forgive her for not being able to cry. Her loyalty and dedication to Willy are such that she wishes to do the expected, appropriate, female supportive behavior even when Willy is no longer there to require it. The two notes sounded alternatively throughout the speech are that she cannot cry and she cannot understand it. Thus part of what she cannot understand is why she cannot cry. On the one hand, Willy's death seems like just another of his absences, when she carries on, managing the bills, etc., as always. She has made the last payment on the house today, and "there'll be nobody home," considering herself, as Willy had, to be nobody. But suddenly a sob rises as she says, "We're free and clear." The idea of freedom releases her to sob more fully: "We're free . . . We're free" (139). What she cannot yet sort out, perhaps, is that she could not cry for Willy because of her unconscious sense of his oppression of her and her sons. She will no longer have to bend under the burden of the masculine ego. Biff is free of the patriarch now, and so is she: free and crying in the emotional intensity that her freedom releases.

Although mystified to seem otherwise, the male American Dream of *Death of a Salesman* is, as the play shows, unbalanced, immature, illogical, lying, thieving, self-contradictory, and self-destructive. Only Willy literally kills himself, but the Dream's celebration of the masculine mythos is inherently self-destructive in its need to obliterate other men or be obliterated, to castrate or be castrated.[36] It prefers to destroy itself rather than to acknowledge the female as equal or to submit to a realistic and balanced feminine value system. This tragedy of the common *man* also wreaks the suffering of the common woman, who has trustingly helped the man to maintain and repair the Dream and has helplessly watched him destroy it and render her sacrifices meaningless. One could argue that Linda as common woman possesses more tragic nobility than Willy.[37] Her only flaw was in harnessing all of her talents and energies to support the self-destructive American masculine mythos that requires Woman's subjugation and exploitation. Yet, at the end of the play, Linda lives—and even, for once, gets the last word. Biff, under her unacknowledged influence, now even shows her some tenderness as they leave the stage. But Happy exits last, alone, with the male music of the flute remaining, reminding us of the perpetuation of the Dream.

Thus the audience and readers are left with a choice between Happy and Linda, as Willy had had a choice between Ben and Linda. We can continue to side with the immature masculine mythos in degrading and ignoring Woman while making her the scapegoat for failures in American male-dominated society, or we can free Woman to rise from her oppression by choosing with her the appreciation of love and compassion, the recognition of the values of human dignity, and the worthwhile contributions of men and women.

From *Feminist Rereadings of Modern American Drama*, ed. June Schlueter (Madison, NJ: Fairleigh Dickinson University Press, 1989): 67-102. Copyright © 1989 by Associated University Presses. Reprinted by permission of Associated University Presses.

Notes

1. See Arthur Miller, "Tragedy and the Common Man" [1949], in *The Theater Essays of Arthur Miller*, ed. Robert A. Martin (New York: Viking Press, 1978), pp. 3–7, and "Introduction" to Arthur Miller, *Collected Plays* (New York: Viking Press, 1957), pp. 3–55, especially pp. 31–36.

2. Much of the criticism on the play involves the question of whether it can properly be called a tragedy. For a summary of the various positions, as well as for a distillation of analysis of the work as social drama and for discussion of its place in theater history, see Helene Wickham Koon, "Introduction" to *Twentieth Century Interpretations of Death of a Salesman*, ed. Helene Wickham Koon (Englewood Cliffs, N.J.: Prentice-Hall, 1983), pp. 1–14.

3. Note the example of "Private Conversations" (produced, directed, and photographed by Christian Blackwood), the 1985 PBS documentary in the *American Masters* series that was a commentary on the filming of the televised version of the 1984 Broadway production of *Death of a Salesman*, starring Dustin Hoffman. In it, the male lead actors, director, Miller, and even male guests made pronouncements on the play, but no comments from Kate Reid, who played Linda, were included, although Dustin Hoffman's flirting with a female stagehand and his remark about the physical endowments of Kathy Rossetter as The Woman were.

4. Arthur Miller, *Death of a Salesman* (New York: Viking Press, 1949), p. 23. Subsequent references are cited parenthetically by page number within the text.

5. Although some mention that Ben has achieved mythic stature in Willy's mind, I seem to be alone among critics in believing, and finding Linda capable of believing, that Ben was just as much of a "fake" as Willy; lying and exaggerations of success do seem to be typical traits in Loman men. Ben keeps his two visits short and gives supposedly profound but actually vague explanations of his wealth. Although he offers Willy a job, he surely knows that there is no danger of Willy's accepting it. His gift of a diamond watch fob to Willy hardly constitutes proof of his success in diamond mines, because he could have simply bought or stolen one to dazzle Willy. If Ben were as rich as he claims to be, he could have made some provision for his only brother in his will (if only to impress him further), even if he did have seven sons. But what Ben really was matters less to Willy than what he believed Ben to be.

6. I use the word "flashback" for convenience; Miller, in "Introduction" to *Collected Plays*, maintains that "There are no flashbacks in this play but only a mobile concurrency of past and present" (p. 26).

7. My interpretation here is directly opposite to that of Lois Gordon, "*Death of a Salesman*: An Appreciation," in *The Forties: Fiction, Poetry, Drama*, ed. Warren French (DeLand, Fla.: Everett/Edwards, 1969), who states that "The first generation (Willy's father) has been forced, in order to make a living, to break up the family" (p. 278).

8. Barclay W. Bates, "The Lost Past in *Death of a Salesman*," *Modern Drama* 11 (Fall 1968): 164–72, suggests that Willy tries to function as the "dutiful patriarchal male intent upon transmitting complex legacies from his forbears to his progeny" (p. 164).

9. Willy's dream of a male patriarchal-fraternal community corresponds to the American Dream of the United States as male-dominated capitalist (patriarchal)/democratic (fraternal) nation.

10. Many critics blame this incident on Linda. For example, Barry Edward Gross, "Peddler and Pioneer in *Death of a Salesman*," *Modern Drama* 7 (February 1965): 405–10, says, "Linda discourages him from accepting the one opportunity which would allow him to fulfill his pioneer yearnings . . . [she] frustrates the pioneer in Willy because she fears it. . . . What Linda does not understand is that Willy was brought up in a tradition in which one had worlds to conquer and that the attempt to conquer them was the mark of a man" (pp. 407–8).

11. Paul Blumberg, "Sociology and Social Literature: Work Alienation in the Plays of Arthur Miller," *American Quarterly* 21 (1969): 291–310, determines that, in sociological terms, Ben represents the nineteenth-century robber baron, "hard, unscrupulous, firm, self-reliant, full of . . . self-confident energy," whereas Willy represents "the new, salaried, pathetically other-directed middle class" (p. 300).

12. Note the Green World implications in the animal images, and in the nature association and sexual pun of the "Bushwick" location, of this woman.

13. Both Richard J. Foster, "Confusion and Tragedy: The Failure of Miller's Salesman," in *Two Modern American Tragedies: Reviews and Criticism of Death of a Salesman and A Streetcar Named Desire*, ed. John D. Hurrell (New York: Charles Scribner's, 1961), pp. 82–88, and Joseph A. Hynes, "Attention Must Be Paid . . .," *College English* 23 (April 1962): 574–78, reprinted in Arthur Miller, *Death of a Salesman: Text and Criticism*, ed. Gerald Weales (New York: Viking Press, 1967), pp. 280–89, note inconsistencies in the play, particularly in the character of Biff, but neither, nor any other critic I have read, detects what is to me a troubling contradiction. When were Biff and Happy together conducting those seductions of "About five hundred women"—before or after the incident in Boston? If Biff, brimming with sexual confidence, had already had several successful experiences and had supervised Happy's initiation *before* he had gone to Boston, he surely would not have been so shocked and devastated at learning of his father's affair. He conceivably could have begun and brought Happy into a rampage of promiscuous sex as a reaction to Willy's adultery, but that interpretation seems to be at odds with Happy's mention here of Biff's mysterious change in character toward bashfulness and loss of "confidence."

14. By calling this woman a "strudel," Happy continues in his habit of self-centered definition of women by projection: when he went to his first woman to satisfy *his* "natural" but "animal" urges, she was framed in natural, animal images; here, as he is in a restaurant, Miss Forsythe is an item on *his* menu—a delicacy to be ordered, "bought," devoured, and digested to provide him with sustenance.

15. Thomas E. Porter, *Myth and Modern American Drama* (Detroit: Wayne State University Press, 1969), like many critics, calls these women "prostitutes" (p. 143). Eric Bentley, *In Search of Theatre* (New York: Knopf, 1953), asks, "Has [Miller] given us a suitable language for his tarts (in the whoring sequence)?" (p. 87), without thinking to question whether the language of the women might be right and the unreliable Happy's assumptions about them wrong.

16. Note that male and female interpretations of female "ruin" do not correspond:

The Woman sees her "ruin" not in being "used goods" but in allowing her job performance to be affected by a sexual relationship.

17. In Arthur Miller, "The Family in Modern Drama" [1956], in *Theater Essays*, ed. Martin, pp. 69–85, Miller postulates that all plays considered "great" or even "serious" examine this problem: "How may a man make of the outside world a home? How and in what ways must he struggle, what must he strive to change and overcome within himself and outside himself if he is to find the safety, the surroundings of love, the ease of soul, the sense of identity and honor which, evidently, all men have connected in their memories with the idea of family?" (p. 73).

18. Whereas I see Linda as the foundation of what is good in Willy as opposed to his "massive dreams," in which he separates himself from association with her, many critics make Linda the foundation for Willy's problems. For example, Guerin Bliquez, "Linda's Role in *Death of a Salesman*," *Modern Drama* 10 (February 1968): 383–86, states that "Linda's facility for prodding Willy to his doom is what gives the play its direction and its impetus" and projects onto Linda the play's thematic "cash-payment fixation" (p. 383). Karl Harshbarger, *The Burning Jungle: An Analysis of Arthur Miller's Death of a Salesman* (Boston: University Press of America, 1980), misappropriates "feminism" to advance his theory that Linda, beneath her "show of the 'perfect' wife," is "attempting to destroy her husband" (p. 7). He twists her statements of support of Willy into attacks (pp. 8–21) and even accuses her of an incestuous desire for Biff (p. 28).

19. Critics often give Linda even less credit than does her family. Henry Popkin, "Arthur Miller: The Strange Encounter," *Sewanee Review* 67 (1960): 34–60, calls Linda "not in the least sexually interesting" (p. 56), forgetting Willy's statement to her that "on the road I want to grab you sometimes and just kiss the life outa you." As Linda is so thoroughly compliant with Willy's other desires, there is no reason to assume her to be otherwise in connection with sex. Similarly, Brian Parker, "Point of View in Arthur Miller's *Death of a Salesman*," *University of Toronto Quarterly* 35 (1966): 144–57, reprinted in *Twentieth Century Interpretations of Death of a Salesman*, ed. Helene Wickham Koon (Englewood Cliffs, N.J.: Prentice-Hall, 1983), pp. 41–55, discounts Linda's "traditional values and her downtrodden, loving loyalty" because they "blind audiences to the essential stupidity of Linda's behavior. Surely it is both stupid and immoral to encourage the man you love in self-deceit and lies" (Koon, p. 54). Yet, as is noted by Irving Jacobson, "Family Dreams in *Death of a Salesman*," *American Literature* 47 (1975): 247–58, "given Loman's inability to accept disagreement from his sons or Charley, it is hard to suppose that he would tolerate a less acquiescent wife" (p. 257). Besides, rather than "encouraging" Willy's "lies," Linda instead balances delicately and skillfully between helping to maintain Willy's self-esteem and trying to keep him grounded in reality.

20. In Arthur Miller, "The American Theater" [1955], in *Theater Essays*, ed. Martin, pp. 31–50, Miller tells the story of Mildred Dunnock's efforts to secure the role of Linda in the original 1949 production: "We needed a woman who looked as though she had lived in a house dress all her life, even somewhat coarse and certainly less than brilliant. Mildred Dunnock insisted she was that woman, but she was frail, delicate, not long ago a teacher in a girls' college, and a cultivated citizen who probably would not

be out of place in a cabinet post. We told her this, in effect, and she understood, and left." She returned the next day, "had padded herself from neck to hem line to look a bit bigger, and for a moment none of us recognized her, and she read again. As soon as she spoke we started to laugh at her ruse; but we saw, too, that she was a little more worn now, and seemed less well-maintained, and while she was not quite ordinary, she reminded you of women who were. But we all agreed, when she was finished reading, that she was not right, and she left." But on every following day, "she was there again in another getup," and "each day she agreed with us that she was wrong; and to make a long story short when it came time to make the final selection it had to be Milly, and she turned out to be magnificent" (pp. 46–47). Thus it seems that Dunnock, better than Miller, understood Linda Loman to be a bright woman "disguising" herself to seem inferior to meet male expectations.

21. Miller had originally written "shrimp," changed it to "walrus" to fit Lee J. Cobb in the original 1949 production, then changed it back to "shrimp" for Dustin Hoffman in the 1984 production.

22. In "Introduction" to *Collected Plays*, Miller mentions having received "innumerable letters asking if I was aware that the fountain pen which Biff steals is a phallic symbol" (p. 28), and some critics continue to interpret the pen thusly, although none to my knowledge have discovered the other phallic symbols that I discuss, nor have they examined the castration theme further than do Schneider and Field, whom I cite below.

23. According to Miller in "Introduction" to *Collected Plays*, one of the "simple images" out of which the play grew was that of "the son's hard, public eye upon you, no longer swept by your myth, no longer rousable from his separateness, no longer knowing you have lived for him and have wept for him" (p. 29).

24. In Olga Carlisle and Rose Styron, "Arthur Miller: An Interview" [1966], in *Theater Essays*, ed. Martin, pp. 264–93, Miller calls the father-son relationship "a very primitive thing in my plays. That is, the father was really a figure who incorporated both power and some kind of a moral law which he had either broken himself or had fallen prey to. He figures as an immense shadow . . . it had a mythical quality to me" (pp. 267–68).

25. Benjamin Nelson, *Arthur Miller: Portrait of a Playwright* (New York: David McKay, 1970), unfairly burdens Linda with responsibility for the Loman men's dichotomizing of women into Madonna/whore categories, in order to blame her for their sexual misconduct: "In her well-meaning prudery and naïveté, and in her unswerving loyalty to Willy, she has unconsciously fostered adolescent sexual attitudes in all three of her men by creating an image of herself as the maternal counterpart of the infallible father. The more she is a paragon of virtue to them the less are they able to relate to her as adult males to a wife and mother. That view of her is pantingly adolescent and distorts all their relationships with women." Thus Happy's "image of Mom as goddess is partially responsible for his shoddy encounters with girls who are never fit to bring home to her, as well as for his father's cheap and pathetic adultery and Biff's traumatic reaction to it" (p. 113).

26. Beverly Hume, "Linda Loman as 'the Woman' in Miller's *Death of a Salesman*," *Notes on Modern American Literature* 9 (1985): item 14, also sees connection between the two characters, but her interpretation finds in Linda an "intense material-

ism" that places her "in league with 'the Woman,'" who "is manipulating Willy only for money (or stockings)."

27. Psychoanalyst Daniel E. Schneider, *The Psychoanalyst and the Artist* (New York: Farrar, Straus, 1950), pp. 246–55, suggests that the dinner was to be a "totem feast in which the sons recognize the father's authority and sexual rights" (p. 250).

28. Eric Bentley, *What Is Theatre?* (New York: Atheneum, 1968), states that "one never knows what a Miller play is about: politics or sex. If *Death of a Salesman* is political, the key scene is the one with the tape recorder; if it is sexual, the key scene is the one in the Boston hotel" (p. 261). To me, the play is not about politics or sex but politics of sex, so even the scene with the tape recorder (actually a "wire recorder") is sexually political. Howard's presentation of the three females in his private life—daughter, wife, and maid—recapitulates in miniature the treatment of women elsewhere in the play. Although Howard had bought the recorder for dictation, he tries it out on his family—testing Business World techniques in the Home. His daughter, the first guinea pig, whistles "Roll out the Barrel," then Howard whistles the same song, perhaps to demonstrate superiority over her. She is seven years old, and her chief value is in being "crazy for" her father. Howard's son, however, is the important one—five years old and reciting the state capitals, in alphabetical order. Father and son are the best performers, with the females only to express devotion, provide entertainment, or demonstrate supposed inadequacy to the male standard. The maid "kicked the plug out," but later Howard will depend on her to support the machine by recording radio programs for his convenience. Howard's wife is bullied into speaking into the machine, but she proves such an embarrassment that he interrupts her dissension by shutting off her voice. Willy's function throughout this episode is to admire but to be interrupted and silenced when the son displays his talents. Willy is thus put into the position of Woman, into the same role that he expects Linda to play. Furthermore, Willy even replays the actions of the wire-recorded women: like the daughter, Willy calls forth the admired father (Howard's father); like the wife, he has no interest in the recorder but is forced to interact with it; and like the maid who accidentally unplugs the machine, Willy (a "servant" of Howard's firm) accidentally turns it on, thereby becoming an embarrassment to be "shut off," again like the wife. Howard the "son" then begins the symbolic castration (completed by Biff) of Willy the "father" by asking him to turn in his samples, his two salesman's cases, representing his testicles.

29. In "Introduction" to *Collected Plays*, Miller relates that "when asked what Willy was selling, what was in his bags, I could only reply, 'Himself'" (p. 28).

30. Schneider, *The Psychoanalyst and the Artist*, labels as "castration-panic" Willy's flight to the bathroom after hearing of Biff's theft of Oliver's pen (p. 250).

31. Cf. the hideous portrayal of Linda's self-assertion by Schneider, *The Psychoanalyst and the Artist*: "Her rage at being old and dried-up is implicit as she fights like a she-tiger against the sons who have cast off the father for their own sexual philandering" (p. 251).

32. B. S. Field, Jr., "*Death of a Salesman*," *Twentieth Century Literature* 18 (1972): 19–24, reprinted in *Twentieth Century Interpretations of Death of a Salesman*, ed. Helene Wickham Koon (Englewood Cliffs, N.J.: Prentice-Hall, 1983), pp. 79–84, interprets Willy's *hamartia* to be his success in making his sons in his own image: "One

may . . . say of Willy that 'he's got no balls.' And neither have his sons. . . . They are morally and socially castrated . . . he has made moral eunuchs of his own sons" (Koon, p. 84).

33. As is noted by Chester E. Eisinger, "Focus on Arthur Miller's *Death of a Salesman*: The Wrong Dreams," in *American Dreams, American Nightmares*, ed. David Madden (Carbondale: Southern Illinois University Press; London and Amsterdam: Feffer & Simons, 1970), pp. 165–74, Biff "cannot and need not rely on a mere symbol of manhood. This conviction transcends the phallic value of the pen and sustains Biff in his honest self-knowledge at the end of the play" (p. 172).

34. Note Parker's explanation in "Point of View": "After thirty-five years of marriage, Linda is apparently completely unable to comprehend her husband: her speech at the graveside . . . is not only pathetic, it is also an explanation of the loneliness of Willy Loman which threw him into other women's arms" (Koon, p. 54).

35. Miller, in "Introduction" to *Collected Plays*, remembers that he "laughed when the line came, laughed with the artist-devil's laugh, for it had all come together in this line, she having been made by him though he did not know it or believe in it or receive it into himself" (p. 30).

36. In Phillip Gelb, "Morality and Modern Drama" [interview, 1958], in *Theater Essays*, ed. Martin, pp. 195–214, Miller states that because he kills himself, Willy cannot be an "average American man," yet he "embodies in himself some of the most terrible conflicts running through the streets of America today. A Gallup Poll might indicate that they are not the majority conflicts; I think they are" (pp. 199–200).

37. In "Introduction" to *Collected Plays*, Miller, recalling some of the widely varying evaluations of the play, says that "The letters from women made it clear that the central character of the play was Linda" (p. 28). But those women were not alone. Several critics have made a case for Biff as the play's tragic protagonist, and one (Schneider) has even done so for Happy. Recent criticism sometimes cites these readings, but it is much less often remembered that some early reviewers sketched in a similar possibility for Linda. Robert Garland, "Audience Spellbound by Prize Play of 1949," *The New York Journal-American*, 11 February 1949, p. 24, reprinted in *Arthur Miller*, ed. Gerald Weales (New York: Viking Press, 1967), pp. 199–201, saw Linda as the "the play's most poignant figure" whose "all-too-human single-mindedness holds *Death of a Salesman* together," and he found the "most tragic tragedy" to be her powerlessness to prevent Willy from being his "own worst tragedy" (Weales, p. 200). Similarly, William Beyer, "The State of the Theatre: The Season Opens," *School and Society* 70 (3 December 1949): 363–64, reprinted in *Arthur Miller*, ed. Weales, pp. 228–30, interpreted the play to be "essentially the mother's tragedy, not Willy Loman's. Willy's plight is sad, true, but he is unimportant and too petty, commonplace, and immature to arouse more than pity, and the sons are of a piece with their father. . . . We can only sympathize since they reflect human frailties all too common among men. Within her circumscribed sphere of living, however, the mother makes of her love a star which her idealism places on high, and when it is destroyed her heavens are wiped out. What the mother stands for is important, and when she goes down the descent is tragic" (Weales, p. 230).

"What's the Secret?": Willy Loman as Desiring Machine

Granger Babcock

Arthur Miller's *Death of a Salesman* (1949) conveys its critique of American capital in a more complex and subtle manner than critics have thus far recognized. Most criticism of the play, as Sheila Huftel points out, is "governed by the need . . . to know and understand Willy Loman" (103). Unfortunately, much of the energy expended to understand Willy has been too narrowly focused on analyzing the individuated character traits of the protagonist and the attendant issue of tragic stature. The play, in fact, suggests just the opposite—that Willy is not autonomous, self-generated, or self-made (even in "failure"), but that he is completely other to himself; he is more puppet than person, more machine than man, and as such he announces the death, or disappearance, of the subject, the death of the tragic hero, and the birth of "the desiring machine."

Most critics recognize that Arthur Miller intends Willy Loman as a victim of "society." But Willy's construction as a victim is interpreted within the parameters of a self-generated individual and is used as the main reason conservative critics deny *Salesman* tragic status. As a victim, the argument runs, Willy has no understanding of his situation; he is, in the words of Dan Vogel, "too commonplace and limited" (91). Unlike Oedipus, Hamlet, or Lear, Willy is incapable of self-knowledge and is, therefore, not tragic but pathetic: "he cannot summon the intelligence and strength to scrutinize his situation and come to some understanding of it" (Jacobson 247). Even liberal critics like Thomas Adler and Ruby Cohn, who are generally sympathetic towards Willy, tend to judge his character harshly; in their estimation, he is either a "victim of himself and his choices," or he "has achieved neither popularity nor success as a salesman, and has failed as a gardener, carpenter, and father" (Adler 102; Cohn 44). Willy's problem (or part of his problem), then, according to these critics, is that he accepts his fate; he does not possess the vision, volition, capacity, strength, knowledge, or pluck to fight against the cultural forces that shape his life.

The underlying assumption of these arguments is that Willy *can* change his life—with a little hard work, perhaps—but that he *will* not. Behind these judgments is a model: the national subject, or what I will call the masculine unconscious. This model can also be described as the autonomous, active male subject that determines and makes itself, as well as the liberal subject, the rugged individual, or the exceptional American. Whatever linguistic sign the masculine unconscious uses to communicate itself, it is wholly other to the subject, and it is given to the subject by the publicity apparatus of capital. Miller calls this other the "law of success":

> The confusion of some critics viewing *Death of a Salesman* . . . is that they do not see that Willy Loman has broken a law without whose protection life is insupportable, if not incomprehensible to him and to many others; it is a law which says a failure in society and in business has no right to live. Unlike the law against incest, the law of success is not administered by statute or church, but it is very nearly as powerful in its grip upon men.
>
> (*Collected Plays* 35; hereafter referred to as *CP*)

In *Dialectic of Enlightenment* (1947), Max Horkheimer and Theodor Adorno identify the "law of success" as an effect of the "technological rationale" which dominates the cultural and economic institutions of modern industrial nations:

> Through the countless agencies of mass production and its culture the conventionalized modes of behavior are impressed upon the individual as the only natural, respectable, and rational ones. He defines himself as a thing, as a static element, as success or failure.
>
> (28)

That is, under what Horkheimer and Adorno call late capitalism, individual behavior is reduced to a series of "protocols" or stereotypical responses found on the job, on the radio, in the movies, and in the then-emerging television industry. For Adorno, these standardized models of behavior signaled the end of the liberal subject, since "motivation in the old, liberal sense" was being appropriated and "systematically controlled and absorbed by social mechanisms which are directed from above" ("Freudian Theory" 136). In other words, the subject's desire for success (e.g., for material wealth, to "get ahead"), which the subject believes is self-generated, is, in fact, his identification with the rationale of the apparatus, which has programmed individual consumption as spontaneous thought or reason or the assertion of individual will.

Viewed in light of Horkheimer and Adorno's discovery, the operations of Willy Loman's mind reflect this change in subjectivity. Specifically, Willy assumes that his desire is spontaneous, when in fact, as Miller suggests in *Timebends* (1987), it has been "hammered into its strange shape by society, the business life Willy had lived and believed in" (182). Willy's desire does not make him autonomous; it makes him "common" since that desire is what motivates all the men in the play and indeed most men in our culture. In constructing Willy, Miller exposes the liberal subject as a fiction, as part of a structure of value that is an effect of the economy. To dismiss Willy as "pathetic" because he does not have the strength of character to understand his situation or because he has made the wrong choices is to recode the play according to the protocols of the apparatus (i.e., a man is either a success or he is a failure). Willy chooses nothing; he merely follows a blueprint. Like a machine, he operates according to plan. The publicity apparatus tells Willy that if he works hard like Edison, that if he perseveres like Goodrich, that if he is "well-liked" like Dave Singleman, then he will rise like Charley and become rich and powerful like J. P. Morgan. The blueprint also tells Willy that if he does not become "a success," that if he does not become like a Gene Tunney or a Red Grange, then he is a failure—and that this is his fault. Willy's question to Ben and to Bernard—

"What's the secret?"—is therefore by design. Willy cannot see that there is no secret—that success or status is largely determined by extrinsic factors.

Conservative critics do not recognize Willy as an effect of the economy because the critical field in which they operate does not permit this. For them, he is a problem, not a cultural symptom. Critics from the left, such as Raymond Williams, Michael Spindler, and John Orr, while they see Willy as a symptom of capitalist culture, have focused more on Willy's objectification than on his relationship to the apparatus that produced him. Williams, for instance, argues that "Willy Loman is a man who from selling things has passed to selling himself, and has become, in effect, a commodity which like other commodities will at a certain point be discarded by the laws of the economy" (104). While Williams's argument concerning Willy is certainly accurate, given Willy's desire to "make an appearance in the business world" (*CP* 146), I would like to suggest a different way to read Willy, which is more in keeping with the model of subjectivity theorized by Horkheimer and Adorno in *Dialectic of Enlightenment*, and which, I believe, more fully represents the rationalization of consciousness brought about by the symbolic apparatus of late capitalism.

In their book *Anti-Oedipus: Capitalism and Schizophrenia* (1983), Gilles Deleuze and Felix Guattari problematize previous models of subjectivity by eliminating the opposition around which the subject is constructed: "There is no such thing as either man or nature now, only a process that produces the one within the other and couples the machines together. Producing-machines, desiring-machines . . . the self and the non-self, outside and inside, no longer have any meaning whatsoever" (2). According to Deleuze and Guattari, the cognitive subject no longer exists since the subject-object split on which its identity is based has collapsed. The boundary between subject and object collapses, they argue, under the weight of the publicity apparatus of late capitalist cultures, which colonizes the subject from without by pouring its narratives inward. They replace the cognitive model with a quasi-cybernetic model, the desiring machine. The desiring machine runs on information from the outside; its goals, writes Jean-François Lyotard, are "programmed into it" and therefore it cannot "correct in the course of its functioning" (16). The man/machine is programmed to fit the body of capital, to adjust to the demands of efficiency of the larger system. Deleuze and Guattari stress that the identity produced by the system is "a producing/product identity" (7). That is, the machine produces, or in Willy's case reproduces, not only biologically but also ideologically, for the system at the same time that it is produced or constructed by the system.

A more effective way to interpret Deleuze and Guattari's "producing/product identity," especially when we consider Willy Loman and the other men in *Salesman*, is to see it as a producing/consuming identity. The male subject desires to reproduce itself (pass itself on) at the same time it desires to consume success narratives, cheese, Chevrolets, Studebakers, aspirin, women, refrigerators, etc. The male subject reproduces itself by having children and acting as a model for those children. Willy, for instance, wants his sons to learn the law of success embodied by his brother Ben: ". . . when I walked into the jungle, I was seventeen. When I walked out I was twenty-one. And, by God, I was rich" (*CP* 159–60). The male subject consumes by buying products. Listen to Happy:

> . . . suppose I get to be merchandise manager? He's a good friend of mine, and he just built a terrific estate on Long Island. And he lived there about two months and sold it, and now he's building another one. He can't enjoy it once it's finished. And I know that's just what I would do. I don't know what the hell I'm workin' for.
>
> (*CP* 139)

Or listen to Howard Wagner talk about his wire recorder: "I tell you . . . I'm gonna take my camera, and my bandsaw, and all my hobbies, and out they go. This is the most fascinating relaxation I've ever found"

(*CP* 178). Willy's desire has also been programmed; just listen to Linda tell us why he bought a Hastings refrigerator: "They got the biggest ads of any of them!" (*CP* 148).

The three passages suggest that Miller is aware that (re)production and consumption are programmed. Desire is mediated by an other, by the publicity apparatus of capital. The "subject" merely occupies a circuit or an outlet, or, to use Lyotard's word, a "post," through which messages or units of information pass (15). Willy (or Happy or Howard Wagner) is reduced to the function of a receptacle/transmitter; information travels through him and in him. In this process, memory (the site of the other) becomes a depository for and a transmitter of the masterprograms or "masternarratives" of the system in which the desiring machine operates. The machine's program can thus be viewed as a metanarrative that is used to reinscribe or recode reality into a pattern that the larger system finds acceptable. The metanarrative acts like the unconscious because it is wholly other to the subject and because it works through the subject to structure social life. This operation is seen in Happy's description of the merchandise manager's mindless consumption, in his building of houses which he soon deserts only to build new houses; his desire spins metonymically out of control, seeking difference or fulfillment in what is essentially the same. Neither man understands why he buys things or why he works, yet they both buy and work without question. Presumably they work to "get ahead," to "accomplish something," but in reality they are, like Willy, programmed for the body of capital; it doesn't matter if they get ahead, if they succeed, or even if they become "number-one man." What does matter, however, is that everybody desire to work so that everybody can afford to consume. Desire, to use Sartre's term, has been "massified."

At this point, we turn our attention to Willy Loman and explore how the dreams of capital have programmed his "life." Throughout the play, Willy consumes and then reproduces models and axioms that are part of the masculine unconscious:

> Be liked and you will never want. (*CP* 146)
>
> A man oughta come in with a few words. (*CP* 149)
>
> I gotta overcome it. I know I gotta overcome it. I'm not dressing to advantage, maybe. (*CP* 149)
>
> Everybody likes a kidder, but nobody lends him money. (*CP* 168)
>
> But remember, start big and you'll end up big. (*CP* 168)
>
> Start off with a couple of your good stories to lighten things up. It's not what you say, it's how you say it—because personality always wins the day. (*CP* 169)

These axioms (and the model they represent) appear in the text as isolated linguistic events, as the recitations of a lone idiolect, but they are in fact "splinters" or units (traces) of the metanarrative of national subject that speak through the subject. Willy consumes these bits of information just as he consumes aspirins and cheese. Their presence indicates that Willy's subjectivity has been "interpellated" by the ideological apparatus.[1] Another indication of Willy's interpellation are his numerous contradictory statements. Early in the play, for instance, Willy calls Biff a "lazy bum" because Biff does not have a steady job. Three lines later, however, after Linda tells Willy that Biff is "lost," Willy replies incredulously, "Biff Loman is lost. In the greatest country in the world a young man with such—personal attractiveness, gets lost. There's one thing about Biff—he's not lazy" (*CP* 134). Willy then reminds Linda that "Certain men just don't get started till later in life. Like Thomas Edison, I think. Or B. F. Goodrich" (*CP* 135).

In this instance, the masterprogram operates to allegorize the experience of the "subject" by making the subject part of the national narrative of progress; the process is therefore synecdochical (*e pluribus unum*). The process reveals itself as a fusion or syndesis of narratives, modes of masculinity from different historical periods, that cover over the reality of the present and mystify history. This fusion is first discovered in the practices of late nineteenth-century advertising, where the consumer ideology is bound together with eighteenth- and nineteenth-century conceptions of masculinity. The adjusted or emergent narrative is deposited on the hegemonic narrative, which in turn lends the newer representation its legitimacy or authority.

However, the crucial thing to note about the masterprogram is the way in which Miller suggests it operates through Willy to reinscribe his family history as part of the success narrative of the national subject. Willy desires to be the same as his father or his brother Ben; he desires to be other than he is, to inhabit earlier periods of capital through an other's body, which is essentialized or universal. By banishing *différance*, Willy hopes to construct a stable subjectivity. He no longer wishes to feel "temporary" (*CP* 159) about himself. He no longer wants to be part of the body of capital, which is always (magically) transforming itself, adjusting itself, expanding itself—like the neighborhood in which he lives. The desire to be successful, then, is the desire to connect himself to a transcendental masculinity that erases the reality of his present social position. This erasure is achieved, however, at a cost. The subject is restored to fullness by transforming extrinsic social factors into personal failure. Willy performs this function to empower himself, to restore the independence of the subject, which has been irretrievably lost. In the process, however, he learns to misrecognize himself (and Brooklyn). At the same time, Willy also learns to marginalize other masculinities, the alternative men he might represent, in favor of the dominant models advocated by the culture industry (i.e., Edison, Goodrich, etc.).

As C.W.E. Bigsby notes, "Willy Loman's life is rooted in America's past" (184). More precisely, his identity is rooted in models from two different periods of American capital, which are conflated in his mind. Willy's father represents the unfettered and unalienated labor of mercantile capital. His brother Ben represents the accumulative processes of monopoly capital. Both figures are mythic; that is, both figures embody an heroic past that is disseminated by the symbolic practices of capital and reproduced in individual men. Together, Miller suggests, they represent the (his)tory (not an history) of the (white) race in America. Or, as Irving Jacobson suggests,

> What Willy Loman wants, and what success means in *Death of a Salesman*, is intimately related to his own, and the playwright's, sense of the family. Family dreams extend backward in time to interpret the past, reach forward in time to project images of the future, and pressure reality in the present to conform to memory [ideology] and imagination.
>
> (248)

The flute "melody" that marks the beginning and the ending of the play, and which is heard periodically throughout, is the emblem or signature of Willy's lost father. According to the stage directions, "It is small and fine, telling of grass and trees and the horizon" (*CP* 130). It is, as numerous critics point out, the aural symbol of his "pioneer virtues" (Parker 33). It is the sound of the unalienated commodity, which later returns (transformed) as the mass-produced "golden" pen that Biff steals. It is the sound of the past in the present, the still active residual model which operates to marginalize the present. It represents the desire for opportunity and mobility associated with westward expansion. Willy's father, as Ben tells him, was a small entrepreneur whose life was determined by the structures of a mercantile economy:

> Father was a very great and very wild-hearted man. We would start in Boston, and he'd toss the whole family into the wagon, and then he'd drive the whole team right across the country; through Ohio, and Indiana, Michigan, Illinois, and all the Western states.
>
> (*CP* 157)

Willy's father was a "great inventor" who would "stop in the towns and sell the flutes he'd made on the way" (*CP* 157). "With one gadget," Ben tells Willy, "he made more in a week than a man like you could make in a lifetime" (*CP* 157).

Ben's last statement seems unlikely, and its hyperbole marks a confusion in Willy's mind produced, or mediated, by the other's desire. Willy desires to be like his father because his father is like other successful men, other "great" inventors; his father is a model citizen—he has amassed a fortune. His father is like America's first model citizen, Ben Franklin, who "invented" electricity and the lightning rod. His father is like Thomas A. Edison and B. F. Goodrich, both rich and famous because of their inventions. Nevertheless, given the mercantile economy in which Miller locates Willy's father, it is unlikely that he could have produced a "gadget" that earned him more in a week than Willy earns in his lifetime. This type of event was more common (but still relatively isolated) in the period of capital Ben represents (monopoly capital) when "great" inventors like Edison and Goodrich did earn more money in a week (by producing technology for an emergent industrial economy) than a salesman could earn in thirty-five years. The figure of Willy's father exists simultaneously in Willy's "mind" with the figures of Edison and Goodrich. The simultaneity of the Franklin-Edison-Goodrich-father Loman narrative produces a fusion of the individual stories, which erases the specific history of the individual figures by marginalizing their differences; this fusion, again, is produced by the publicity apparatus of capital. Through the other, that is, Willy plugs himself into the success narrative as he rereads his family history.

A more elaborate example of this type of conflation is found when we examine Ben Loman. On one level, Miller uses the figure of Ben to link the formation of the national subject to the founding of the Republic—that is, Miller clearly chooses the name Ben to remind his readers of Ben Franklin's paradigmatic American masculinity. Ben's continual repetition of the rags to riches story—"Why, boys, when I walked into the jungle, I was seventeen. When I walked out I was twenty-one. And, by God, I was rich" (*CP* 157)—is a deliberate echo of Franklin's *Autobiography*, in which Franklin tells his readers that he walked into Philadelphia with the clothes on his back and within a few years became rich and famous. Notably, Miller conflates the Franklin myth with another version of masculinity from a later stage of American capital, not to differentiate the two, but to suggest that they are both operative, and that the latter version is just a rearticulation of the former. The phrase "acres of diamonds," which Ben continually uses, alludes to a series of lectures and books written by the evangelist Russell Conwell in the 1890s "to spread the gospel of material wealth" (Innes 64–5; Porter 24–7). Conwell's writings, which included *The Safe and Sure Way to Amass a Fortune and Be a Benefactor and Achieve Greatness*, were typical of the "success cult" that dominated American magazine and popular book culture around the turn of the century (Greene 111).

The assumptions about masculinity at the core of Franklin's *Autobiography* are present in Conwell's writings as well. Both writers construct masculinity in very ahistoric ways by insisting that "success" is the result of personal agency or character. Miller uses Ben's speech, which Willy is remembering, to illustrate that language has a history. The traces of Franklin's and Conwell's stories survive as moments of the past in the present, and because they have been decontextualized by the operations of the publicity apparatus, they exist only as ideology within memory (i.e., devoid of their cultural context, they become part of the same moment, the typology of American maleness—not products of specific historical periods and circumstances). These representations do, however, bear the mark of their history and, as such, their difference can only be recognized when their history is restored. The conflation of Franklin and Conwell in Ben's speech is recognized when we try to account for the fact that Ben Loman and Russell Conwell inhabit an America radically different from Franklin's. Ben's ascendancy to what Willy calls "success incarnate" (*CP* 152) takes place in the late 1880s, a period marked by intense imperial expansion and expropriation of native labor and resources. As what Ruby Cohn calls a "ruthless adventurer" (41), Ben represents the accumulative processes of monopoly capital (roughly 1880 to 1910).

Further, the mode of masculinity that Ben represents is radically out of place in the America of the late 1940s (as is Willy's father's "pioneer" masculinity). Willy's desire to be like Ben and like his father manifests itself as a nostalgia that seals him off from the present. As a result, Willy cannot recognize "reality," and he therefore engages in the success fantasy given to him by the other. In addition, Miller also suggests that the nostalgia for previous models or paradigms is constituted by their ability to provide ready-made (read: reductive) interpretations of the world; this operation, however, as Hayden White suggests, is disabling (and therefore destructive) because it prevents individuals and societies from imaginatively confronting the problems of the present (39).

One result of Willy's interpellation is that he cannot see Brooklyn as it is—that is, he is not satisfied with seeing it the way it is; he desires to see it as other, as the old west or the frontier. As he tells Ben, "It's Brooklyn, I know, but we hunt too" (*CP* 158). Willy's desire to see Brooklyn as other is also a symptom of the machine in crisis. The flute melody that represents the fiction of infinite space and unfettered masculine autonomy of the frontier (i.e., the mobility that most Americans expect and desire) is an ideological formation directly at odds with Willy's "reality." Willy can see the "towering, angular shapes" that surround his house "on all sides" (*CP* 130), and he is aware of the changes in his neighborhood:

> The way they box us in here. Bricks and windows, windows and bricks. . . . The street is lined with cars. There's not a breath of fresh air in the neighborhood. The grass don't grow anymore, you can't raise a carrot in the backyard. They should've had a law against apartment houses. Remember those two beautiful elm trees out there? When I and Biff hung the swing between them. . . . They should've arrested the builder for cutting those down. They massacred the neighborhood. . . .
>
> (*CP* 134–35)

Yet the cultural processes that allow the "they" to box him in, to massacre the neighborhood, go unrecognized because his models program him for "oversight." In other words, his knowledge of the world is produced by models that act to exclude or screen out disruptive bits of information. Willy's knowledge of his world represents a desire for older modes that reduce his understanding of his social position.

His models also prevent him from seeing the history of his present (ultimately they push his vision inward, which leads to annihilation). His question to Linda that concludes the diatribe about the neighborhood—"How can they whip cheese?"—outlines the contour or boundary of his knowledge about the operations of capital; this question marks the limits of his awareness, outside (or inside) of which he cannot see or transgress. The question represents his limit as a subject. The salesman, ironically, does not understand how products are made. They appear to him, as they sometimes did to Marx, "as autonomous figures endowed with a life of their own" (165). Willy's seemingly trivial question reveals how effective the publicity apparatus (with its fetishization of consumption) is in marginalizing the effects of technological change. As William T. Brucher points out, Willy's "unexpected, marvellingly innocent question about whipping cheese reveals an ambivalence toward technology livelier and more interesting . . . than a simple dichotomy between farm and factory, past and present" (83–4). Willy's "marvellingly innocent question" reveals a complete ignorance of the cultural processes that affect his life, that cause him to lose his job. Willy's life is, in fact, a denial of the transformative powers of capital. Any recognition of change is subverted by the transcendent (fetishized) models that he worships, which do not record or reflect any change. Celebrity—the lives of B. F. Goodrich and Thomas A. Edison and Dave Singleman—has replaced history. The consumption of technological "progress," as Willy's broken cars, refrigerators, fanbelts, and leaky shower and roof attest, has replaced "real" social relations.

A second result of Willy's interpellation is that he "embues" his sons with the values of the other, what he calls "the spirit of the jungle." These values are mediated through the figure of Ben Loman. "There was the only man I ever met who knew the answers," says Willy (*CP* 155). "There was a man started with the clothes on his back and ended up with diamond mines" (*CP* 152). How does Ben achieve this goal? According to Willy, "The man knew what he wanted and went out and got it. Walked into the jungle, and comes out, the age of twenty one, and he's rich!" (*CP* 152). And this triumph is just what Willy wants for his boys; when Ben comes to visit, Willy brags to him that "That's just the spirit I want to embue them with! To walk into the jungle!" (*CP* 160). He's bringing them up to be "rugged, well-liked, all-around" (*CP* 157). Ben, of course, approves: "Outstanding, manly chaps!" (*CP* 159). Willy's desire is therefore reproduced through and in Biff and Happy; because of Willy's pedagogy, they become carriers of the program. Willy wants them, as Ben advises him, to "Screw on your fists and . . . fight for a fortune. . . ." (*CP* 183). He doesn't want them to be "worms," like Bernard (*CP* 151). But as Brian Parker points out, the aggressive practices Ben represents while "admirable in combatting raw nature [become] immoral when turned against one's fellow man" (33).

I suggest above that Ben's aggressiveness represents a brutality that Miller equates with American imperialism. Another way to read Ben's aggressiveness—this time, within the boundaries of the nation—is as competition. Historically, as C. Wright Mills notes, "for men in the era of classical liberalism, competition was never merely an impersonal mechanism regulating the economy of capitalism, or only a guarantee of political freedom. Competition was a means of producing free individuals, a testing field for heroes; in its terms men lived the legend of the self-reliant individual" (11). Whether or not what Mills argues is historically representative, it is safe to assume that in a decentralized economy (an economy without the hierarchy of industrialized structures), individual competition through labor was a way for many to create mobility and wealth. However, as the economy became more centralized and hierarchical, competition, as Willy says, became "maddening" because it did not yield the same results (imagined or otherwise) as it did for men of Willy's father's and Ben's generations.

In Willy's time, in fact, competition has become warlike. After returning from a selling trip, for instance, Willy tells his family he "Knocked 'em cold in Providence, slaughtered 'em in Boston" (*CP*

146). Willy's gift to his sons on his return from this same trip is a punching bag with "Gene Tunney's signature on it." "[I]t's the finest thing for the timing," he tells his apprentices (*CP* 144). Elsewhere, Willy describes business as "murderous" (*CP* 159). When Biff goes to ask Bill Oliver for a loan, Willy's advice is "Knock him dead, boy" (*CP* 170). The violence of Willy's language echoes the ruthlessness of his model, Ben—the same man who attacks Biff: "Never fight fair with a stranger, boy. You'll never get out of the jungle that way" (*CP* 158). Willy's desire to emulate Ben's power thus leads him to bring "the spirit of the jungle" into his home, where it reveals itself as what Sartre calls "counter-finality." His positive intention of providing his boys with a model for success results in the negative legitimation of theft and fantasy.

Miller problematizes Willy's pedagogy by suggesting that even sanctioned expressions of masculinity involve theft. In the scene which follows Ben's fight with Biff, for example, Willy has his sons start to rebuild the front steps because Willy doesn't want Ben to think he is just a salesman; he wants to show Ben that Brooklyn is not Brooklyn ("we hunt too" [*CP* 158]); he wants to show Ben what kind of stock his sons come from: "Why, Biff can fell any one of these trees in no time!" (*CP* 158). Instead of providing the materials to rebuild the front stoop, however, Willy directs his sons to "Go right over where they're building the apartment house and get some sand" (*CP* 158). Charley warns Willy that "if they steal any more from that building the watchman'll put the cops on them" (*CP* 158). Willy responds, addressing Ben, "You shoulda seen the lumber they brought home last week. At least a dozen six-by-tens worth all kinds of money" (*CP* 158). This, of course, is a parody of Ben's logging operations in Alaska, but it also suggests that the individualism that the success ideology sanctions legitimates theft, just as that ideology legitimates the expropriation of foreign land and mineral resources. This is made even clearer in the following lines, when Willy excuses his sons' behavior because, as he says, "I got a couple of fearless characters there" (*CP* 158). Charley counters: "Willy, the jails are full of fearless characters" (*CP* 158), and Ben responds, "And the stock exchange, friend!" (*CP* 158). Again, these lines suggest that Miller recognizes that even legitimized expressions of masculine behavior, practices and beliefs that the American publicity apparatus valorizes, involve theft.

A further example of Miller transforming the success ideology into theft is found in the scene where Biff "borrows" a football from his high school locker room so that he can practice with a "regulation ball" (*CP* 144). Willy, predictably, laughs with Biff at the theft and rewards the action by saying, "Coach'll probably congratulate you on your initiative!" (*CP* 144). Initiative, even in Franklin's day, is one of the key elements of masculine autonomy, and here Miller insists that initiative is a form of theft. Later in the same scene, Biff tells his father, "This Saturday, Pop, this Saturday—just for you, I'm going to break through for a touchdown" (*CP* 145). Happy then reminds Biff that he is "supposed to pass" (*CP* 145). Biff ignores Happy's warning and says, "I'm *taking* one play for Pop" (*CP* 145; italics mine). This taking is a pattern that will eventually take over Biff's life, for as Biff tells Willy at the end of the play, "I stole a suit in Kansas City and I was in jail. . . . I stole myself out of every good job since high school!" (*CP* 216). More important for Miller, however, is that this one moment of taking represents a typical moment in the dominant version of American masculinity. Biff's "theft" of the play is another instance of his initiative, another example drawn from the headlines which celebrate individual achievement. For a moment in Willy's mind, Biff is like Red Grange or Gene Tunney. As he tells Charley, "When this game is over . . . you'll be laughing out the other side of your face. They'll be calling him another Red Grange. Twenty-five thousand a year" (*CP* 186). What is lost in Biff's taking, however, is the team. Biff's initiative, and his desire to place himself above the goal of the team, jeopardizes the collective goal of the team—to win the City Championship.

Miller addresses the counter-finality of fantasy in the climax of the play, which is organized around Biff's trip to Bill Oliver's office where he plans to ask Oliver to stake him in a new business venture, "The Loman Brothers," a line of sporting goods. This fiction has been created as a way to deflect Willy's fury at learning that Biff plans to "[s]crew the business world!" and return to the West, because in the West he can do as he pleases. That is, he can swim in the middle of the day and, working as a carpenter, he can whistle on the job; he also tells Happy that "we don't belong in this nuthouse of a city! We belong mixing cement on some open plain. . . ." (*CP* 166). At the same time, Biff expresses his hatred of the business world because "They've laughed at Dad for years. . . ." (*CP* 166). Willy responds in a characteristic manner: "Go to Filene's, go to the Hub, go to Slattery's, Boston. Call out the name Willy Loman and see what happens!" (*CP* 166). At this point, to quell Willy's anger, optimistic Happy starts the familiar story ("He's going to see Bill Oliver, Pop" [*CP* 167])—that quickly develops into a success fantasy before the fact: Happy's "feasible idea" is to borrow money from Bill Oliver to start a line of sporting goods (*CP* 167). Of course, Happy's idea is neither feasible nor sensible; it is in fact absurd that Biff believes he can borrow ten thousand dollars from a man he has not seen in fifteen years and from whom he stole merchandise.

At the end of the second act, however, Happy's pipe dream comes apart as Biff begins to insist on the truth; Biff tells Willy that he "was never a salesman for Bill Oliver," that he was a shipping clerk. Willy insists that Biff was a salesman for Oliver, and when Biff tries to correct Willy by asking him to "hold on to the facts," Willy says he's not interested in the facts (*CP* 198–99). What he is interested in is another story, and Willy and Happy begin to work to reimpose the success fantasy they have constructed at the end of the first act, but the fantasy is interrupted by Biff's announcing that he has stolen Bill Oliver's fountain pen.

The final confrontation occurs two scenes later when Biff tells Willy "you're going to hear the truth—what you are and what I am" (*CP* 216). Biff rejects Willy's "phony dream" because

> I ran down eleven flights with a pen in my hand today. And suddenly I stopped. . . . I saw the things that I love in this world. The work and the food and time to sit and smoke. And I looked at the pen and said to myself, what the hell am I grabbing this for? Why am I trying to become what I don't want to be? What am I doing in an office, making a contemptuous, begging fool of myself, when all I want is out there, waiting for me the minute I say I know who I am!
>
> (*CP* 217)

This is an assertion of Biff's desire against Willy's desire and the fantasy that Willy's desire constructs. Because Biff recognizes that his father's dream is false, that his father has been positioned by the law of success to believe in the autonomous male, he is in a position to resist (at least partially) the ideology. Biff does not believe in the version of universal citizenship that Willy believes in. Biff recognizes that he is "a dime a dozen" (*CP* 217), that he will never be B. F. Goodrich or Thomas Edison or Red Grange or J. P. Morgan or Gene Tunney. He attempts to resist the ideology of the success narrative because he doesn't want to be other; he doesn't want to be number one: "I am not a leader of men, Willy, and neither are you. . . . I'm a dollar an hour, Willy. . . . A buck an hour" (*CP* 217). Willy, a believer to the bitter end, insists that he is exceptional: "I am Willy Loman, and you are Biff Loman" (*CP* 217). At this point there is a complete repudiation of the success fantasy: Biff screams, "Pop, I'm nothing! I'm nothing, Pop" (*CP* 217), and he begins to hug his father and cry.

Commenting on this scene, Miller writes that Biff embodies "an opposing system which . . . is in a race for Willy's faith, and it is the system of love which is the opposite of the law of success" (*CP* 36). However, Miller claims that "by the time Willy can perceive [Biff's] love, it can serve only as an ironic comment upon the life he sacrificed for power and for success and its tokens" (*CP* 36). Biff rejects the law that makes men compete with each other and steal from each other in order for them to be successful. Instead, through his characterization of Bernard, Charley, and (at the end of the play) Biff, Miller seems to offer the possibility of a system where men love each other and try to help one another, rather than exploit one another. His solution to the problem of individualism is moral rather than revolutionary, for as he points out, the "most decent man" in the play "is a capitalist (Charley) whose aims are not different from Willy Loman's" (*CP* 37). The difference between Willy and Charley "is that Charley is not a fanatic": "he has learned how to live without that frenzy, that ecstasy of spirit which Willy chases to the end" (*CP* 37). Likewise, "Bernard . . . works hard, attends to his studies, and attains a worthwhile objective" (*CP* 37). Miller also notes that these people all come from the same social class (*CP* 37), yet Charley and Bernard do not succumb to the frenzy because, in Miller's view, they manage to resist the law of success and can act like decent men. What makes their resistance possible? Miller offers no specific answer. The play suggests that some men are able to do this while others are not; it offers hope, but no specific program: "What theory lies behind this double view? None whatever. It is simply that I knew and know that I feel better when my work is reflecting a balance of the truth as it exists" (*CP* 37).

Nevertheless, because the play is organized around the consciousness of Willy Loman, the play does not reflect the balance that Miller seems to have intended. Because Willy is such a strong presence, he pushes Bernard and Charley to the margins of the play. Willy's is the dominant voice, and it is through this voice that Miller maps the discourse of national identity as it interpellates the "low man." Through this process, Miller attempts to construct a counter discourse by exposing the contradictions within the dominant understanding of the social world. The power of the dominant discourse lies in the ability of its codes and protocols to regulate understanding of the social world; they allow individuals to interpret their experience only in previously elaborated paradigms. In *Salesman*, Miller shows how these codes and protocols are reproduced through memory as they are recirculated and repeated in the texts and representations of the publicity apparatus. The epilogue of the play also suggests that we are free of these representations only in death. When Linda says "We're free. . . . We're free" (*CP* 222), Miller is not just ironically commenting on the paid-up mortgage; he is also suggesting that Willy is free from the law of success only in death.

D. L. Hoeveler suggests that Linda's lines are ironic for another reason. Reading the drama as a "psychomachia," Hoeveler stresses that the *Requiem* functions as a final comment on Willy's dream: "All the characters who had previously functioned as parts of Willy's dream or nightmare are now supposedly free of him. . . . But each of the characters continues to embody the values that Willy demanded of them" (80). These "parts," however, to revise Hoeveler, not only embody the values that Willy demands of them, but also they embody the values of the dominant mode of production and the cultural apparatus which reproduces that mode by reproducing its values. Willy is a part of the body of capital, just as are Happy, Biff, Charley, Bernard, Howard Wagner, and Linda; and as Mark Poster writes, the capitalist mode of production forces human beings not only to become "things . . . in appearance," but also "They undergo . . . a profound interior alteration" (53). They become desiring machines, or as Sartre stresses in *Critique of Dialectical Reason*, they become other to themselves. They embody the values of the Other (the publicity apparatus) that programs them to see others as rivals. The irony of this operation, as Sartre points out, is that in attempting to be different (in attempting to be number-one, to earn the most money, to conquer the world) everyone's desire is the same. Desire, therefore, organizes individuals so that it can isolate them. Sartre calls this formation serial, or unified, alterity.

Ultimately, all the men in the play labor in alterity programmed by the other (or others) as parts of the machine of capital. Their desire and their isolations are expressions of the larger machine. Their "prefabricated being" (being as other-than-itself) is fixated on consumption by the publicity apparatus of capital (Sartre 227). The system of value that the play represents permits no true relationship between men; it permits only isolation through competition. The dissatisfaction of the desiring machine can therefore only express itself through nostalgia, an eternal return to previous models and their (pre)determining goals. The consequence of this interpellation is that solidarity is nullified by the desire of the other, thereby ensuring that men will continue to be exploited by their desire. As Deleuze and Guattari point out, "Desire can never be deceived. . . . It happens that one desires against one's own interests: capitalism profits from this. . . ." (257). In the end, then, "attention must be . . . paid" (*CP* 162) to Willy Loman not because he is somehow exceptional (by being an aberration) but because his repression is paradigmatic. Willy has not, as Michael Spindler points out, "seized upon the notion of success as a substitute for genuine identity" (206). Willy, again, seizes nothing; his gods are given to him. Attention must be given to such a man by readers of *Salesman* who would fetishize masculine autonomy, since Miller powerfully suggests that masculine desire is an instrument used by the publicity apparatus of American capital to organize and to regulate social relations and the economy.

From *American Drama* 2, no. 1 (Fall 1992): 59-83. Copyright © 1992 by the American Drama Institute. Reprinted by permission of the American Drama Institute.

Note

1. In the work of Louis Althusser (162–70) *interpellation* denotes the process by which human subjects come to recognize themselves as such by identifying themselves with the subjects referred to by an impersonal "apparatus" of ideological statements: For instance, as the *free* and the *brave* in the phrase "the land of the free and the home of the brave."

Works Cited

Adler, Thomas. *Mirror on the Stage: The Pulitzer Plays as an Approach to American Drama*. West Lafayette: Purdue UP, 1987.

Adorno, Theodor. "Freudian Theory and the Pattern of Fascist Propaganda." *The Essential Frankfurt School Reader*. Ed. Andrew Arato and Eike Gebhardt. New York: Continuum, 1985. 118–37.

Althusser, Louis. *Lenin and Philosophy and Other Essays*. Trans. Ben Brewster. London: NLB, 1971.

Bigsby, C.W.E. *A Critical Introduction to Twentieth-Century American Drama, Vol. 2: Tennessee Williams, Arthur Miller, Edward Albee*. Cambridge: Cambridge UP, 1984.
Brucher, Richard T. "Willy Loman and The Soul of the New Machine: Technology and the Common Man." *Journal of American Studies* 17 (1983): 325–36.
Cohn, Ruby. "The Articulate Victims of Arthur Miller." *Arthur Miller's Death of a Salesman*. Ed. Harold Bloom. New York: Chelsea House, 1988. 39–46.
Deleuze, Gilles, and Felix Guattari. *Anti-Oedipus: Capitalism and Schizophrenia*. Minneapolis: U of Minnesota P, 1983.
Green, Theodore P. *America's Heroes: The Changing Models of Success in American Magazines*. New York: Oxford UP, 1970.
Hoeveler, D. L. "*Death of a Salesman* as Psychomachia." *Arthur Miller's Death of a Salesman*. Ed. Harold Bloom. New York: Chelsea House, 1988. 77–82.
Horkheimer, Max, and Theodor Adorno. *Dialectic of Enlightenment*. 1947. London: Allen Lane, 1973.
Huftel, Sheila. *Arthur Miller: The Burning Glass*. New York: The Citadel Press, 1965.
Innes, Christopher. "The Salesman on the Stage: A Study in the Social Influence of Drama." *Arthur Miller's Death of a Salesman*. Ed. Harold Bloom. New York: Chelsea House, 1988. 59–75.
Jacobson, Irving. "Family Dreams in *Death of a Salesman*." *American Literature* 47 (1975): 247–58.
Lyotard, Jean-François. *The Postmodern Condition: A Report on Knowledge*. Minneapolis: U of Minnesota P, 1984.
Marx, Karl. *Capital*, vol. 1. New York: Vintage, 1977.
Miller, Arthur. *Arthur Miller's Collected Plays*. New York: Viking, 1957.
___________. *Timebends: A Life*. New York: Grove Press, 1987.
Mills, C. Wright. *White Collar: The American Middle Classes*. New York: Oxford UP, 1951.
Orr, John. *Tragic Drama and Modern Society: Studies in the Social and Literary Theory of Drama from 1870 to the Present*. London: Macmillan, 1981.
Parker, Brian. "Point of View in Arthur Miller's *Death of a Salesman*." *Arthur Miller's Death of a Salesman*. Ed. Harold Bloom. New York: Chelsea House, 1988. 25–38.
Porter, Thomas. "'Acres of Diamonds': *Death of a Salesman*." *Critical Essays on Arthur Miller*. Ed. James J. Martine. Boston: G. K. Hall, 1979. 24–43.
Poster, Mark. *Sartre's Marxism*. London: Pluto, 1979.
Sartre, Jean-Paul. *Critique of Dialectical Reason*. London: New Left Books, 1976.
Spindler, Michael. *American Literature and Social Change: William Dean Howells to Arthur Miller*. London: Macmillan, 1983.
Vogel, Dan. *The Three Masks of American Tragedy*. Baton Rouge: Louisiana State UP, 1974.
White, Hayden. *Tropics of Discourse: Essays in Cultural Criticism*. Baltimore: Johns Hopkins UP, 1978.
Williams, Raymond. *Modern Tragedy*. London: Verso, 1979.

Shame, Guilt, Empathy, and the Search for Identity in Arthur Miller's *Death of a Salesman*

Fred Ribkoff

Among other things, tragedy dramatizes identity crises. At the root of such crises lie feelings of shame. You might ask: what about guilt? There is no question that guilt plays a major role in tragedy, but tragedy also dramatizes the way in which feelings of shame shape an individual's sense of identity, and thus propel him or her into wrongdoing and guilt. In fact, Bernard Williams examines the relation and distinction between shame and guilt in his study of ancient Greek tragedy and ethics, *Shame and Necessity*. He "claim[s] that if we can come to understand the ethical concepts of the Greeks, we shall recognise them in ourselves."[1] In the process of establishing a kinship between the Greeks and ourselves, Williams provides an excellent foundation upon which to build an argument on the dynamics of shame, guilt, empathy, and the search for identity in Arthur Miller's modern tragedy *Death of a Salesman*. Williams states that

> We can feel both guilt and shame towards the same action. In a moment of cowardice, we let someone down; we feel guilty because we have let them down, ashamed because we have contemptibly fallen short of what we might have hoped of ourselves. . . .
>
> . . . It [guilt] can direct one towards those who have been wronged or damaged, and demand reparation in the name, simply, of what has happened to them. But it cannot by itself help one to understand one's relations to those happenings, or to rebuild the self that has done these things and the world in which that self has to live. Only shame can do that, because it embodies conceptions of what one is and of how one is related to others.[2]

In order to understand the identity crises of Miller's tragic characters in *Death of a Salesman*, and especially the late, climactic scene in which

Biff confronts Willy with the truth, it is necessary to understand shame's relation to guilt and identity. It is the confrontation with feelings of shame that enables Biff to find himself, separate his sense of identity from that of his father, and empathize with his father. Moreover, it is the denial of such feelings that cripples Willy and the rest of the Loman family.

Until Biff stops to examine who he is, while in the process of stealing the fountain pen of his old boss, Bill Oliver, feelings of shame determine his self-perception as well as his conduct. Even before discovering his father with "The Woman" in Boston, Biff's sense of self-worth, like that of his brother Happy, is dependent on his father's conception of success and manhood and on his father's approval. In fact, because Willy is abandoned at the age of three by his father, his elder brother, Ben, becomes the measure of success and manhood for his sons to live up to. Ben is, in Willy's own words, "a great man!" "the only man I ever met who knew the answers."[3] "That's just the way I'm bringing them up, Ben—rugged, well liked, all-around," says Willy while reliving Ben's visit in the past (49). Early in the play, we see Biff through the proud memory of his father. Willy asks Biff, "Bernard is not well liked, is he?" and Biff replies, "He's liked, but he's not—well liked" (33). Biff inherits from his father an extremely fragile sense of self-worth dependent on the perceptions of others. "Be liked and you will never want," says the proud father of two sons who are, in his own words, "both built like Adonises" (33). But according to the true Loman heroic creed, it is not good enough simply to be "liked." As Willy points out to Happy earlier, "Charley is . . . liked, but he's not—well liked" (30).

Shame, together with the sense of inadequacy and inferiority manifest in the need to prove oneself to others, is evident in both Loman sons, and of course, in the fatherless father, Willy. The Loman men's shame propels them into wrongdoing and guilt.[4] In Act One, Willy begs Ben to stay "a few days" more, and, in the process of doing so, reveals the degree to which he feels incomplete and inadequate:

WILLY, *longingly*: Can't you stay a few days? You're just what I need, Ben, because I—I have a fine position here, but I—well, Dad left when I was such a baby and I never had a chance to talk to him and I still feel—kind of temporary about myself.

(51)

The fact that Willy feels "kind of temporary about" himself is reflected in his inability to complete a thought after he has raised the issue of his identity—the "I." This confession is riddled with dashes—or, in other words, uncomfortable, self-conscious pauses. While in the presence of his god-like brother, Ben, Willy, out of shame, constantly attempts to cover up the sense of failure and inferiority that threatens to expose his sense of inadequacy and weakness every time he is about to say what the "I" really feels.

Willy is driven to commit his greatest wrong by feelings of shame that arise out of his sense of inadequacy as a man. His adulterous affair with "The Woman" in Boston, which haunts both him and his son Biff, is a desperate attempt to confirm and maintain his self-esteem.[5] In the middle of Act One, while reliving the past. Willy confesses to his wife that "people don't seem to take to me" (36), that he "talk[s] too much. A man oughta come in with a few words. One thing about Charley. He's a man of few words, and they respect him" (37). After this confession, "The Woman" appears "*behind a scrim*" as his feelings of guilt for betraying his wife surface in his words to her. Just prior to "The Woman's" first spoken words and interruption, Willy attempts to make sense of his betrayal without mentioning it:

WILLY, *with great feeling*:

> You're the best there is, Linda, you're a pal, you know that? On the road—on the road I want to grab you sometimes and just kiss the life outa you.
>
> (38)

"*The Woman has come from behind the scrim . . . laughing*," and Willy continues:

> 'Cause I get so lonely—especially when business is bad and there's nobody to talk to. I get the feeling that I'll never sell anything again, that I won't make a living for you, or a business, a business for the boys.
>
> (38)

Willy believes that he turns to another woman out of loneliness for his wife, Linda. But at the root of his loneliness and his need of a woman are feelings of shame he cannot face. He is driven by feelings of inadequacy and failure to seek himself outside of himself, in the eyes of others. "The Woman" makes him feel that he is an important salesman and a powerful man. After she interrupts Willy with the words, "I picked you," Willy immediately asks, "*pleased*," "You picked me?" (38). Again, on the same page, after she says, "And I think you're a wonderful man." Willy asks, "You picked me, heh?" (38). Just prior to leaving, "The Woman" makes a point of saying exactly what Willy wants to hear. "I'll put you right through to the buyers," she says, and, feeling full of masculine power, "*slapping her bottom*," Willy responds, "Right. Well, bottoms up!" (39).

The father's bravado is the son's shame. At the root of Biff's wrongdoing and feelings of guilt lie shame and feelings of inadequacy and inferiority. But, unlike his father, he faces, and learns from, his shame. Consequently, the play suggests that he can rebuild his sense of self-worth and re-establish his relation to others on healthier grounds. He makes sense of his guilt by confronting the shame buried deep in his sense of identity. Ultimately, the ability to do so enables him to empathize with his father.

Biff's inherited sense of inadequacy and inferiority send him "running home" (22) in springtime from the outdoor life out West—a life that reflects his own desires and needs. And yet, it is his father's wrong, a shameful act of adultery, coupled with Biff's failure to pass math and go to university to become a football star (as he and his father had hoped), that shatters Biff's already fragile sense of identity and sends him out West in the first place. His own desires and needs cannot hold him still. He is plagued by his father's, and his society's, measure of a person—the mighty dollar, the dream of "building a future" (22). Until Biff discovers his father with "The Woman" in Boston, Willy is as good as a god to him. So, rather than expose his father's shame, which, at some level, he experiences as his own, Biff runs, and attempts to hide, from the collapse of the ideal, invulnerable, infallible image of his father. Thus the source of his sense of identity in shame goes unquestioned. He continues to steal and to move from job to job, not so much because he feels guilty but because he feels ashamed of himself for not living up to an image of success that has already been proven to be a "fake." After he witnesses his father give "The Woman" in Boston "Mama's stockings!" Biff calls his father a "liar!" a "fake!" and a "phony little fake!" (121). He does not, however, reconcile this image of his father with his sense of himself. Not, that is, until he is in the process of stealing a fountain pen belonging his old boss, Bill Oliver. As he says to his father, "I stopped in the middle of that building and I saw—the sky" (132)—the same sky that is obscured from view by the "*towering, angular shapes . . . surrounding*" the Loman home "*on all sides*" (11), and which also forms part of the "inspiring" outdoor world Biff has left behind (22). Biff goes to see Oliver in a futile attempt to fit his, if you will, circular self into an "angular" world—a world in the process of crushing both the son and the father, men far more adept at using their hands than at using a pen. Biff reveals to his father that he has taken Oliver's pen, and that he cannot face Oliver again, but Willy accuses him of not "want[ing] to be anything," and Biff, "*now angry at Willy for not crediting his sympathy*," exclaims, "Don't take it that way! You think it was easy walking into that office after what I'd done to him? A team of horses couldn't have dragged me back to Bill Oliver!" (112–13). There is no question that Biff feels guilty for what he has "done to" Oliver, first, by stealing "that carton of basketballs" (26) years ago, and second, by stealing his fountain pen. On the other hand, he also feels extremely ashamed of himself.

Biff's inherited sense of shame drives him to steal and to perform for his father. The fact that he steals does not, however, bother his father too much. Guilt can be concealed and, perhaps, forgiven and forgotten. Willy suggests as much when he advises Biff to say to Oliver: "You were doing a crossword puzzle and accidentally used his pen!" (112). But Biff's sense of himself is at stake, and he knows it. He knows that he cannot bear to be seen (the classic sign of shame) by Oliver. He can no longer separate his sense of himself from the act of stealing. Biff says to his father. "I stole myself out of every good job since high school!" (131). But, in essence, as Biff now realizes, his self was stolen by his inherited, shame-ridden sense of identity. He never had a chance to see himself outside his father's point of view. Willy feels attacked by Biff's confession that he "stole" himself "out of every good job," and responds: "And whose fault is that?" Biff continues: "And I never got anywhere because you blew me so full of hot air I could never stand taking orders from anybody! That's whose fault it is!" (131).

Biff understands his relation to others, notably his father, only after he literally goes unnoticed and unidentified by someone he thought would recognize him: Bill Oliver. Biff comes to the realization that there is no reason why Oliver should have recognized him, given that he couldn't recognize himself. That is, as Biff says to Happy, "I even believed myself that I'd been a salesman for him! And then he gave me one look and—I realized what a ridiculous lie my whole life has been! We've been talking in a dream for fifteen years. I was a shipping clerk" (104). Unlike his father's true self, which is immersed in shame and guilt, Biff's self surfaces and stays afloat because he learns about his guilt from his shame.

Willy's insistence that Biff is "spiting" him by not going to see Oliver prompts Biff to voice what he sees as the meaning behind his theft and his inability to face his old boss again: "I'm no good, can't you see what I am?" (113). In this case, it is not simply Biff's wrongdoing that makes him identify himself as "no good"; he has now grasped the fact that behind his habit of breaking the law lie feelings of shame. This question, "can't you see what I am?" represents the beginnings of Biff's separation of his own identity from that of his father. By the end of Act Two, Biff is certain, as he says to his brother, that "[t]he man don't know who we are!" At this point he is determined to force his father to "hear the truth—what you are and what I am!" (131, 130). He knows who he thought he was and, thus, why he stole Oliver's pen. As he reveals to his whole family,

> I stopped in the middle of that building and I saw—the sky. I saw the things that I love in this world. The work and the food and time to sit and smoke. And I looked at the pen and said to myself, what the hell am I grabbing this for? Why am I trying to become what I don't want to be? What am I doing in an office, making a contemptuous, begging fool of myself, when all I want is out there, waiting for me the minute I say I know who I am! Why can't I say that, Willy? *He tries to make Willy face him, but Willy pulls away and moves to the left.*
>
> (132)

"Willy," the father who has been transformed from "Dad" into simply a man in his son's eyes, cannot bear to have his dreams, and his heroic vision of his son, himself, and his own brother and father—the vision by which he lives and dies—exposed. Therefore, he "*pulls away*" in shame, before standing his ground and yelling, "*with hatred, threateningly,*" "The door of your life is wide open!" (132). Unlike the scene in the restaurant, in which Biff presents Happy with "*the rolled-up hose*" with which Willy intends to commit suicide and tells his brother that he "can't bear to look at his [father's] face!" out of shame (115), this time Biff does not turn away from his father. He insists on the truth being truly heard by his father. It is only after he realizes that this is an impossibility that "*he pulls away*" (133): "There's no spite in it any more. I'm just what I am, that's all" (133), says the son to his father. He now knows that he is "nothing" only under the umbrella of his father's destructive vision.

By the end of Act Two, Biff has a relatively clear understanding of who he is or, at the very least, who he is not. "I am not a leader of men," he says to his father in a "*fury*," before "*he breaks down, sobbing*" (132–33). But his father cannot empathize with him because he is incapable of facing his own feelings of guilt and shame. To Willy, Biff's tears symbolize simply his son's love, and not, in any way, the struggle to separate from him. Biff demonstrates that he does in fact love his father, but, at the same time, this love is balanced by the recognition that if there is any chance of saving himself and his father he must leave home for good. The complexity of his feelings for his father goes unrecognized, however. Willy's response to Biff's breakdown is, "Oh, Biff! *Staring wildly*: He cried! Cried to me. *He is choking with his love, and now cries out his promise*: That boy—that boy is going to be magnificent!" (133).

What Biff wants from his father he ends up giving, without getting it back. He wants not only love, but empathy. Moreover, after confronting his own shame and discovering who he is not—that is, not the "boy" his father believes him to be—Biff demonstrates his ability to separate from his father and, consequently, his ability to empathize with him. In his dictionary of psychoanalysis, Charles Rycroft defines empathy as "[t]he capacity to put oneself into the other's shoes. The concept implies that one is both feeling oneself into the object and remaining aware of one's own identity as another person."[6] Biff does exactly this. In tears, he asks his father, "Will you let me go, for Christ's sake? Will you take that phony dream and burn it before something happens?" (133). He is not simply asking for his own freedom from the shame produced by not living up to the dream of success and being "well liked"; he is asking for his father's freedom from shame and guilt as well. He feels for his father and recognizes how "that phony dream" tortures him, at the same time that he retains his own sense of identity. But nothing can save Willy from his inability to accept the failure to live up to his own expectations—not even his son's empathy and forgiveness. Both are powerless in the face of shame.

In "Requiem," the final moments of Miller's tragedy, Biff is alone in his empathic understanding. Even Charley does not understand the meaning of Biff's final words about his father. "He had the wrong dreams. All, all, wrong. . . . He never knew who he was" (138, intervening dialogue omitted). Happy is "*ready to fight*" after these words, and Charley responds by saying to Biff, "Nobody dast blame this man. You don't understand: Willy was a salesman." But, as Linda suggests prior to this statement by Charley, "He was so wonderful with his hands," and it is this very suggestion that triggers Biff's final words about his father (138). Willy Loman was more himself, relatively free of guilt and shame, when he worked with his hands than at any other time in his life.

Driven by shame, he kills himself in order to preserve his dream of being "well liked" and a successful father and salesman. Of course, the irony is that because of his suicide the odds are very good that neither of his sons will benefit from his sacrifice, and nobody from his world of sales comes to his funeral. Linda's words at the end of the play, and especially the words, "We're free and clear" (139), reveal the degree to which she and her husband lived in denial, in fear of exposing the man who hid in shame behind the idea of being a successful salesman and father. To be "free and clear" is, ultimately, an impossibility for Willy Loman. His vision of success perpetuates crippling feelings of inferiority and inadequacy that drive him to destroy himself.

Unlike Biff, Willy does not confront and come to terms with his shame, and therefore he can never understand his guilt, nor his son's pain and his own responsibility for it. In "Tragedy and the Common Man," Miller states that "In [tragedies], and in them alone, lies the belief—optimistic, if you will, in the perfectibility of man."[7] In *Death of a Salesman*, he suggests, perhaps unintentionally, that the path to "perfection" lies in a confrontation with feelings of shame that enable one to understand guilt and arrive at a clearer sense of identity, as well as to empathize with others.

From *Modern Drama* 43, no. 1 (Spring 2000): pp. 48-55. Copyright © 2000 University of Toronto Press Inc. Reprinted by permission of University of Toronto Press Inc.

Notes

1. Bernard Williams, *Shame and Necessity* (Berkeley and Los Angeles: U of California P, 1993), 10.
2. Ibid., 92–94.
3. Arthur Miller, *Death of a Salesman: Certain Private Conversations and a Requiem* (New York: Penguin, 1987), 48,45. Subsequent references appear parenthetically in the text.
4. In addition to *Shame and Necessity*, Helen Merrell Lynd's *On Shame and the Search for Identity* has been influential in shaping my understanding of the distinction and relation between guilt and shame. Lynd states that "[a] sense of guilt arises from a feeling of wrongdoing, a sense of shame from a feeling of inferiority. Inferiority feelings in shame are rooted in a deeper conflict in the personality than the sense of wrongdoing in guilt." Helen Merrell Lynd, *On Shame and the Search for Identity* (New York: Harcourt, 1967), 22.
5. In *On Shame and the Search for Identity*, Lynd defines shame as "a wound to one's self-esteem, a painful feeling or sense of degradation excited by the consciousness of having done something unworthy of one's previous idea of one's own excellence" (23–24). See note 4.
6. Charles Rycroft, *A Critical Dictionary of Psychoanalysis* (London: Penguin 1989). 42.
7. Arthur Miller, "Tragedy and the Common Man," in *The Theater Essays of Arthur Miller*, ed. Robert A. Martin (New York: Viking, 1978), 7.

The Ironic Hercules Reference in *Death of a Salesman*

Terry W. Thompson

Although not an educated, erudite, or worldly man, Willy Loman does, on a few occasions during *Death of a Salesman*, offer modest literary or contemporary allusions. For example, when he conjures up a vivid memory of Biff—the favorite of his two sons—back in the glory days of his youth, Willy visualizes the superb young athlete with a large capital "S" on his letterman's sweater, alluding, of course, to Superman, the popular comic book and movie serial hero. As the star football player on his high school team, Biff certainly was a local super hero of sorts—good-looking, charismatic, athletically gifted, clearly destined for future greatness in professional sports, politics, business, anything and everything he chose to tackle after high school. In praise of Biff's youthful promise, Willy offers an important if brief mythological allusion to one of the most beloved of all Greek heroes, but, like the aging salesman himself, the reference is rather shallow, ignorant, and uninformed, proving that Willy Loman knows as little about classical mythology as he does about business or management or public relations.

At the end of Act One, as he engages in another of his emotionally draining recollections of the family's rose-tinted yesterdays when all things were possible, Willy describes how Biff looked as a muscular teenage heartthrob, boasting that his older boy was "Like a young god, Hercules—something like that."[1] Without even realizing it, Willy has made an ironic yet appropriate mythological allusion, one that he sees as fitting on the surface, but one that is complex, even profound, when examined more closely. As Willy mentions this comparison to Linda, his wife, he intends for the simile to conjure up only the heroic image of Hercules as a strong, fearless, universally admired figure, and certainly the revered Greek demigod embodied all of those positive attributes along with a multitude of others. However, Willy does not, perhaps cannot, comprehend the deeper, darker meanings of his comparison as well as the ironic suitability of his paralleling of Biff with "the greatest of all the Greek heroes."[2]

Born half divine, Hercules was the son of Zeus by a mortal woman, Alcmene of Argolis. Immediately after the birth of Hercules, Zeus neglected the boy and the mother—embarrassed by the consequences of his philandering and also unwilling to accept the daunting responsibilities of full-time fatherhood. In addition, Zeus's duties as king of all the Olympian gods caused much of his time to be taken up with the demands of his high position. As a result, Hercules, "the strongest man on earth," spent almost all of his childhood and formative years without a father figure, without an older, wiser male to give advice, to answer questions, in short, to teach him how to be a man.[3] Raised by a concerned mother who loved but could not control her son, the myths of Hercules are rich with the many problems and difficulties of the boyish giant trying to grow up on his own without a father around to provide male guidance and, when necessary, strong masculine discipline. In effect, Hercules grows up without limits, without corrections on his misbehavior, since no one dares to tell him "No."

Likewise, Biff Loman grows up without a full-time father in his life, especially during his rebellious adolescent years when he was stealing footballs, cheating on exams, driving illegally, and roughing up school girls until, according to Linda, "All the mothers [were] afraid of him!" (Miller 40). During much of Biff's childhood, Willy was off in his Studebaker or Chevrolet, traveling the back roads and byways of New England, leaving his two muscular and headstrong sons to fend for themselves. On one of Willy's much-anticipated arrivals back home, Biff greets him with "Where'd you go this time, Dad? Gee, we were lonesome for you. . . . Missed you every minute" (30). Willy's dedication to breadwinning for the family is, of course, completely admirable, but his habitual absences—as well as his Zeus-like infidelity while in Boston—have a traumatic effect on his two boys, but most especially on Biff. Willy's homecomings are extremely special events in the childhood of young Biff, but they are infrequent and not enough to keep the boisterous young boy on the straight and narrow path. Willy promises Biff that "Someday I'll have my own business, and I'll never have to leave home any more" (30). That admirable vow, however, never comes to pass, and Biff's self-guided childhood and rebellious adolescence prove to have a negative effect on him as he tries—without success—to become a mature, responsible man. Similarly, Zeus did, on rare occasions, come down from high Olympus to aid or encourage his wayward, troublesome son, and though much appreciated, these few visits were no replacement for a full-time father during Hercules's important formative years.

Throughout his tragic and troubled life, the powerful Greek hero failed at practically everything he attempted since, although incredibly athletic and supernaturally strong, "Intelligence did not figure largely in anything he did and was often conspicuously absent" (Hamilton 160). Handsome, well-built, charismatic, likable, all the attributes that Willy Loman believes guarantee success, these were present in Hercules as well as in the young Biff, but they are merely surface qualities, and unfortunately Willy can never get beyond that surface—in the business world or in the greater world at large. Modern television and movie treatments notwithstanding, when the myths of Hercules are studied in their entirety in Ovid, Virgil, Pindar, Plautus, et al., the tales are often poignant and forlorn, quite moving in their sadness and their pathos. For instance, Hercules married, sired several healthy children, but then he murdered his entire family in a fit of madness. He married a second time, and the wife from that union unintentionally caused him to suffer the agonizing, flesh-eating wounds that would drive him to commit suicide. Realizing what she had done, she hanged herself in despair. During his short life, Hercules also killed a number of people by accident, some of them close friends and companions, causing him tremendous guilt and shame. For the most part, he wandered through the classical world alone, failing at almost every turn to fit in, to find his place. Assigned by the gods as penance for his many sins, the infamous

Twelve Labors took Hercules far and wide—and when accomplished gave him great fame—yet he died alone without family or friends to comfort him. His days were punctuated by occasional brief periods of contentment, but overall his life was filled with loneliness and pain, depression and disappointment, so much so that in the end, the "earth's champion," as Ovid describes him, decided to cremate himself on the summit of Mount Oeta in central Greece.[4]

At the end of Act One, when Willy tosses off his clichéd and cursory allusion to the famous Greek hero-athlete, he understands nothing of the darker elements of the Hercules myths, yet they are the very ones that so closely correspond with Biff's unhappy life and his failure to find a place in the world. Willy's own mythological allusion is presumably over his head, demonstrating the shallowness of his erudition and insight and echoing his lack of real acumen about the business world in which, after a lifetime of work, he has proven so inept and unsuccessful. At the age of sixty-three, at a time in his life when he should be able to offer sage and mature counsel to Biff, Willy remains simplistic and superficial, well intentioned and caring, yet still woefully ignorant of almost all things, even his own allusions.

From *English Language Notes* 40, no. 4 (June 2003): pp. 73-77. Copyright © 2003 by *English Language Notes.* Reprinted by permission of *English Language Notes.*

Notes

1. Arthur Miller, *Death of a Salesman: Certain Private Conversations in Two Acts and a Requiem* (New York: Viking, 1949) 68. All further references will be documented parenthetically within the text.
2. Lillian Feder, *Crowell's Handbook of Classical Literature* (New York: Harper Colophon, 1964) 161.
3. Edith Hamilton, *Mythology: Timeless Tales of Gods and Heroes* (New York: Mentor, 1969) 160.
4. Ovid, *The Metamorphoses*, trans. Mary M. Innes (New York: Penguin, 1955) 209.

Masculine and Feminine in *Death of a Salesman*

Heather Cook Callow

No one disputes the importance of Arthur Miller's *Death of a Salesman* in the American drama canon. It is, as Gayle Austin has observed, "the Oedipus Rex of American drama for many people" (63). As such it has occasioned a good deal of critical wrangling, particularly over the nature and stature of its protagonist Willy Loman. Several critics, Harold Bloom among them, consider Miller himself to be confused as to his intentions or at least their execution (*Loman* 1–2; Driver 22–23), and certainly the play's conclusion may be read as unclear regarding what specific values it condemns or advocates. In the Requiem, Biff condemns Willy's dreams as "all wrong" while Charley, elsewhere a realistic and trustworthy friend to Willy, excuses him, saying a salesman has to dream. I suggest that part of the confusion stems from the melange of typically "masculine" and "feminine" interactional traits, values, and achievements that Miller gives to his characters. In his opening stage directions, Miller describes the imaginary wall lines of Willy's house, pointing out that their boundaries will be broken by the characters as they move into the past. Even so, I suggest, set boundaries between "masculine" and "feminine," as traditionally construed, have also been broken within the play. An examination of these broken boundaries in light of Deborah Tannen's *You Just Don't Understand: Men and Women in Conversation*, a study of gender associated linguistic patterns and the values they reflect, leads me to suggest that readers have found Willy Loman lacking, in part, because the values he espouses are, strangely enough, primarily "feminine," those that Tannen finds women bring to interaction and to the workplace.

To set the stage, I need first to catalog briefly specific criticisms raised against Willy Loman that correlate with Tannen's gender paradigm. The first series focuses upon Willy's concept of the necessary criteria for success. Henry Popkin observes that "Willy . . . believes, with Dale Carnegie, that success is the reward of making friends and influencing people" (*Loman* 12). Ivor Brown reports that in England Willy was taken as "a poor, flashy, self-deceiving little man," whose obsession with popularity was more contemptible than natural (*Loman* 5). Arthur Ganz says, "Willy is a man so foolish as to believe that success in the business world can be achieved not by work and ability but by being 'well-liked,' by a kind of hearty popularity that will open all doors and provide favors and preferential treatment" (*Loman* 22). Robert N. Wilson labels these beliefs "Willy's warped dicta for success" (80). In a more psychological vein, Wilson observes, "Willy attempts to be the person he thinks others desire" (81), and Raymond Williams similarly declares, "Loman is a man who from selling things has passed to selling himself and has become in effect a commodity" (*Loman* 15).

The last few quotations emphasize what Miller himself identified as a playwright's central problem—bridging "the deep split between the private life of man and his social life" (Overland 53). Commenting on Willy's attempt to secure an office job from his boss, Paul Blumberg remarks, his "appeal—so strange and incongruous for a hard headed salesman—is an appeal to 'family relations'" (58). Stephen Lawrence, observing a similar breakdown of the boundary between private and public life says:

> Perhaps what is wrong with society is not that it has implanted the wrong values in him, values which finally do not lead to success anyway, but that it has lost touch with values which should never be relegated only to the personal sphere or the family unit. . . . Willy's problem is that he is human enough to think that the same things that matter in the family—especially his love for his son—matter everywhere, including the world of social success.
>
> (57)

Finally, and perhaps reflecting upon all of these "shortcomings," John Beaufort insists that Willy is not tragic but sad and that he "will not for one minute accept Willy Loman as the American 'Everyman'" (*Loman* 45).

"Warped," "unnatural," "foolish," "incongruous," inadequate as an American "Everyman"—these are the terms used to characterize Willy's values, his desire to be the person others wish him to be, his wrongheaded confusion of the private and the public, with Lawrence's caveat that perhaps society could benefit from a more personal approach to public intercourse. What may seem warped, unnatural and incongruous coming from a male speaker may, however, as Tannen's study reveals, be quite acceptable coming from a female speaker.

The sociolinguistic approach that Tannen employs shows, through a series of recorded and reported conversations and examples, that American girls and boys grow up in different cultures and that talk between American men and women is consequently cross cultural communication, with each group's patterns of speech showing distinguishable characteristics. Her study provides several observations that are pertinent to *Death of a Salesman* which, one must remember, is subtitled *Certain Private Conversations in Two Acts and a Requiem*. Tannen finds that men view the world hierarchically and that to them in any interaction, conversational or behavioral, one is either one up or one down from the others involved (24–25). This certainly fits Willy and his boys. It is this sentiment that prevents Willy from accepting a job from Charley and that feeds Happy's notion that "to come out number one man" is "the only dream you can have" (139). Linda, in contrast, asks, "Why must everyone conquer the world?" (85) Willy also appears to fit the masculine model that Tannen finds in his practice of boasting of his personal accomplishments (Tannen 219). In several other respects, however, his talk and his behavior better fit the feminine model. Tannen asserts that women approach the world as a network of connections and that when they pursue status, it is in the guise of connection. She states, "Girls and women feel it is crucial that they be liked by their peers. . . . Boys and men feel it is crucial that they be respected by their peers. . . ." (108).

The number of lines Willy speaks that testify to the importance to him of personal connections and being "well-liked" are legion. He asserts, "personality always wins the day" (65) and tries to bring that to bear in his conversation with his boss Howard. His appeal is to personal relations—his relationship with Howard's father, that he remembers the day Howard was born and named—but Howard's approach is hierarchical. He calls Willy "kid" and says "where am I going to put you . . . ?" (80) To his older brother Ben, who achieved his own financial success mining for diamonds and is suspicious of intangible assets, he asserts, "It's not what you do. . . . It's who you know and the smile on your face! It's contacts, Ben, contacts!" (86) Even when he speaks of his professional hero, Dave Singleman, he speaks not of Singleman's wealth, but of his being "remembered and loved and helped by so many different people" (81). Singleman's clients were not purchasing a product, they were helping and loving Dave Singleman. In like manner, Willy envisions his own funeral as a testimony to Biff of his personal popularity. These qualities—helping and being helped, being connected and remembered, experiencing and demonstrating solidarity—are all qualities Tannen finds valued more by women than by men.

Willy tells Ben, "That's the wonder . . . of this country that a man can end with diamonds here on the basis of being liked" (86). Granted Willy is speaking in the context of diamond mines, but if one substitutes the word *woman* for *man* here, the statement is not only perfectly understandable but actually truer. Diamonds are a glamorous choice as a commodity, but the association with women's engagement and anniversary jewelry, the feminine jewelry of personal connection and promise is inescapable. Willy's belief that personal attractiveness and personality are his most important assets is much more a traditionally socialized "feminine" attitude than a "masculine" one. Willy comments frequently on Biff's "personal attractiveness," and, when he learns that Biff has gone to see Bill Oliver about a business deal, asks, "How did he dress?" (72), traditionally a quintessentially "feminine" question. When he ponders his own disappointments in the business world he likewise speculates, "I'm not dressing to advantage, maybe" (37). The parlaying of external attractiveness and charm into economic success has historically been a socially acceptable and indeed inculcated "feminine" objective, but one readers are unaccustomed to hearing from a male speaker. Indeed Charley, at one point, exclaims in exasperation to Willy, "Why must everyone like you? Who liked J. P. Morgan?" (97). Charley's focus, like that of the men in Tannen's study, is upon respect not popularity.

The commodification of the self that results from Willy's emphasis upon personal attractiveness has been observed by Raymond Williams (*Loman* 15). Willy very much wishes to be the person others desire him to be and has been selling himself for years. His suicide is simply his final commodity exchange. That transaction is prompted by the emotional revelation at the end of act 2 that, as Willy expresses it, "Biff—he likes me!" But this moment of personal, private value is translated almost immediately in Willy's mind over to the hierarchical business realm as he savors the suicide money-making scheme which he joyously exclaims will put Biff "ahead of Bernard again!" (135). Willy here seems to employ traditionally "feminine" means, the commodification of the self, to reach "masculine" ends—being number one man. One remembers his admiration for Biff when he discovers "the girls pay for you?"—a situation that simultaneously involves Biff in a gender role reversal and makes him, in Willy's eyes, a huge success (28).

Willy very definitely exhibits a mixture of typically "masculine" and "feminine" speech and values. This contradictory mixture is evident in his own stated definitions of manhood. On the one hand, he boasts and states unequivocally the qualities a man must exhibit: "A man can't go out the way he came in . . . a man has to add up to something," (125) and "A man who can't handle tools is not a man" (44). On the other hand, he denigrates physical labor saying, "Even your grandfather was better than a carpenter" (61) and asserts, "The man who makes an appearance in the business world, the man who creates personal interest, is the man who gets ahead. Be liked and you will never want" (33). A partial explanation of Willy's mixed aspirations and values may be sought in the sketchy history Miller provides of Willy's childhood. His father, an itinerant flute maker, left the family when Willy was a baby, and his older brother Ben followed suit when Willy was only four. Willy was thus raised by his mother and as a result, he says, still "feels kind of temporary" about himself (51). He expresses his uncertainty about the values he developed to Ben saying, in relation to his own sons, "sometimes I'm afraid I'm not teaching them the right kind of—" (52).

Kay Stanton and Jan Balakian have noted Mother Loman's seeming invisibility in Willy's world (Stanton 68–69; Balakian 120). She appears to have reared Willy alone and yet there are no grand character stories about her in Willy's memories, only mythologized stories of Dad. One wonders about the source of these stories. It is hard to imagine a woman abandoned by both husband and eldest son and left to raise a four year old with apparently no financial help from either one (Ben, when he visits Willy, is unaware that their mother has been dead a long time) telling glowing stories of her husband. Perhaps the stories come, like much else in Willy's world, only from his imagination, fortified by Ben's few details and projected from Ben's success backward to his father. June Schlueter raises the possibility that Ben himself is Willy's fabrication (148–149), though I tend to credit Ben's existence, if not the enormity of his success. In any case, Willy does seem to have emerged from this fatherless, "feminine" environment with a craving for personal admiration and a talent for self-deception, developed perhaps in response to truths too hard to absorb. His sense of who he should be and how be should behave is a confused mixture of pioneer machismo, belief in the power of personal ingratiation and, it would seem, a genuine desire for love.

Even Willy's relation to Linda in the play, which some critics have seen as frozen into rigid gender roles (Kintz 108), actually shows each of them exhibiting a curious mixture of Tannen's designated "masculine" and "feminine" conversational and behavioral traits with one another. Certainly, Willy frequently dominates their conversations, accusing Linda of interrupting (64) and insisting that she let him talk (when in fact she has not interrupted) until Biff protests angrily, "Don't yell at her, Pop" (65). A moment later, when Linda begins a sentence, the stage directions indicate that Willy interrupts "going right through her speech" (67). Interruptions of this kind and Willy's false perception that Linda is interrupting him match the findings of studies Tannen cites showing that men tend to interrupt women, but perceive women as more talkative than themselves (Tannen 188–89). However, elsewhere in their dialogue one finds Linda taking a conversational role—that of problem solver—that Tannen identifies as typically "masculine" (51–53). Consider the following exchange:

> LINDA: . . . Did something happen, Willy?
>
> WILLY: No, nothing happened.
>
> LINDA: You didn't smash the car, did you?
>
> WILLY, *with casual irritation*:
> I said nothing happened. Didn't you hear me?
>
> LINDA: Don't you feel well?
>
> WILLY: I'm tired to the death. . . . I couldn't make it. I just couldn't make it, Linda.
>
> LINDA, *very carefully, delicately*:
> Where were you all day? You look terrible.
>
> WILLY: I got as far as a little above Yonkers. I stopped for a cup of coffee. Maybe it was the coffee.
>
> LINDA: What?
>
> WILLY, *after a pause*:
> I suddenly couldn't drive anymore. The car kept going off the shoulder, y'know?
>
> LINDA, *helpfully*:
> Oh. Maybe it was the steering again. I don't think Angelo knows the Studebaker.

WILLY: No, it's me, it's me. Suddenly I realize I'm goin' sixty miles an hour and I don't remember the last five minutes. I'm—I can't seem to—keep my mind to it.

LINDA: Maybe it's your glasses. You never went for your new glasses.

WILLY: No, I see everything. I came back ten miles an hour. It took me nearly four hours from Yonkers.

LINDA, *resigned*:

Well, you'll just have to take a rest, Willy, you can't continue this way.

WILLY: I just got back from Florida.

LINDA: But you didn't rest your mind. Your mind is overactive, and the mind is what counts, dear.

(12–13)

Here Linda begins by questioning Willy's veracity, and then as he begins to open up and reveal his feelings, rather than responding sympathetically and drawing him out, she begins to suggest further reasons for and solutions to his problems. Though it is true, Willy begins by suggesting bad coffee as a reason for his problems, he rapidly shifts his focus within himself while Linda continues to offer up possible external solutions to his difficulties. Tannen reports this problem-solving conversational behavior to be typically masculine. She finds that for most women telling a problem is a bid for an expression of understanding or mutuality and that women resent men's tendency to respond with offers of solutions (51–53). Here with Willy and Linda we find the typical gender roles reversed as Linda offers a series of solutions while Willy looks within.

Interestingly, when Linda confides to her sons her discovery of Willy's rubber pipe—his provision for suicide—she also describes Willy and his life's endeavors in a curiously "feminine" fashion. "It sounds so old-fashioned and silly, but I tell you he put his whole life into you and you've turned your back on him" (60). Surely in 1949 it was more usual to speak of an old-fashioned mother as putting her whole life into her children rather than a father. Yet in the Loman family flashbacks it is always Willy and his boys who are featured spending time together, though in actuality, given Willy's hours on the road, the majority of the boys' time must have been spent under Linda's supervision. In Willy's own family, as in the family his parents created, though the women may pass more time with the sons, it is the father's input that seems to loom largest.

Gender roles are also atypically aligned in the Loman family when it comes to mathematical ability. Biff's failure in math is a watershed event in the play, redirecting not only his immediate future (he loses his college football scholarship) but also precipitating the break in his relationship with his father, since it is while seeking advice from his father about the problem that he discovers Willy's infidelity. But his inability makes him curiously "feminine" and dependent upon the femininely perceived (by Willy) "anemic" Bernard. Even today, male achievement on American standardized math tests has been documented as significantly higher than female achievement, but in the Loman household it is the "anemic," femininely portrayed Bernard and Linda who skillfully handle the math. It is Linda who is always calculating Willy's commission in response to his wild estimates of sales and Linda who is minutely aware of the amount due on all their debts.

Linda is also, simultaneously, treated as a stereotypical "weaker vessel" who needs to be shielded from harsh realities by the men of the play on many occasions. When Willy has been fired and is pressing Biff concerning his appointment with Bill Oliver, he makes shielding of Linda his excuse saying, "I'm looking for a little good news to tell your mother, because the woman has waited and the woman has suffered" (107). While this is true, it is not Linda who needs the good news. Similarly, when he presents his suicide scheme to Ben in his imagination, although he envisions the resulting insurance money going to Biff and not Linda, he still makes her the cause: "Cause the woman has suffered, Ben, the woman has suffered. You understand me?" (125). Biff, too, when Willy is talking aloud to himself about events of the past, shows concern that Linda not know, exclaiming, "Doesn't he know Mom can hear that?" (26) But she has known for a long time. It is Linda who has uncovered the silent testimony of the gas hose attachment and while she shows it to her sons, she ironically feels she must shield Willy from her knowledge of him. She thus clearly contributes to Willy's view of herself as someone who is unaware of the extent of his failure and must be protected from such knowledge. All of this shielding of one another in the family seems in many instances really to be self-protection and surely an example of what Biff means when he says, "We never told the truth for ten minutes in this house" (131).

With regard to the gender issues of truth-telling and truth-shielding, Willy gives interesting advice to the young Biff. He cautions, "Be careful with those girls, Biff, that's all. Don't make any promises. No promises of any kind. Because a girl, y'know, they always believe what you tell them . . ." (27). The advice is meant both to shield Biff from trouble and to shield the girls, but it reveals two interesting operating assumptions. One is that whatever promises Biff might make would be untrue and the other is that girls believe everything boys tell them. One wonders who his models are for this dictum—his father and mother, Linda and himself? He certainly seems to believe that Linda is unaware that Charley has been loaning him his salary. In any case, he presents a view of men as always deceiving and women as always vulnerable to deception, but also perhaps capable of making trouble by calling men on their promises—like the woman in his hotel room in Boston who insists on receiving her promised stockings (119). Her insistence and refusal to disappear foil Willy's attempt to deceive Biff about his marital infidelity, so that her actions are central to the plot. As a character in the play, however, she barely exists. Though she asserts to Willy's evident pleasure that she "picked" him, not he her (38), their sexual exchange follows a traditional gender pattern—she offers sex in return for economic gain (in this case, stockings), and Willy feels he can evict her at will.

The basic unimportance of women in this play to the central thoughts and action of the characters is startling. As Austin, Stanton and Balakian have observed, women's role in the work is primarily to provide men with what they need, whether it be sex, children, power over other men, or simply convenient scapegoats. Mother Loman is entirely absent. Ben's wife, who produces seven sons and manages to outlive Ben, has no individual presence in the play. Linda, who Willy at one point calls his "foundation and support" (18), is not invited to the men's celebratory dinner, and Biff observes at one point that Willy "always wiped the floor with [her]" (55). Indeed, as Barbara Lounsberry points out, even the furniture in the stage directions—"a kitchen table with three chairs" rather than four—seems to leave Linda out. In addition, both Willy and Biff attempt to use female receptionists and secretaries to reach the more powerful men behind them, and Happy continually boasts that he will provide women for Biff, any kind and any time he wants. As Eve Kosofsky Sedgwick has demonstrated in her theory of "male homosocial desire," women in these sorts of interactions are exchanged among men to facilitate men's relation with each other. The women themselves are incidental. As Happy observes about the executives' fiancees he sleeps with, "I don't want the girl, and, still, I take it . . . maybe I just have an overdeveloped sense of competition or something" (25). These women also become Happy's scapegoats—he can't marry because they demonstrate that there are no "good" women except Linda. But Linda too, he thinks, can be appeased by a superficial offering of roses to make up for bad behavior.

The absence of women as active subjects in the play has made the high regard in which the play is held in the American canon problematic for feminist critics. As Austin has observed, the lack of a daughter in this quintessential two-son family leaves only the role of wife, mother, girlfriend or secretary for women to portray and makes the weight of attention fall on the male characters' interrelationships (61). Miller's original title for the work—*The Inside of His Head*—certainly seems to indicate that characters loom only as large in the play as they do in

Willy's mind. Linda's role is secondary and supportive. She doesn't talk about herself or her feelings, only about the men of the play and their attitudes and actions. Though at least one critic comments on "the depth of her own failure to understand the man she has loved" (Bigsby 89), in a tone that suggests that she has terribly and pathetically missed her purpose in life, no one asks if Willy has understood her. It is not one of his objectives nor a focus of the play. As Miller himself observes, "My women characters are of necessity auxiliaries to the action, which is carried by male characters . . ." (Roudané 370). Indeed, as Schlueter notes, we rely for the version we are given of the Linda of the past entirely upon Willy's remembered reconstruction of her attitudes and remarks.

But while it is true men dominate the play, it is also true, as I have been documenting, that a good measure of the concerns, values and expressions of the chief male character may be termed typically "feminine," according to Tannen's study. Indeed I suggest the critical controversy that swirls around the character of Willy Loman is, in part, generated by the tension between the "masculine" and "feminine" components Miller has given to him—his conflation of the private and the business world, the importance to him of personal relationships and one-up-manship, his desire to be loved and to be "number one." This is not to say that because Willy's espoused values of appearance, charm and personal relations may be labeled "feminine" that they are not also superficial. Willy's interest in being "well-liked," in linking the private and the public, in making and sustaining connections, has not produced in his life the kind of close relations women with this focus would typically expect. Ironically, this espouser of connections has very few connections in his private or public life—none with mother, father, brother or brother's family, only sporadic, tumultuous ones with his sons, none in the business community but with his neighbor Charley and with his wife, a relation based upon fantasies both avoid confronting. So he is, in a sense, a failure in this respect also. But it is not his failure in this area that has produced negative critical views of him—no critics berate him for not having influential friends. It is not his failure to succeed, but, I assert, the curiously androgynous nature of his goals and methods that adds fuel to critics' dispute over his right to the title of American Everyman.

Several critics do suggest that uniting the private and public domain could be beneficial and might produce a more humane society, and Balakian offers up Charley as a possible representative of feminized capitalism (a businessman with compassion who still turns a profit) (124). But the union of the two domains remains, on the practical level, an unrealized ideal. As Tannen has noted, linguistically speaking, the public domain is still male-dominated and women consequently sometimes experience difficulty because their conversational patterns and focus on personal relations and solidarity may be misunderstood or falsely assessed in the workplace. Simply speaking and behaving conversationally as a man, however, is not a successful remedy; for, as Tannen observes, women who talk like men in the workplace are not judged as men would be, they are judged differently and harshly (Tannen 188). I suggest that in Willy Loman's case we have evidence that the reverse is also true. Willy's continual talk of the importance of appearance, charm and friends to success has elicited harsh judgments from critics unused to finding such sentiments on masculine lips.

From *"The Salesman Has a Birthday": Essays Celebrating the Fiftieth Anniversary of Arthur Miller's* Death of a Salesman, ed. Stephen A. Marino (Lanham, MD: University Press of America, 2000): 65-77. Copyright © 2000 by University Press of America. Reprinted by permission of University Press of America.

Works Cited

Austin, Gayle. "The Exchange of Women and Male Homosocial Desire in Arthur Miller's *Death of a Salesman* and Lillian Hellman's *Another Part of the Forest*." *Feminist Rereadings of Modern American Drama*. Ed. June Schlueter. Rutherford: Fairleigh Dickinson UP, 1989.

Balakian, Jan. "Beyond the Male Locker Room: *Death of a Salesman* from a Femi-

nist Perspective." *Approaches to Teaching Miller's Death of a Salesman*. Ed. Matthew C. Roudané. New York: MLA, 1995.
Bigsby, C.W.E. *Modern American Drama, 1945–1990*. Cambridge: Cambridge UP, 1992.
Bloom, Harold. "Introduction." *Willy Loman*. Ed. Harold Bloom. New York: Chelsea House, 1991.
Blumberg, Paul. "Work as Alienation in the Plays of Arthur Miller." *Arthur Miller: New Perspectives*. Ed. Robert A. Martin. Englewood Cliffs: Prentice-Hall, 1982.
Driver, Tom F. "Strength and Weakness in Arthur Miller." *Arthur Miller*. Ed. Harold Bloom. New York: Chelsea House, 1987.
Kintz, Linda. "The Sociosymbolic Work of Family in *Death of a Salesman*." *Approaches to Teaching Miller's Death of a Salesman*. Ed. Matthew C. Roudané. New York: MLA, 1995.
Lawrence, Stephen A. "The Right Dream in Miller's *Death of a Salesman*." *Twentieth Century Interpretations of Death of a Salesman*. Ed. Helene Wickham Koon. Englewood Cliffs: Prentice-Hall, 1983.
Lounsberry, Barbara. "'The Woods Are Burning': Expressionism in *Death of a Salesman*." *Approaches to Teaching Miller's Death of a Salesman*. Ed. Matthew C. Roudané. New York: MLA, 1995.
Miller, Arthur. *Death of a Salesman*. New York: Viking, 1967, © 1949.
Overland, Orm. "Arthur Miller's Struggle with Dramatic Form." *Arthur Miller*. Ed. Harold Bloom. New York: Chelsea House, 1987.
Roudané, Matthew C. *Conversations with Arthur Miller*. Jackson: UP of Mississippi, 1987.
Schlueter, June. "Re-membering Willy's Past: Introducing Postmodern Concerns through *Death of a Salesman*." *Approaches to Teaching Miller's Death of a Salesman*. Ed. Matthew C. Roudané. New York: MLA, 1995.
Sedgwick, Eve Kosofsky. *Between Men: English Literature and Male Homosocial Desire*. New York: Columbia UP, 1985.
Stanton, Kay. "Women and the American Dream of *Death of a Salesman*." *Feminist Rereadings of Modern American Drama*. Ed. June Schlueter. Rutherford: Fairleigh Dickinson UP, 1989.
Tannen, Deborah. *You Just Don't Understand: Women and Men in Conversation*. New York: Ballantine, 1990.
Wilson, Robert N. "The Salesman and Society." *Willy Loman*. Ed. Harold Bloom. New York: Chelsea House, 1991.

The Psychological Politics of the American Dream: *Death of a Salesman* and the Case for an Existential Dialectics

Lois Tyson

In "Ideology and Ideological State Apparatuses," Louis Althusser argues that in order for any social system to survive, its conditions of production must be reproduced in the individual psyche. This task, he observes, is accomplished by ideology: "ideology has the function (which defines it) of 'constituting' concrete individuals as [social] subjects" (171). To choose the simplest example, members of a capitalist society must believe, among other things, that private enterprise, individual ownership of property, and competition for wages and markets is right or natural or in their best interest; members of a communist society must believe the same about collective regulation of these economic entities. Without such ideological collusion on the part of individual members, the society as a whole could not maintain its status quo. How ideology fulfills its purpose—what psychological processes are involved and why they usually succeed on such a large scale—has remained, however, an open question.

This question is one that we can begin to answer through literary analysis. Because literature is a repository of both a society's ideologies and its psychological conflicts, it has the capacity to reveal aspects of a culture's collective psyche, an apprehension of how ideological investments reveal the nature of individuals' psychological relationships to their world. While it is reasonable to assume that our national literature can suggest some promising hypotheses concerning the interaction of the psychological and ideological dimensions of American life, critics of American literature—despite the theoretical focus, over the last two decades, on the social origins of subjectivity—have kept these two domains separate. Instead, an archaic notion of the individual in society has remained the dominant model for American literary criticism. From F. O. Matthiessen's portrait of American Renaissance writers as literary revolutionaries committed to exploring the possibilities of a self-expression inspired by the lack of a specifically American literary tradition, to Donald Pease's provocative reconsideration of the motives of American Renaissance writers in terms of their desire for community and continuity, critics of American literature have treated the individual and the socius as interactive but discrete entities. Indeed, a good deal of American literary criticism places the two in a polarized opposition in which the individual is seen primarily as the victim of an antagonistic American society, without considering the ways in which psyche and socius are dialectically related. That is, such criticism doesn't consider the ways in which the individual psyche and its cultural milieu inhabit, reflect, and define each other in a mutually constitutive symbiosis. In this context, psychology is always cultural psychology and politics is always psychological politics, not because, as post-structuralism would have it, the structures of consciousness are inscribed within the processes of signification, but because both the structures of consciousness and the processes of social signification are inscribed within the same dialectics of desire. That is, both terms of the dichotomy are constituted by desires that neither originate in nor grant predominance to either term, but collapse them together within a cultural amnion that makes the separation of psyche and socius an untenable theoretical construct.

While the victim model certainly has value, it is, at best, incomplete and, at worst, reductive. For the large body of American literature that focuses on the relationship between the individual and the socius, the traditional Americanist paradigm of subjectivity has produced a canon of criticism dominated by the question, "Who is responsible for the protagonist's problems, the protagonist or society?"—a question that precludes our seeing the dialectical connections between psyche and socius that such works reveal. This state of affairs is less surprising, however, when we consider that recent theories of subjectivity have not provided a dialectical paradigm for subjectivity and, therefore, have not offered Americanists a real alternative to the traditional model.

While it has foregrounded the ways by which the notion of an autonomous subject has been used to veil society's ideological operations, the post-structuralist view of subjectivity as nothing more than a collection of cultural identifications has merely swung the theoretical pendulum away from the modernist emphasis on free will to a post-modern social determinism, without radically altering the terms of the dichotomy or undermining their influence. And, for obvious reasons, theories of subjectivity grounded in social determinism can do little to undermine a victim model of the individual's relation to the socius. With the growing popularity of so-called ethical criticism[1]—which seeks, among other things, to reestablish the autonomous subject—we are in danger of merely continuing to swing back and forth between these two theoretical poles.

The source of our problem, however, is not our inability to choose between two theoretical extremes, but the narrowness of the models of subjectivity offered by each side. Once we begin to see the ways in which the individual subject is neither wholly an autonomous agent nor merely a social product, the conceptual space thereby opened makes room, not for a return to the autonomous subject the ethical critics want to construct, but for a return to and dialectical reformulation of the existential subject, arguably the most rich and useful notion of subjectivity available, but one that was popularly misunderstood when it was initially disseminated and that has been largely neglected since the advent of post-structuralism.

As Walter Davis explains in *Inwardness and Existence: Subjectivity in/and Hegel, Heidegger, Marx, and Freud*, existentialism, properly conceived, "transcends the social-individual dichotomy" (375 n12) that informs ongoing debates between deconstruction and traditional humanism and between Marxism and psychoanalysis. For, according to an existential model, social factors may largely establish our initial identity, but, as we shall see, they do not freeze us at that stage without our daily consent. To summarize Davis, the individual is an historically situated (Marxist) subject of (psychoanalytic) desire, "condemned" to his or her own (existential) freedom to be either in collusion with social forces—consciously or unconsciously—or to resist. And this subjectivity is informed by what might be called a destabilized Hegelianism: the dialectical relationship between the individual and the socius—like that among the Marxist, psychoanalytic, and existential realities that constitute subjectivity—does not issue in some reified *Geist*, but remains in a state of contingency and flux, anchored in the real world, utterly existentialized.[2] If we apply Davis's dialectical model of existential subjectivity to American literature, the question for literary critics ceases to be, "Is the individual a free agent or a social product?" and becomes instead, "How are the individual and the socius cut from the fabric of the same desire?" In other words, what are the dialectics of desire that constitute our psychological politics? What psychological payoffs, conscious or unconscious, do we seek through our acceptance of any given ideology whether articulated or not? Such a theoretical perspective might be termed an existential dialectics, and this essay will attempt to illustrate its efficacy as a framework for re-reading American literature. As a case in point, I will offer a reading of Arthur Miller's *Death of a Salesman* aimed at answering the question, "How do psychology and ideology intersect in this drama to make the traditional Americanist separation of psyche and socius an untenable theoretical construct?"

Despite the play's rather obvious psychoanalytic content—the drama is structured by a series of detailed descriptions of the stages in Willy Loman's psychological breakdown—most literary critics treat the work's psychological dimension in terms of its tragic, rather than psychoanalytic, function, and the play's psychological dimension is viewed in opposition to its ideological dimension. The psychological drama, the argument goes, foregrounds the protagonist's responsibility for his failure as a husband and father and is thematically centered on the scene in which Willy commits adultery in a Boston hotel room; the play's Marxist critique of capitalist culture foregrounds the protagonist's victimization by an uncaring society obsessed with material success and is thematically centered on the scene in which Willy is coldbloodedly fired by Howard Wagner.[3]

This polarization of the work's psychological and political dimensions misunderstands, I believe, the nature of the overarching myth that, as everyone ironically acknowledges, informs Miller's play: the myth of the American dream, the belief that, because one's socioeconomic success in America is limited only by one's ability and ambition, socioeconomic success is the measure of one's value as a person. It is in the American dream—specifically, in its ideological relation to commodification[4]—that the play's psychological and political strands are inextricably entwined. For the American dream serves as the "ore" from which Willy fashions the ideological armor he uses to disguise and deny his true psychological state, and that of his family, in order to escape what such a self-awareness would force upon him: existential inwardness, that anxious awareness of oneself as a creature "whose very being is at issue" (Heidegger 67) in a world filled with physical and emotional uncertainties. This dialectical relationship between psyche and socius is manifest at those points where the play's psychological and ideological content intersect most clearly: Willy's commodification of personal image; his five so-called "memory" scenes, which, I will argue, are regressive episodes the structural similarities of which underscore their psychological importance; and the Loman family's sexuality, which is an important, though critically neglected, aspect of this work. In addition, I will suggest that the intersection of psychology and ideology can be observed, in more speculative terms, in the rather one-sided reading of Willy Loman that has dominated the criticism of this play.

* * *

Certainly, the most obvious example of Willy's ideological armor, and the one that informs all the psychological events that structure the play, is his commodification of personal image. For him, the road to the

American dream is paved with a winning personality: "[T]hat's the wonder, the wonder of this country," the protagonist tells his young sons, "that a man can end with diamonds here on the basis of being liked!" (79; Act II). Because, as Willy observes, a rich man is always well liked, being well liked, he concludes, must be how poor men become wealthy. For this reason, the protagonist believes that being well liked is the necessary and sufficient currency for purchasing success in the business world. Of course, Willy's logic depends on a very superficial view of what it means to be well liked. Because he substitutes form for content—"It's not what you say, it's how you say it" (58; Act I)—he mistakes the image of popularity for the reality, ignoring, for example, the obvious fact that, for some rich men, being "well liked" is not the source of their wealth but its effect: as Charley next door says of financial scoundrel J. P. Morgan, "with his pockets on he was very well liked" (90; Act II). It's the image of success Willy tries to project by joking with his customers and by exaggerating his sales prowess, and it's the image of success—the appearance of being well liked—that Willy teaches his sons is the necessary and sufficient commodity to ensure their future success in the business world, the world that Willy is certain will fulfill his dreams.

As Biff observes, however, and most critics agree, Willy "had the wrong dreams" (132; Requiem). We must wonder, although the question is rarely raised, why the protagonist chooses—and why, at all costs, he clings to—his dream of business success when his ability and his pleasure clearly lie in working with his hands. The answer can be found in the American dream's promise to remediate Willy's ontological insecurity, his lack of "any unquestionable self-validating certainties" (Laing 39), which has apparently plagued him since his abandonment in early childhood by his father and older brother Ben. The early loss of these two role models,[5] with whose idealized memory Willy could never compete, has left the protagonist, in his own words, feeling "kind of temporary about [him]self" (46; Act I) or, in psychoanalytic terms, narcissistically wounded—humiliated by his own powerlessness. The resulting need for a reassuring father explains the otherwise mystifying importance for Willy of the Dave Singleman story: the old salesman, whose popularity and resourcefulness allowed him to make a good living even at the age of eighty-four, fits Willy's idealized image of his own father. The protagonist's obsession with image throughout the play underscores his narcissism, for it bespeaks the man who must continually bolster the surface of his personality by finding its positive reflection in the world around him because that surface has no firm ground of its own to support it from within. Narcissism also explains why Willy refuses to relinquish, no matter what the cost to himself or his family, the personal image of the successful salesman he has manufactured from the ideological fabric of the American dream. It is not merely shame he fears, but the loss of a coherent self, for an idealized self-image is the sine qua non of the narcissist's identity.[6] Such a shaky structure requires the kind of ego reinforcement Willy desires: the admiration of financially successful, powerful men like his brother, the admiration one receives for achieving the American dream's rags-to-riches metamorphosis. Thus, Willy's failure to see the obvious unscrupulous underside of Ben's financial success, like the rest of his apparent moral confusion concerning his and his sons' success-oriented ethics, is not the result of innocence or ignorance, but of selective perception.[7] The protagonist's overwhelming psychological need for ontological reassurance doesn't permit him to see anything that might inhibit his pursuit of the business success that promises to supply that reassurance.

The only place Willy ever was able to successfully market his personal image was in his home. As we see in the protagonist's memories of his boys' high school days, Willy's young sons, Biff and Happy, adored their father. They believed all his stories about his popularity, his sales achievements, and the business of his own that he would have someday so that he'd be able to stay home with his family instead of spending his work week on the road as he had done all his life. In their eyes, he was the success he pretended to be, and their belief in him helped him to deny the reality of his small sales commissions. If young Biff and Happy kept their father's image shining for him, Linda, Willy's wife, has always kept it in good repair. However, she is not, as Dennis Welland claims, "too good for Willy and thus too good for the play" (49). Rather, she exacerbates her husband's illness. As we can see in the following memory scene, which closely resembles her behavior in the play's present-tense action, Linda refused to acknowledge any of Willy's weaknesses and wouldn't let him acknowledge them either:

WILLY: My God, if business don't pick up . . .

LINDA: Well, next week you'll do better.

WILLY: Oh, I'll knock 'em dead next week. I'll go to Hartford. I'm very well liked in Hartford. . . . [T]he trouble is . . . people don't seem to take to me.

LINDA: Oh, don't be foolish.

WILLY: I know it when I walk in. They seem to laugh at me. . . . I talk too much.

LINDA: You don't talk too much, you're just lively.

WILLY, *smiling*:
Well, I figure, what the hell, life is short, a couple of jokes. . . .

(30–31; Act I)

If Linda provides "the spiritual glue that holds together [Willy's] rickety frame" (Schlueter and Flanagan 59), it's nevertheless a service of dubious value she performs. By functioning, in effect, as a manic defense against the physical and psychological realities that continually threaten to invade her husband's awareness, Linda prevents him from challenging his own self-delusions and thereby helps preclude the possibility of his psychological growth.

It is Willy's struggle with those realities, brought to the fore by the double trauma of mounting pressures at the office and Biff's visit home, that constitutes the five expressionistic episodes in which the protagonist seems to remember or imagine events from his past. However, these episodes are not a function simply of memory or imagination. They are, rather, psychological regressions, which, in pathological cases like Willy's, involve "a full hallucinatory cathexis of the perceptive systems" (Freud 496). As D. W. Winnicott explains, regression involves not the imagining but the "*reliving* of dream and memory situations" (288; my emphasis) that opens the psyche to new possibilities. Although in the therapeutic encounter the regressed subject relives early childhood episodes, Winnicott's description of regression closely parallels, and illuminates, Willy Loman's behavior.

Like Winnicott's patients, Willy has developed a "false self" (Winnicott 281)—his successful-salesman persona—to defend against what Winnicott calls an "original environmental-failure situation" (287), in this case, Willy's childhood loss of father and older brother. The existence of this false self "results in [a] sense of futility" (Winnicott 292), which the protagonist recurrently manifests throughout the play. Furthermore, regression can involve a return either to a pleasant past experience, such as Willy's return to happier times with his young family, or to a painful episode from the past, such as his return to the initial falling-out with Biff in the Boston hotel room. Most important for our understanding of the protagonist, "regression is distinct from the other defence organizations in that it carries with it . . . a new opportunity for an unfreezing of the [failure] situation and a chance for . . . spontaneous recovery" (Winnicott 283). Because regression involves a return to the experience that lies at the bottom of a current conflict, as it does in each of Willy's five regressive episodes, it allows the regressed person to become aware of the concrete source of a heretofore baffling psychological condition. Recovery, in this context, means the acquisition of a new attitude toward oneself and one's problems based on the insight gained during the regression. Thus, in offering the opportunity to live an authentic relationship to one's conflicts, regression always offers the opportunity to acquire or deepen existential inwardness. From this perspective, Willy's five regressive episodes represent five opportunities for the protagonist to alter his course, both psychologically and existentially, and it is significant that his response, in each case, is the same. For, as we shall see, the pattern formed by his responses to regression reveals a systematic, if only partly conscious, effort on Willy's part to eschew the existential inwardness increasingly pressed upon him by the accumulated refuse of his psyche.

The first three regressive episodes follow roughly the same pattern: each time Willy is confronted with a traumatic reality in the present, he regresses to a time when his American-dream fantasies could still convince himself and his family that he was the success he wanted to be. Thus, as we see in Willy's first regression, which occurs shortly after his return home from his aborted attempt to drive to New England (20–34; Act I), the protagonist tries to escape the present reality of having been taken off salary and put on commission by regressing to a time when his young sons, still in high school, polished his car and hung on his every word, a time when Willy could still look to the future with hope. In his second regression, which occurs during and after his card game with Charley later that night (38–46; Act I), Willy tries to escape his present pain over Biff's life as a drifter and his own inability to help his son by regressing to a time when he was able to show off his boys' high-spiritedness and filial devotion in front of his brother Ben: the protagonist imagines sending the boys off to steal sand from a nearby construction site in order to rebuild the front stoop. In his third regression, which occurs in Howard Wagner's office (77–83; Act I), the protagonist tries to escape the present trauma of being fired by regressing to a time when he had the opportunity to superintend Ben's Alaskan timberland: "God, timberland! Me and my boys in those grand outdoors!" (78; Act I).

None of these three visions of the past, however, provides the escape Willy seeks. For it is during such regressive experiences that repressed conflicts tend to erupt.[8] Thus, the protagonist's first regressive vision of his happy young family is inevitably interrupted by the memory that

Biff had been a petty thief whose behavior was often wild and selfish: he cheated on his math exams, stole a football from the high school athletic department, and was so rough with the girls that their mothers complained to Linda (33–34; Act I). Similarly, Willy's second pleasant regression is interrupted by his fear that he didn't raise his sons right, as he imagines telling Ben, "Sometimes I'm afraid that I'm not teaching them the right kind of—Ben, how should I teach them?" (46; Act I). Finally, Willy's third regressive episode is interrupted by the memory that he had refused the opportunity to manage Ben's Alaskan timberland: Linda's repetition of his story about Dave Singleman convinced him to keep his job.

In terms of Willy's psychological experience, readers' concern over whether or not the past events he recalls are accurately reported according to some standard of objective reality is irrelevant. What matters is that the conflicts' emergence reveals Willy's experience of them; it is subjective reality that is revelatory here. For these eruptions of repressed conflicts are a product of Willy's present psychological state as well as a reflection of his former condition. During a traumatic period, conflicts that have been long buried tend to surface and demand attention or discharge. This is, of course, why regression often functions as a tool of psychological growth: it brings forward into consciousness and gives the subject the opportunity to work on conflicts that have heretofore inhabited the unconscious.

In Willy's case, however, the opportunity is never taken: the play does not dramatize the protagonist's "progression to enlightenment" (Jackson 17). Instead of using the knowledge offered by his regressive episodes to achieve what George S. Klein terms "active reversal," Willy tries to repress the conflicts anew by clinging to the American-dream myths and fantasies he used to deny and submerge the conflicts in the first place. Thus, when his pleasant picture of his sons' adoration is interrupted by his memory of Biff's misconduct, he defines the boy's behavior as spiritedness, which, we may recall, is the basis upon which Willy believes socioeconomic success is founded: "There's nothing the matter with [Biff]! . . . He's got spirit, personality. . . . Loaded with it. Loaded!" (34; Act I). Similarly, when self-doubt about his parenting interrupts his vision of showing off his boys for Ben, he imagines receiving Ben's reassurance that he was raising them to be "outstanding, manly chaps" (46; Act I), perfectly suited to fulfill their father's dreams of success. And when the memory of his refusal to accept an outdoor job from Ben interrupts his vision of receiving the job offer, Willy remembers Biff's Ebbets Field game—evidence that Biff had what it takes to be a success in Willy's competitive world and that the protagonist had therefore made the right decision in turning down Ben's offer.

Even Willy's fourth regressive episode, in which he relives the unhappy time young Biff discovered him in a Boston hotel room with another woman (102–14; Act II), does not "ope[n] the salesman's eyes" (Szondi 23) and force him to recognize "his own responsibility for what has happened to his family" (Welland 47), for the protagonist refuses to accept the painful awakening this regression offers him. As Willy recalls, young Biff flunked his high school math course and rushed off to Boston to ask his father to pressure the math teacher into giving him the four points he needed to pass. Finding Willy with a woman in his room, the boy refused, from that point on, to carry out any of Willy's plans for him: he gave up on graduating from high school and attending college, and he became a drifter. Willy represses his awareness of his role in Biff's difficulties, however, telling himself that Biff's flunking the math course is the source of his son's problems. It is noteworthy that Willy's awareness of the importance of the hotel incident is itself an attempt to sidestep the real issue: Willy's failure as a parent in general. As Biff finally admits, his father had so raised his expectations of success—and provided him with so little real basis for them—that, because instant success didn't come his way, he "stole [himself] out of every good job since high school" (124; Act II). Willy's immediate flight from the restaurant where this regression occurs, to buy seeds for the plot of sterile land behind his house—an obvious escape into a time before the hotel episode occurred—underscores the protagonist's repression of the psychological insight this regression provides.

It is part of the nature of conflict, however, that repression merely increases its force. Therefore, Willy's conflicts get more out of control with every attempt he makes to deny and re-submerge them. In this context, his decision to kill himself, which occurs during his fifth and final regression at the end of Act II (119–20, 127–29), is not "an act of affirmation" (Heyen 50) nor, as many critics would have it, a misguided attempt to secure his son's future.[9] Rather, Willy's suicide is his ultimate act of denial. Having bought the seeds he had run off to get when he left the restaurant earlier that evening, Willy is now pacing off a garden plot in his back yard. Unable to face the day's accumulated disappointments, Willy is frantically seeking a way out of his despair, and he thinks he has found one: he will kill himself in a way that appears to be an accident—in a car wreck—and Biff will collect twenty thousand dollars in life insurance. With this financial backing, Willy reasons, Biff will achieve the business success of which his father believes him capable. In both segments of this regression, Willy imagines himself discussing his idea with Ben, and the deeper motive for Willy's intended suicide quickly surfaces: the protagonist wants to regain Biff's esteem so that he can regain in his son's eyes the personal image that used to impress the boy so much. As Willy tells Ben,

> This [Willy's death] . . . changes all the aspects. Because he thinks I'm nothing, see, and so he spites me. But the funeral–*Straightening up*: Ben, that funeral will be massive. They'll come from Maine, Massachusetts, Vermont, New Hampshire! . . . [T]hat boy will be thunder-struck, Ben, because he never realized—I am known.
>
> (120–21; Act II)

The blunt revelations and accusations with which Biff interrupts his father's imaginary conversation with Ben—Biff's claims that Willy raised him to be the thief he is and that he and Happy, like their father, are failures who lie about their success—have no lasting effect on Willy. The only thing the protagonist takes from this experience is the fact that Biff cries to him, that Biff loves him. "That boy . . . is going to be magnificent!" (126; Act II) is Willy's final response to his interaction with Biff, and he returns immediately, his suicide project unchanged, to his conversation with Ben.

"Can you imagine that magnificence with twenty thousand dollars in his pocket?" Willy asks Ben during the second half of his final regression (128; Act II). This vision of Biff holds such charm for Willy, as does every success Biff has ever had, because Willy feels it is his own success he is experiencing in Biff's success. This is something other than healthy parental pride in a son who makes good, pride in one's success as a father—Charley's pride in his son, not Willy's, is of this kind. Willy's pride is projection, a very personal and intense form of vicarious experience. And, if he can just keep this vision intact until he kills himself, Willy will not have to face the repressed awareness of his failed life that keeps threatening to break through into his consciousness and overwhelm him. Thus, the protagonist's self-destruction is a last-ditch act of repression; the twenty thousand dollars in life-insurance money intended for Biff provides both his excuse for killing himself and the fantasy he needs in order to keep self-knowledge at bay until he can accomplish it. The conflicts that constitute his psyche have come to such an impasse that ordinary forms of denial and avoidance are nothing but ineffective stop-gap measures. The only way to shut this psyche off is to kill it. Like all his other defenses, Willy's suicide draws on the same American dream in which personal and financial success are at once wed in and transcended by social status. For, as we have seen, Willy's suicide is grounded in his vision of the increased prestige a showy funeral and a life-insurance legacy will purchase for him in the eyes of Biff, who has long been the repository of his father's self-image.

* * *

The play's psychological and ideological dimensions are fused even more clearly in the Loman family's sexuality. As Walter Davis observes, human sexuality is primarily a matter of meanings (*Inwardness and Existence* 80–87 and passim): through one's sexuality one enacts one's conscious and unconscious attitudes and motives toward others and thereby reveals, as Merleau-Ponty puts it, one's "manner of being towards the world" (158). In the Lomans' case, not only are the family's sexual attitudes compatible with the commodifying ideology of the American dream, but, like that dream, the family's sexual mores help them disguise and deny their own psychology and thereby avoid existential inwardness. In order to see how the Lomans' apparently diverse sexual natures achieve a single, ideologically saturated psychological end, we must first briefly review some key elements in the sexual characterization of each family member.

To begin with, Willy's extramarital affair, a natural focal point for any consideration of the protagonist's sexuality, reveals neither "the hollowness of [Willy's] affection for Linda" (Aarnes 96), nor his unhappiness over "his failure to impress her" (Hayman 51), nor the paucity of Linda's comprehension of Willy (Parker 108). For the protagonist's infidelity was not a function of his relation to his wife, but of his relation to his work. As we can see in the following scene, Willy's memory of his inadequacy in business is replaced by the memory of his lover:

> WILLY [to Linda]:
>
> . . . I get so lonely—especially when business is bad and there's nobody to talk to I get the feeling that I'll never sell anything again, that I won't make a living for you, or a business, a business for the boys. . . . *The Woman primps at the "mirror."* There's so much I want to make for—

THE WOMAN:

Me? You didn't make me, Willy. I picked you.

WILLY, *pleased*:

You picked me?

THE WOMAN:

. . . I've been sitting at that desk watching all the salesmen go by, day in, day out. But you've got such a sense of humor, and we do have such a good time together, don't we?

WILLY: Sure, sure. *He takes her in his arms.* Why do you have to go now?

(31–32; Act I)

Clearly, Willy's strong positive response to The Woman was elicited by her preference for him over the other salesmen who came through her office. Finally, someone in the business world liked him better than his competitors. For Willy, this woman was a commodity, the acquisition of which conferred upon him a status, at least in his own eyes, he was unable to otherwise attain.

For Happy, as well, women are commodities used to boost his self-image. He is not, as Brian Parker suggests, "compulsively competitive in sex and business for no reason at all" (32). Happy uses women to make him feel that he is able to "get" something that he cannot get from his career. Because he covets the attention his father has always lavished on Biff, Happy has invested a good deal of his identity in following in Willy's footsteps, in achieving the business success his father desired for both boys. Happy lives in the town in which he grew up and works in sales: he's one of two assistants to the assistant buyer for a local firm. Though he makes enough money to support his apartment, car, and social life, he has not achieved the big success—the wealth, power, and prestigious title—that Willy's dreams had reserved for his sons. Therefore, Happy feels disappointed, cheated: a world in which he must take orders from men he "can outbox, outrun, and outlift" (17;

Act I) is, he feels, an unjust world. For this reason, he compulsively seduces the fiancees of executives in his firm: he can't have their jobs, so he'll have their women.[10] We can see the connection between Happy's feelings of inadequacy in business and his womanizing when he tells Biff about his struggle to compete with his co-workers and follows immediately with, "But take those two we had tonight. Weren't they gorgeous creatures?" (18; Act I).

For both Willy and Happy, the achievement of financial success is tied to masculine self-image. This is why, as is typical in America, their metaphors for success involve winning fights and killing opponents. "Knocked 'em cold in Providence and slaughtered 'em in Boston," Willy tells his young sons upon returning home from a sales trip (27; Act I), using the same kind of language his brother Ben had used in advising him to go to Alaska: "Screw on your fists and you can fight for a fortune up there" (78; Act II). This link between business success and masculinity is, of course, one reason why both men use women to assuage their egos, to make up for their disappointments in the business world. It is no mere coincidence, then, that Happy abandons his father in the restaurant, to pursue women, directly upon learning that the plan for a Loman Brothers sporting-goods company is down the drain.

Of course, Happy's sexual pattern has strong Oedipal overtones as well. Raised within a family dynamic in which Dad's attention was focused on Biff, who was an authority figure for the younger child, it is no wonder that Happy's struggle for identity and recognition early took the form of masculine competitiveness. "I lost weight, Pop, you notice?" (44; Act I) is this character's pathetic boyhood refrain as he undertakes the impossible task of competing with his brother-the-football-hero for paternal esteem. While Willy frequently embraces Biff, in flashback as in the present, he never touches Happy. And the younger brother must listen to Dad's continual boasting about Biff without ever himself being the object of his father's pride. Happy is, thus, the perpetual benchwarmer, the onlooker at the lives of his father and brother, just as Willy had been before him.

Mother's neglect of the younger brother adds insult to injury and fans the flame of an already unhealthy Oedipal situation. While Linda frequently addresses Biff using the same language and tone she uses to address Willy—"I know dear" (47; Act I), "Please, dear" (59; Act I), "Thanks, darling" (69; Act II)—she uses such terms for Happy only to express contempt: "You never asked, my dear!" she responds angrily to Happy's remark that he was unaware of his father's demotion to straight commission work (50; Act I). Indeed, Happy barely exists for his mother. She frequently acts as if he were not there, as we see when the brothers return home after the restaurant scene. Although Happy does all of the talking as he and Biff enter the house, Linda ignores him to vent her emotion on Biff: "*Linda, cutting Happy off, violently to Biff*: 'Don't you care whether he lives or dies?'" (116; Act II). Only Biff's feelings matter. Only Biff's behavior can change anything. "I'm gonna get married, Mom" (61; Act I) is Happy's new hopeless bid for attention and approval. And it is in his attitude toward marriage and women that we find his Oedipal symptomology most clearly revealed.

Happy's compulsion to seduce the fiancees of executives he works with is a rather obvious enactment of his Oedipal desire: he wants to compete with his father and brother and, especially, punish his mother for ignoring him. For Happy is a psychologically castrated man who has to use his penis to assert his existence and value. The executives he works with are, like his father and brother, authority figures. They're wealthier and more successful than he is and each has won the (symbolically) exclusive attention of a woman. He can't compete with these men in the marketplace any more than he has been able to compete with Biff and Willy in the home. So he punishes them by "ruining" their fiancees. Happy can't find a girl "with resistance," a girl "like Mom" (19; Act I) that he could marry, because he doesn't want to. By sticking to his pattern of one "easy" woman after another, he can continue simultaneously to fulfill two conflicting Oedipal needs: he can continue, symbolically, to preserve his mother (no woman can take her place), and he can continue, symbolically, to soil her (to seduce a woman is to seduce his mother).

There is in Biff's psyche, as in his brother's, an important Oedipal layer. However, for young Biff, the Oedipal object was not Linda, but Willy, and the relationship between father and son was a symbiotic one: each fulfilled the other's narcissistic and masturbatory phallic projection. For Willy, Biff was, of course, the star athlete, admired by the boys and pursued by the girls, as Willy had never been. For Biff, Willy was the successful businessman, universally respected and given "red-carpet treatment" by everyone everywhere he went, as Biff looked forward to being when the time came for him to take his place in the business world. Father and son saw in each other, and became for each other, an idealized phallus.

The love that bound these two characters resembled that of lovers rather than that of father and son. Linda's reminiscence with Biff certainly sounds like a description of sweethearts: "How you used to talk to him on the phone every night! How lonely he was till he could come home to you!" (51; Act I). Similarly, when Linda reminds young Biff, during Willy's flashback, that there is a cellar full of boys waiting for him, her son responds, "Ah, when Pop comes home they can wait!" (28; Act I). Biff put his father ahead of his pals, as most seventeen-year-old boys put their girlfriends. In fact, Biff put his father ahead of—or in place of—his girlfriends as well. For it was not the young girls Biff dated who received his chivalrous attentions. As we see in Willy's Ebbets Field flashback, it was Willy who basked in the warmth of Biff's courtly love: as the family left for the game, it was Willy's hand that Biff took, ignoring Happy's comment about his brother's popularity with the girls (Willy's hopeless rivals for Biff's attention), and it was to Willy that Biff dedicated a special touchdown (25; Act I).

Thus, when Biff found his father in a Boston hotel room with another woman, it was not his mother's betrayal for which the boy suffered; it was his own. Willy and Biff, in fact, sound as if they're having a lovers' quarrel:

BIFF, *his weeping breaking from him*:

Dad . . .

WILLY, *infected by it*:

Oh, my boy . . .

BIFF: Dad . . .

WILLY: She's nothing to me, Biff. I was lonely, I was terribly lonely. . . . *Grabbing for Biff.*

BIFF: Don't touch me, you—liar!

(114; Act II)

Biff's outrage at Willy's betrayal of Linda—"You—you gave her Mama's stockings!" (114; Act I)—was a displacement of the boy's outrage at Willy's betrayal of himself, Biff. So deep was Biff's hurt and anger, his sense of personal betrayal, that he rejected the relationship with his father the two had enjoyed until this point. That is, he rejected both his own and Willy's role as idealized phallus. This does not mean, however, that Biff evolved into a delayed Oedipal relationship with his mother. For one thing, he could not quite leave the idealized Willy behind—he couldn't "kill" the father—and this is why Biff, unable to wholly reject the paternal belief that business success is the only success, has remained vaguely dissatisfied with the outdoor ranch-life he loves.

Finally, Linda's sexuality, like her dreams for the family's future, belongs rather to her husband than herself. She is the devoted, sexless wife that "good" women were required to be in the patriarchal society of her time and place; she is the woman, as we saw Happy put it earlier, "with resistance" (19; Act I). Even her frequent use of dear and darling in addressing her husband bespeaks a motherly, rather than wifely, affection. For, as we have seen, she frequently addresses Biff using the same language and tone she uses to address Willy. This is the same motherly caretaking that shows itself in her concern over Biff's remembering to take his comb to his interview with Bill Oliver and over Willy's remembering to take his glasses, handkerchief, and saccharine to his interview with Howard Wagner. Given the dearth of sexual content in

Linda's behavior throughout the play, the similarity of her dialogue with husband and older son does not suggest the eroticization of her relationship with Biff, but the de-sexualization of her marital discourse.

The Lomans' sexual attitudes intersect in what is known in common parlance as the "good girl/bad girl" view of women. "Good girls" are virgins until marriage; therefore, they are the girls men marry. "Bad girls" do not confine their sexual activity to marriage; therefore, they are the girls men sleep with, hold in contempt, and sooner or later abandon. Obviously, the salesman and his sons enact this attitude in their talk about and behavior toward women. And Linda, who is herself a "good girl" and who calls the women Happy sleeps with his "lousy rotten whores" (117; Act II), certainly concurs with this classification system. The obvious premise underlying "good girl/bad girl" is that sex is "dirty" or evil and that women are marriage commodities whose exchange value is measured by their willingness to put their sexuality in the hands of men. Part of achieving the American dream, from this perspective, must include marriage to a "good girl" like Linda Loman, the kind of girl Willy dreams his sons will bring home—and the kind of girl Happy and Biff are unable to find. This is the pre-1960s sexual attitude associated with the social and political conservatism of post–World War II America, and, clearly, it served the patriarchal status quo by maintaining male domination over women physically and psychologically. However, the "good girl/bad girl" classification supports a conservative status quo in a subtler and more powerful manner as well: it masks the psychosexual structures informing relations between the sexes and, in so doing, masks the merger of the psychosexual structures of human consciousness with the ideological structures of the socius.

"Good girl/bad girl" defines Linda's sexless, mindless devotion to Willy as virtue and thereby permits her to ignore her role in Willy's self-delusion and in her self-delusion about him. And "good girl/bad girl" offers the Loman men an excuse for their behavior with women without making any of them responsible for their own psychological sub-texts.[11] Willy doesn't have to ask himself why he cheated on his wife; Happy doesn't have to probe too deeply into his motives for stealing other men's fiancees; Biff doesn't have to wonder why he used to be so rough with the girls who threw themselves at him in high school or why he has always been rather disinterested in women. The rationalization, as we all know, is that "bad girls" don't deserve better treatment—they probably don't even want better treatment—and it is "natural" for men to respond to them as objects to be used. By validating the Loman men's unexamined displacements—displacements of ontological insecurity, of career anxiety, of Oedipal desire, of phallic projection—"good girl/bad girl" helps keep them looking at the surface of their behavior, their motives, the meaning of their lives.

The conservative era during which *Death of a Salesman* was written and in which the play is set is directly related to the sexual attitudes expressed by the Loman family. For the repression of psychosexual awareness is a product of the same unconscious desire that informs the repression of political awareness: the desire to restrict the growth of critical thinking—thinking that examines motives and sub-texts—which, as Horkheimer and Adorno were the first to observe, is always a threat to a conservative status quo. A conservative society's restriction of psychosexual awareness (which, as the history of the 1950s and 1980s illustrates, is accompanied by a policy of sexual conservatism on the part of America's political leadership) can be seen as an unconscious symbol of what that society really wants to repress: knowledge of ideology, of how the social/political/economic machinery runs. If we can be kept forever "innocent," forever ignorant of our own psychology and of the ways in which that psychology constitutes and is constituted by the sociopolitical domain, we will remain, like Willy, in childlike awe of the powers that be, forever seeking access to the realm of the chosen without ever questioning the terms on which that realm exists.

The relationship I have posited between ideology and sexuality might be termed an Althusserian interrogation of Lacan: the question isn't merely "How does psychosexual development mark the individual's programming within the symbolic order?" but "How does the individual's psychosexual programming within the symbolic order reproduce the society's conditions of production?" In other words, as Miller's play reveals, sexuality hasn't become public; it has always been public. As we see in the case of the Loman family, unexamined, repressive attitudes toward sexuality are part of the larger symbiotic relationship between the individual psyche and the socius that finds its most self-destructive expression in the ideological armor of the American dream, the armor Willy has constructed to hide himself and his family from their own psychology.

* * *

Considered as a labor to avoid and deny existential possibility, *Death of a Salesman*'s psychological/ideological content—Willy's commodification of personal image, his five regressive episodes, and the Loman family's sexuality—can be seen as a kind of psychological death-work. As a concept applicable to the drama of everyday life, death can be seen as a labor we perform whenever we refuse the Nietzschean daily task of reconquering our humanity. As Davis explains,

> Insofar as we are dramatic beings defined by certain core conflicts, each day presents a task that will involve some expenditure of [psychological] energy . . . either to confront or avoid oneself. Such energy is bound to . . . emotional patterns of behavior which define . . . our field of possible action. Life is the effort to make that situation the emergence of existential possibility. Death is the effort to protect us from same.
>
> (*Get the Guests* n. pag.)

This is the real death, the most meaningful death, in *Death of a Salesman*: death seen not as an instinct or a drive, but as an effort to avoid existential inwardness. From this perspective, the play's title gains added bite: the death in *Death of a Salesman* no longer refers merely to the way Willy ends his life, but to the way he lives it as well.

This kind of death-work should not be wholly unfamiliar to most readers. Few of us can honestly assess our own family histories without seeing the same kind of avoidance and denial we see in Willy. And don't we ourselves regularly practice the kind of death-work that traps us, perhaps unconsciously but certainly not unwillingly, in static careers and interpersonal relationships? Ironically, I believe it's the familiarity of Willy's death-work that informs many readers' blindness to it. Willy Loman's sympathetic qualities are foregrounded in the criticism while his weaknesses are often either marginalized or blamed on external forces, and the reason is, I suspect, that the protagonist's psychological/ideological project is compatible with those of his critics. As Esther Merle Jackson notes, "the story of Willy Loman" has an "intimate association with our aspirations" (8).

As Christopher Innes observes, "Brooks Atkinson's judgment [in 1949] that Willy 'represents the homely, decent, kindly virtues of middle class society' . . . was typical" of the critical response of that period (61), and it has remained representative of most of the critical response since that time. Eric Mottram, for example, believes that Willy's failure to succeed in business is based on the protagonist's failure "to learn that business ethics . . . oppose the traditions he assumed were still in action: the personal ethics of honour, the patriarchal nature of a basically benevolent society and family, and neighborhood relations" (30). Mottram doesn't seem to notice that Willy's personal ethics are, at best, very problematical. Similarly, June Schlueter and James K. Flanagan ignore the difficulties involved in any assessment of Willy's values in their apparent nostalgia for the mythical period they feel the character represents: "Willy's little house in Brooklyn stands as a symbol of time past, when the world still had room for vegetable gardens and for salesmen who carried on their trade on the strength of a smile" (57). Harold Bloom, too, believes that Willy "is a good man, who wants only to earn and to deserve the love of his wife and of his sons" (15).

Even among those critics who see Willy's life and death as "a continual commitment to illusion" (Bigsby 120), there is a desire to romanticize this commitment. C.W.E. Bigsby, for example, views Willy's self-delusion as "an attempt to sustain a sense of personal dignity and meaning . . . in a life which seems to consist of little more than a series of contingent events" (117). Similarly, although William Heyen notes that Willy "die[s] lying" (49), he nevertheless calls the decision to commit suicide rather than face the truth about his life an affirmative choice of "meaning over meaninglessness" because the character thus chooses, "in effect, to insist that he had lived, to defend his life as it was" (50).[12] And while Gerald Weales observes that much of Willy's behavior is geared to "keep him from questioning the assumptions that lie beneath his failure and his pretence of success" (134), this critic believes that the play's only positive possibility lies "in Willy's vitality, in his perverse commitment to a pointless dream, in his inability simply to walk away" (135–36).

The desire to see Willy Loman in as positive a light as possible has, I think, also led some readers to interpret other aspects of the play in a way that supports the reading they want to have of the protagonist. As a case in point, Bigsby asserts that Charley does not offer a positive alternative to Willy because Charley believes "that human concerns can play no role in business" and "boasts that his son's success had been a consequence of his own lack of concern" (121). However, Charley does not ignore the role of human concerns in business; he merely rejects the sentimentalization of business—and the trivialization of human concerns—apparent in Willy's attempt to substitute superficial personal interaction for meaningful business service and productivity. Furthermore, Charley's claim that he was a disinterested father, to which Dennis Welland also points as an example of this character's difference from Willy (42), is obviously not to be taken at face value. Charley's oft-quoted "My salvation is that I never took any interest in anything" (89; Act II) is followed immediately with his gift of fifty dollars to Willy and a job offer. Charley continually underplays his concerns—his love for Bernard, of whom he is clearly very proud, and his interest in Willy's well-being, which he shows throughout the play—

but he has these concerns nonetheless. Behind the attempt to contrast Charley with Willy in this manner is, I think, the desire to canonize Willy as the repository of familial love in order to romanticize his motives. And it is the romanticization of Willy's motives that leads, for example, Bigsby to say that "Miller's portrait of Bernard—moral, hard-working, successful, attractive—is perhaps in danger of validating the dreams which Willy had for Biff" (122) without recognizing that Willy's dreams for Biff involve the image rather than the reality of such values. Thus, like the protagonist—and, perhaps, for similar reasons—his critics focus, in Barthes's terms, on the surface of reality, or the appearance of meaning, rather than on its sub-text, or the meaning of appearances (143).[13]

* * *

The collapse of the psychological and ideological dimensions of Miller's play implies a cultural psychology grounded in a thoroughly existentialized dialectics of *psyche* and *socius*, for, as I suggested earlier, it shows that the structures of consciousness and the processes of social signification are inscribed within the same dialectics of desire and that this inscription does not fit the victim model of the relationship between the individual and the socius that, explicitly or implicitly, informs most readings of *Death of a Salesman* and most American literary criticism in general. If Willy Loman is a man manipulated by the ideology of the American dream, it is because that ideology is so easily manipulated to serve his own psychological ends. And surely it is here—in the nature of the psychological pay-offs offered by the adherence to a belief system—that the seductive power of ideology in general, and of the American dream in particular, really lies.

If we want to continue to examine the ways in which American literature places the individual in opposition to society, we must interrogate this dichotomization of psyche and socius by analyzing the ways in which our literature reveals the dialectical complexities of their inexorable existential symbiosis. For, as *Death of a Salesman* illustrates, an existential understanding of the dialectics of psyche and socius opens the text, and the culture it represents, to a new domain for American literary and cultural criticism strikingly relevant to the current theoretical deadlock in conceptualizing subjectivity and the social crisis it reflects. Without such a model of subjectivity, our understanding of American literature and culture will remain sorely limited.

From *Essays in Literature* 19, no. 2 (Fall 1992): 260-278. Copyright © 1992 by Western Illinois University. Reprinted by permission of Western Illinois University.

Notes

1. Among the best known of the numerous publications promoting ethical criticism are probably Allan Bloom's *The Closing of the American Mind*, Wayne Booth's *The Company We Keep*, and Gerald Graff's *Literature Against Itself.*

2. Of course, there have been a number of significant attempts to account for the interaction of the individual and society in terms of the relationship between psychology and ideology, among them Habermas's *Communication and the Evolution of Society*, Jameson's *The Political Unconscious*, Luhman's *The Differentiation of Society*, and, earlier, Horkheimer and Adorno's *Dialectic of Enlightenment* and Fromm's *Escape from Freedom*. However, such texts do not provide the kind of dialectical conception of psyche and socius necessary to a full understanding of their existential - symbiosis. Such efforts have usually been circumscribed by their reliance upon categories too discrete and static to illuminate the subtle ways in which the terms they separate overlap; or they have been limited by a teleology that inevitably issues in some form of reification reminiscent of Hegel's *Geist*. These forms of reification include *a priori*, rationalist structures of communication; structuralist semiotics; psychological structures based on the dominance of the ego; essentialist theories of human nature; and the like.

3. June Schlueter and James K. Flanagan, C.W.E. Bigsby, Leonard Moss, and Brian Parker, among others, see the play primarily as a psychological, or tragic, drama; Richard T. Brucher, Dennis Welland, and Christopher Innes, among others, view it primarily as a Marxist critique of capitalist culture. William Aarnes, Orm Overland, M. W. Steinberg, and Eric Bentley suggest that the play is flawed by the logical incompatibility of its psychological and Marxist dimensions. While Raymond Williams believes that the psychological and Marxist components are fused in the play, he doesn't analyze the nature of this fusion.

4. Karl Marx's analysis of value distinguishes between use value (value based on the uses to which an object is put) and exchange value (value based on the money or other objects for which an object can be traded). French semiotician Jean Baudrillard extends Marx's theory to include sign-exchange value (value based on the social status

an object's ownership confers). A commodity, by definition, is judged only in terms of its exchange value or sign-exchange value. Commodification, then, is the act or condition of seeing something in terms of its exchange value or sign-exchange value to the exclusion of other considerations.

5. Eugene R. August notes the importance of Willy's abandonment by his father and suggests that his early lack of a male role model is responsible for many of the male role problems he has as an adult.

6. For a complete discussion of the cultural manifestations of narcissism (including useful comparisons of the work of Freud, Melanie Klein, Heinz Kohut, Otto Kernberg, Christopher Lasch, and others), see C. Fred Alford.

7. Giles Mitchell's interesting analysis of Willy's narcissism misses this point when he concludes that Loman is "a victim of a pathetic ignorance of the world and of a naivete so colossal as to amount to a kind of innocence" (406). Mitchell sees Willy's failures as "pre-eminently personal" (394) rather than inextricably bound, as I see them, to the socius.

8. Daniel E. Schneider discusses "the return of the repressed" in the play, but he focuses his analysis on what he claims is Willy's guilty hatred of Ben and on Biff and Happy's Oedipal murder of their father.

9. See, for example, C.W.E. Bigsby (56), Peter Szondi (21), Eric Mottram (13), and Esther Merle Jackson (16).

10. Of course, Happy's success with the easy "pick ups" in the restaurant scene is more believable than the rather outrageous success he claims to have with the fiancees of his executive co-workers. However, whether or not these seductions are the product of macho exaggeration is not at issue; the point is that the character's desire turns to sexual exploitation whenever he feels inadequate in the business world.

11. While Ronald Hayman notes that Miller uses sex to forward his social argument, he believes that the Loman men's sexuality "reflects their social conditioning and expresses their resentment of the role society forces them to play" (51).

12. Leah Hadomi also notes that Willy's suicide is an "act of self-deception" (157). While she doesn't romanticize his suicide, neither does she analyze the motives behind it. She believes that Willy kills himself simply because "in his mind suicide becomes . . . equated with success" (168).

13. As I argue elsewhere, Miller's *Theatre Essays* reveal that he too can be numbered among the critics who identify with Willy Loman's dream and who, therefore, interpret the play in a way that supports the most positive reading possible of the protagonist. I also use his essays, in tandem with an examination of the play's formal elements, to suggest that Miller unconsciously manipulated the play's realist, or present-tense, episodes in order to close down the interpretive possibilities opened up by the play's expressionist, or past-tense, episodes.

Works Cited

Aarnes, William. "Tragic Form and the Possibility of Meaning in *Death of a Salesman*." Bloom, *Modern Critical Interpretations*. 95–111.

Alford, C. Fred. *Narcissism: Socrates, the Frankfurt School, and Psychoanalytic Theory*. New Haven: Yale UP, 1988.
Althusser, Louis. "Ideology and Ideological State Apparatuses." 1970. *Lenin and Philosophy and Other Essays*. Trans. Ben Brewster. New York: Monthly Review, 1971. 127–86.
Atkinson, Brooks. Rev. of *Death of a Salesman*, by Arthur Miller. *New York Times*, 11 Feb. 1949, sec. 2: 27.
August, Eugene R. "*Death of a Salesman*: A Men's Studies Approach." *Western Ohio Journal* 7.1 (1986): 53–71.
Barthes, Roland. *Mythologies*. 1957. Trans. Annette Lavers. New York: Hill, 1979.
Baudrillard, Jean. *For a Critique of the Political Economy of the Sign*. 1972. Trans. Charles Levin. St. Louis: Telos, 1981.
Bentley, Eric. "Back to Broadway." *Theatre Arts* 33 (1949): 10–19.
Bigsby, C.W.E. "*Death of a Salesman*: In Memoriam." Bloom, *Modern Critical Interpretations*. 113–28.
Bloom, Allan. *The Closing of the American Mind*. New York: Simon, 1987.
Bloom, Harold. Introduction. Bloom, *Modern Critical Interpretations*. 1–15.
___________, ed. *Modern Critical Interpretations: Arthur Miller's Death of a Salesman*. New York: Chelsea, 1988.
Booth, Wayne. *The Company We Keep*. Berkeley: U of California P, 1989.
Brucher, Richard T. "Willy Loman and The Soul of a New Machine: Technology and the Common Man." Bloom, *Modern Critical Interpretations*. 83–94.
Corrigan, Robert W., ed. *Arthur Miller: A Collection of Critical Essays*. Englewood Cliffs: Prentice, 1969.
Davis, Walter. *Get the Guests: The Play of Aggression in Modern American Drama*. Madison: U of Wisconsin P, forthcoming.
___________. *Inwardness and Existence: Subjectivity in/and Hegel, Heidegger, Marx, and Freud*. Madison: U of Wisconsin P, 1989.
Freud, Sigmund. "The Psychology of the Dream Processes." *The Basic Writings of Sigmund Freud*. Trans. Dr. A. A. Brill, ed. New York: Modern Library, 1938. 180–549.
Fromm, Erich. *Escape from Freedom*. New York: Holt, 1961.
Graff, Gerald. *Literature Against Itself*. Chicago: U of Chicago P, 1979.
Habermas, Jürgen. *Communication and the Evolution of Society*. Trans. Thomas McCarthy. New York: Beacon, 1979.
Hadomi, Leah. "Fantasy and Reality: Dramatic Rhythm in *Death of a Salesman*." *Modern Drama* 31 (1988): 157–74.
Hayman, Ronald. *Arthur Miller*. London: Heinemann, 1970.
Heidegger, Martin. *Being and Time*. 1927. Trans. John Macquarrie and Edward Robinson. New York: Harper, 1962.
Heyen, William. "Arthur Miller's *Death of a Salesman* and the American Dream." Bloom, *Modern Critical Interpretations*. 47–58.
Horkheimer, Max, and Theodor Adorno. *Dialectic of Enlightenment*. 1944. Trans. John Cumming. New York: Continuum, 1982.

Innes, Christopher. "The Salesman on the Stage. A Study in the Social Influence of Drama." Bloom, *Modern Critical Interpretations*. 59–75.

Jackson, Esther Merle. "*Death of a Salesman*: Tragic Myth in the Modern Theatre." Bloom, *Modern Critical Interpretations*, 7–18.

Jameson, Frederic. *The Political Unconscious: Narrative as Socially Symbolic Act*. Ithaca: Cornell UP, 1982.

Klein, George S. *Psychoanalytic Theory: An Exploration of Essentials*. New York: International Universities, 1976.

Laing, R. D. "Ontological Insecurity." *The Divided Self*. 1959. Baltimore: Penguin, 1970. 39–61.

Luhmann, Niklas. *The Differentiation of Society*. Trans. Stephen Holmes and Charles Larmore. New York: Columbia UP, 1982.

Marx, Karl. "Commodities." *Capital*. 1867. Trans. Samuel Moore and Edward Aveling. Ed. Frederick Engels. London: Sonnenschein, 1886. 1–35.

Merleau-Ponty, M. *Phenomenology of Perception*, 1945. Trans. Colin Smith. London: Routledge, 1962.

Miller, Arthur. *Death of a Salesman*. 1949. *The Portable Arthur Miller*. Ed. Harold Clurman. New York: Viking, 1971. 3–133.

___________. *The Theatre Essays of Arthur Miller*. Ed. Robert A. Martin. New York: Penguin, 1978.

Mitchell, Giles. "Living and Dying for the Ideal: A Study of Willy Loman's Narcissism." *Psychoanalytic Review* 77 (1990): 391–407.

Moss, Leonard. *Arthur Miller*. New York: Twayne, 1980.

Mottram, Eric. "Arthur Miller: The Development of a Political Dramatist In America." Corrigan, 23–57.

Overland, Orm. "Arthur Miller's Struggle with Dramatic Form." *Modern Critical Views: Arthur Miller*. Ed. Harold Bloom, New York: Chelsea, 1987. 51–63.

Parker, Brian. "Point of View in Arthur Miller's *Death of a Salesman*." Corrigan, 95–109.

Schlueter, June, and James K. Flanagan. *Arthur Miller*. New York: Ungar, 1987.

Schneider, Daniel E., M.D. "Play of Dreams." *Theatre Arts*, Oct. 1949: 18–21.

Steinberg, M. W. "Arthur Miller and the Idea of Modern Tragedy." Corrigan 81–93.

Szondi, Peter. "Memory and Dramatic Form in *Death of a Salesman*." Bloom, *Modern Critical Interpretations*. 19–23.

Tyson, Lois M. *The Psychological Politics of the American Dream: The Commodification of Subjectivity in Twentieth-Century American Literature*. Columbus: Ohio State UP, forthcoming.

Weales, Gerald. "Arthur Miller's Shifting Image of Man." Corrigan, 131–42.

Welland, Dennis. *Miller: A Study of His Plays*. London: Methuen, 1979.

Williams, Raymond. "The Realism of Arthur Miller." Corrigan, 69–79.

Winnicott, D. W. "Metapsychological and Clinical Aspects of Regression within the Psycho-Analytic Set-Up." *Collected Papers: Through Paediatrics to Psycho-Analysis*. New York: Basic 1975. 278–94.

Death of a Salesman and the Poetics of Arthur Miller

Matthew C. Roudané

Death of a Salesman is a deceptively simple play. Its plot revolves around the last twenty-four hours in the life of Willy Loman, the hard-working sixty-three-year-old traveling salesman whose ideas of professional, public success jar with the realities of his private desires and modest accomplishments. Subtitled "Certain private conversations in two acts and a requiem," the play has a narrative which unwinds largely through Willy Loman's daydreams, private conversations revealing past family hopes and betrayals, and how those past experiences, commingled with entropic present circumstances, culminate in Willy's death. Realizing that in death he may provide for his family in ways he never could during his lifetime, Willy commits suicide, hoping that his insurance will grant Biff a "twenty-thousand-dollar"[1] deliverance, an extended period of grace. He hopes the insurance money will somehow expiate, or at least minimize, the guilt which he feels for his affair at the Standish Arms Hotel a lifetime ago. The simplicity of the play, however, quickly dissolves into filial ambiguity, civic paradox, and philosophic complexity.

Mythologizing America

Death of a Salesman presents a rich matrix of enabling fables that define the myth of the American dream. Indeed, most theatregoers assume, on an a priori level, that the principles Willy Loman values—initiative, hard work, family, freedom, consumerism, economic salvation, competition, the frontier, self-sufficiency, public recognition, personal fulfillment, and so on—animate American cultural poetics. The Founding Fathers, after all, predicated the US Constitution on the belief that every citizen possesses an inalienable right to the unfettered pursuit of the American Dream. No wonder Benjamin Franklin's practical 1757 essay on how to achieve Salvation, *The Way to Wealth* (whose title would have prompted Willy Loman to buy a copy), attracted the common working person. Although Willy Loman, inspired by a mythologized Dave Singleman and a desire to build a future for his boys through hard work, endorses such values, it is an endorsement foisted upon him less by personal choice than by a malevolent universe whose hostility mocks his every pursuit. Well-meaning yet lacking, a fatherless father, a salesman no longer capable of selling, Willy Loman can only cling to idyllic fables that baffle as they elude him. In the past, the ever talkative Willy has lived by "contacts" and "who you know and the smile on your face!" (*Death of a Salesman*, p. 86); in the present, Willy's talk reaches a Beckettian decrescendo, "Shhh!" (p. 136) being his last utterance before he speeds off to his suicide.

In its text and subtext, then, *Death of a Salesman* replicates a model of community and of citizenship to which most theatregoers—regardless of gender, race, nationality, or ideology—respond. The nature of that popular and intellectual response varies greatly, to be sure. The play embodies, for many, the *peripeteia*, *hamartia*, and *hubris* that Aristotle found essential for all great tragedies. For many feminist critics, on the other hand, the play stages "a nostalgic view of the plot of the universalized masculine protagonist of the Poetics";[2] it presents a grammar of space that marginalizes Linda Loman and, by extension, all women, who seem Othered, banished to the periphery of a patriarchal world. *Death of a Salesman*, the universalists counter, seems beyond philosophical limits or gendered subjectivity, and thus is a play to which all—social constructionists, Jungians, Marxists, poststructuralists, and so on—react. *Death of a Salesman* presents a constellation of conflicting views and warring narratives, and has become what Walter Benjamin would call a "cultural treasure." This explains its enduring appeal. Within a year of its premiere, *Death of a Salesman* was playing in every major city in the United States. As early as 1951 it was viewed by appreciative audiences in at least eleven countries abroad, including Great Britain, France, Israel, and Argentina. As Brenda Murphy observes, "since its premiere, there has never been a time when *Death of a Salesman* was not being performed somewhere in the world."[3]

This is not to imply that the play has received universal praise. For decades, artistic terrorists (to borrow Frank Zappa's term) masquerading as theatre reviewers, as well as serious scholars, have taken Miller to task. The charges are familiar. The play sentimentalizes experience. Its Hallmark Card flourish at the end dismantles the play's moral seriousness. The rhetoric of clichés diminishes its riposte. The play's protagonist is an unfit subject of tragedy, an unworthy man incapable of carrying the tragic burdens its author places on him. An implicit sexism somehow dates the play. And, among other charges, Miller in this play and in selected theatre essays presents a flawed essentialistic humanism. But the critical challenges, sometimes eloquently and convincingly argued, often seem much to do about little. The emotional impact of the play remains so strong that the response of most theatregoers, despite the occasional dissenting voice of some academics, has been overwhelmingly favourable for half a century.

Such praise comes from the notion that most in the audience relate to as they rebel against the Lomans. The adulterous father. The marginalized mother. Wayward children. A family's battles to pay bills. Unemployment. The child's quest. Spite. Loss. Felt but unexpressed love. Guilt and shame. Self-reliance. Theatregoers see themselves, their parents, or their children in the play. As David Mamet said to Miller after watching the play in 1984, "that is *my* story—not only did you write it about me, but *I could go up on stage right now and act it.*"[4] A play concerning the most public of American myths, *Death of a Salesman* lays bare the private individual's sensibility, a sensibility neutralized by those very myths. Dustin Hoffman revealed that after he read the play at the age of sixteen, he "had a kind of small breakdown for about two weeks." Hoffman, who read Bernard's lines in a 1966 record version of the play and then played Willy in the celebrated 1984 Broadhurst Theater revival in New York, says of Miller: "He's my artistic father."[5] In an era when many scholars question precisely what constitutes American essentialism, most theatregoers still regard *Death of a Salesman* as the quintessential American play.

But the play also transcends its own American heritage and claims to American essentialism. As C.W.E. Bigsby suggests, the play has "had no difficulty finding an international audience, often being produced in countries whose own myths are radically different, where, indeed, the salesman is an alien and exotic breed. . . . Certainly, no country seems to have been baffled by a play in which an individual creates his own fate while believing himself to be an agent of social process. No audience seems to have had difficulty in responding to the story of a man distracted from human necessities by public myths."[6] Many audience members watching the 1950 Vienna production wept, as did the Chinese audiences after seeing the 1983 Beijing run. The play "has been played before a native audience in a small Arctic village with the same villagers returning night after night to witness the performance in a language they did not understand."[7]

Death of a Salesman continues to engage audiences on an international level, not only because it traverses intercultural borders, but also because it brings audiences back to the edges of prehistory itself. Postmodern in texture, reifying a world in which experience is "always ready" for the Lomans, the play gains its theatrical power from ancient echoes, its Hellenic mixture of pity and fear stirring primal emotions. Miller himself believes that

> it's a well-told, paradoxical story. It seems to catch the paradoxes of being alive in a technological civilization. In one way or another, different kinds of people, different classes of people apparently feel that they're in the play. . . . It seems to have more or less the same effect everywhere there is a dominating technology. Although it's also popular in places where life is far more pretechnological. Maybe it involves some of the most rudimentary elements in the civilizing process: family cohesion, death and dying, parricide, rebirth, and so on. The elements, I guess, are rather fundamental. People *feel* these themes no matter where they are.[8]

Audiences feel such themes because, despite the play's modernity, tribal undercurrents animate the narrative. Although critics have long questioned Miller's conception of tragedy, and understandably so, the playwright nonetheless places in useful perspective his views regarding the tragic textures of *Death of a Salesman*. In Willy Loman, Miller writes in "Tragedy and the Common Man" (1949), "we are in the presence of a character who is ready to lay down his life, if need be, to secure one thing—his sense of personal dignity." Despite the deep irony of his life choices, Willy Loman represents, for many, the commonplace "individual attempting to gain his 'rightful' position in his society"; in "his willingness to throw all he has into the contest, the battle to secure his rightful place in his world," Willy's struggle defines his Sisypheian heroism.[9] Audiences experience, in other words, the afterwash of the tragic.

The Set and the Stage Directions

Miller underpins the tragic power of the play through the wonderfully multivalent set and setting. When theatregoers settled into their seats at the packed Morosco Theatre on opening night in 1949 and waited for the play to begin, they heard the melody of a flute. The aural dissolves (like Willy's dreams) to the visual as the curtain rises and the salesman's skeletal house comes into focus. Elia Kazan and Miller worked meticulously with Jo Mielziner, who developed the set, and Eddie Kook, the lighting engineer. Miller provides one of the best-known opening stage directions in American drama, directions on which Kazan, Mielziner, and Kook based their collaborative efforts. Functioning as a kind of prose-poem, the initial stage directions prefigure many of the play's major dynamics.

The stage directions function in at least two important ways. First, they delineate the spatial and physical machinery of the play, including the basic layout of props, the importance of the forestage, the use of such kinesic devices as music and lighting, and, above all, the centrality of the salesman's house. Mielziner filled the stage with realistic props: a kitchen table with three chairs, a small refrigerator, telephone, wastebasket, stairs, three beds, an athletic trophy, and a chest of drawers. But these realistic props were placed within a highly expressionistic set. No solid walls separated Willy and Linda's bedroom, situated slightly elevated and stage right from the kitchen, or the boys' bedroom, located on the second floor, from the kitchen. Instead of a solid roof, only gabled rafters angling upwards, silhouetting a roof line, were used. The back of each room had walls of sorts, but they were translucent backdrops. Since no walls separated the rooms, characters were not necessarily confined spatially or, in the daydream sequences, temporally. When the action occurs in time present, for instance, the actors observe the imaginary wall-lines. But, Miller's stage directions indicate, "*in the scenes of the past these boundaries are broken, and characters enter or leave a room by stepping 'through' a wall onto the forestage*" (*Death of a Salesman*, p. 12).

Audiences gazed at another backdrop behind the house, which featured two trees and images of towering buildings. During Willy's daydreams about the past, Mielziner bathed the stage in a soft amber light, its golden hues suggesting the glory of a past in which the Lomans' neighborhood was filled with grass, trees with green leaves, and a beautiful horizon. The past was a time of freshly painted cars, homes, and soaring hopes. Biff proudly donned his golden football uniform before adoring fans. It was a time when Linda smiled easily. The idealism and happiness of the past have been leeched from the Lomans' present, however. Now, Linda enamels herself with her "*iron repression*" (p. 12). Often during the present scenes, lights from the rear cover the stage with an ominous reddish orange glow. These lighting gradations permit the spatial, the temporal, and the thematic to inhabit the stage simultaneously, and in ways that perfectly suggest the interiority of the characters. The shifts in lighting, if subtly done, not only make for a spatial fluidity, but also register through direct sensory experience the cohering of social, psychic, and actual time.

A particularly foreboding scene illustrates Miller's dramaturgy. The menacing gas heater, located behind a translucent backdrop, visually seems to come alive at the end of Act One. The time is in the present as Biff enters that darkened kitchen, lights a cigarette, and walks downstage into "*a golden pool of light*" (p. 68). At the same time Willy and Linda are in their bedroom, reminiscing about the charisma Biff exuded in high school; Willy says that his son was

> Like a young god. Hercules—something like that. And the sun, the sun all around him. Remember how he waved to me? Right up from the field, with the representatives of three colleges standing by? And the buyers I brought, and the cheers when he came out—Loman, Loman, Loman! God Almighty, he'll be great yet. A star like that, magnificent, can never fade away!
>
> (p. 68)

When Willy utters the "never fade away" lines, however, Kook slowly dimmed the lights that were pointed at Willy, a haunting visual intimation that Linda is helping her husband to bed for the last time. Miller's stage direction accentuates the effect as the "*gas heater begins to glow through the kitchen wall, near the stairs, a blue flame beneath red coils*" (p. 68). Moments later a horrified Biff discovers the rubber tubing Willy hides behind the gas heater. Visually, such stage atmosphere makes for brilliant theatrics. With props, lighting, body movement, and language operating contrapuntally, Miller draws the audience into the Lomans' holy storm.

The initial stage directions function in a second important way. They foreground, through metaphor, many of the play's deeper ambiguities and conflicts. The flute music sounds "*small and fine, telling of grass and trees and the horizon*" (p. 11). The music holds important past references for Willy: his father made and sold flutes as a traveling salesman; through a kind of free associative pattern, the music reveals something of Willy's past desires and dreams, when all things seemed possible to him. Once the music fades, the stage directions concentrate on the house itself, a "*small, fragile-seeming home*," a home dwarfed by the "*solid vault of apartment houses*" (p. 11). The vault allusion, whether referring ironically to a site of banking, investing, and finance, or to a site of entombment, entrapment, a place of no exit, clearly draws attention to the fragility of the Loman home. Miller creates a trope for the decline of the natural world. Towering apartments, radiating "*an angry glow of orange*" (p. 11), surround the home, allowing only a minimal amount of blue light from the sky to fall upon their property. Later, Willy fondly reminisces about lilacs, wisteria, peonies, and daffodils. He tries to plant seeds, impossible though such an effort to reconnect himself with the organic rhythms of the universe proves to be. The plight of the Lomans, then, finds its parallels in the architecture and urban space of their home. In text and performances, Miller insists on maintaining the drama's essential contrariety: "*An air of the dream clings to the place, a dream rising out of reality*" (p. 11), though reality ensures that Willy never fulfills his dreams, and his dreams never fully square with reality. Miller juxtaposes an imploding urban landscape of time present—"Smell the stink from that apartment house!" (p. 18)—with Willy's longings for a pastoral landscape, one necessarily reconstructed only in time past.

Images of the Fall, Falling, and the Fallen

Miller's stage directions provide insight into what Kazan (and Stanislavsky before him) calls the characters' spines, or their fundamental nature. When Willy enters carrying two large valises, symbolically filled with sixty-odd years of Willy's existence, he "*thankfully lets his burdens down*" (p. 12). His physical and spiritual exhaustion obvious, Willy "*hears but is not aware of*" the flute music. Joseph Hirsch's original poster used in advertizing the play in New York City in some ways visually prepared audiences for a troubling image of a troubled salesman: Willy's rear view is pictured, his slumping shoulders outlined through his business suit. Head bowed, dress hat on, he carries his sample cases, the image of an exhausted if not defeated man. Miller heightens our sense of Willy's physical and spiritual depletion by selectively fading the lights on him.

Miller presents no fewer than twenty-five scenes in which Willy's body language and dialogue create images of the fall, the falling, or the fallen. While Charley repeatedly asks his neighbor if he is ever going to grow up, Willy usually appears "*beaten down*" (p. 65). Willy often seeks relief by collapsing into a chair, where he "*lies back, exhausted*" (p. 67). He also sits down in a chair after Howard fires him. Indeed, Miller places special emphasis on the chair in Howard's office: he felt that "the chair must become alive, quite as though his old boss were in it as he addresses him." Mielziner and Kook "once worked an entire afternoon lighting a chair," Miller reports, and, in performance, the result was a highly effective expressionistic moment, one in which, "rather than being lit, the chair subtly seemed to begin emanating light."[10] During the restaurant scene he "*tries to get to his feet*" several times as Biff, "*agonized, holds Willy down*" in his chair (*Death of a Salesman*, p. 112).

Miller fills the daydream scene in Boston with images of a fall, moving from the chair at Frank's Chop House to the bed in the Standish Arms. In the Volker Schlöndorff version (1985), Willy (played by Dustin Hoffman) and the Woman (played by Linda Kozlowski, resplendent with Marilyn Monroesque hair and body) embrace as they *fall* in a slow motion sequence into bed. After hearing Biff's knocking on the door, she pleads, "Willy, Willy, are you going to get up, get up, get up, get up?" (p. 114) while the audience watches a man in the process of falling down, down, down, down. After Biff discovers his father with the Woman, Willy, "*getting down beside Biff*" (p. 120), explains his loneliness. A shattered Biff exits while "*Willy is left on the floor on his knees*" (p. 121); as Willy's mind returns to the present, he remains huddled down against the toilet, abandoned by his sons. During his famous "Spite, spite is the word of your undoing!" speech,

Willy is "*sinking into a chair at the table, with full accusation*" (p. 130). Willy's verbal scattershots, increasingly detached from deeds, reinforce his impotence: he snaps his fingers while giving Biff orders, but his directives are ignored. Biff blots out his father. Willy insists that Linda throw away her worn stockings, but, unknown to Willy, she keeps them.

Miller also reinforces the falling and fallen imagery through the dialogue. When Willy begs his boss for a salary, we hear that he once averaged, in 1928, a salary of a hundred and seventy dollars per week; now he begs for sixty-five, then fifty per week, the regressive monetary requests paralleling Willy's downward spiral. From Biff's running *down* eleven flights of stairs to his realization that he was not a salesman with Oliver but merely a shipping clerk; from Biff's idolizing his father to calling him a "phony little fake!" (p. 121); from Linda's announcement that she will cook a big family breakfast to her throwing the flowers to the floor, images which suggest fallen hopes and expectations dominate the text. Fittingly, at the funeral, Linda "*lays down the flowers, kneels, and sits back on her heels. All stare down at the grave*" (p. 136). The sound of loud, frenzied music lowers to the "*soft pulsation of a single cello string*" (p. 136). In a case of the watchers watching the watchers watch, the audience and the Loman family remember stories of Dave Singleman's massive funeral and cannot help but compare it to Willy's sparsely attended burial ceremony. From page to stage, Miller meticulously structures *Death of a Salesman* upon a cluster of retrogressive images, images that correspond directly with the Lomans' fall.

Family Backgrounds

Miller worked assiduously to create the Lomans' fall. Although written in about six weeks in 1948, *Death of a Salesman* had a long gestation period. Some years after the first production of the play, Miller discovered a college notebook he used as a student at the University of Michigan in the 1930s. Miller had "totally forgotten that ten years earlier I had begun a play in college about a salesman and his family but had abandoned it" (*Timebends*, p. 129). Further, Miller recalls his teenage encounters with his "two pioneer uncles," Manny Newman and Lee Balsam (*Timebends*, p. 121). From them he sought advice about carpentry, a trade that would become a life-long vocation for the playwright. Working with Uncle Balsam on a porch design as a teenager, Miller writes that this "was my first experience with the fevers of construction, and I could not fall asleep for anticipation of tomorrow; and it was exactly the same one cold April in 1948 when I built a ten-by-twelve studio near my first house in Connecticut where I intended to write a play about a salesman" (*Timebends*, p. 121). The relative dynamics of carpentry and the stagecrafting of *Death of a Salesman* would be strong. In each, planning, interconnections, and designs are crucial, while in the case of carpentry Arthur Miller has written that "the idea of creating a new shadow on the earth has never lost its fascination" (*Timebends*, p. 121). While Miller's studio would cast a private shadow, a work space for the individual artist, the end-product, *Death of a Salesman*, cast a very long public shadow.

The impact of his uncles ultimately had less to do with carpentry, however, and much more to do with *Death of a Salesman*. Both were salesmen. Tellingly enough, Miller regarded Uncle Manny and Uncle Lee, like Ben and Willy's father, as pioneering men. It was Manny Newman, especially, who entranced Miller for years, and whose contradictions shaped Miller's conception of Willy Loman and his family. Miller's recollection of the Newman home, for example, parallels the Lomans'. "There was a shadowy darkness in their [the Newmans'] house, a scent of sex and dream, of lies and invention, and above all of contradictions and surprise" (*Timebends*, p. 122). Admitting that his memories of the Newman household were the product of a teenage experience, Miller still remembers "the lure and mystery with which my mind unaccountably surrounded the Newmans. I could never approach their little house without the expectation that something extraordinary was about to happen in there, some sexual lewdness, perhaps, or an amazing revelation of some other kind." Their house "was dank with sexuality" and "was secretly obsessed, as though they were obscenely involved with one another—a fantasy of mine, of course" (*Timebends*, p. 12,4). No wonder the Loman house is a home in whose structure linger secret obsessions.[11]

One of Manny Newman's sons, Abby, told Miller, "'He wanted a business for us. So we could all work together. . . . A business for the boys'" (*Timebends*, p. 130).[12] For the playwright, who had now been thinking about writing *Death of a Salesman* for ten years, this revelation was a galvanizing moment. Miller would interfold the family business motif throughout *Death of a Salesman*. Early in the play, for instance, Willy hopes that "Someday I'll have my own business" (*Death of a Salesman*, p. 30), and after his young boys volunteer to help, Willy marvels, "Oh, won't that be something! Me comin' into the Boston stores with you boys carryin' my bags. What a sensation!" (p. 31). Late in the play, Stanley, the waiter at Frank's Chop House, learns that Happy and Biff might be "going into business together" (p. 100). In repartee encoded with layers of rich ironies, Stanley replies, "Great! That's the best for you. Because a family business, you know what I mean?—that's the best." He quickly adds, "'Cause what's the difference? Somebody steals? It's in the family. Know what I mean?" (p. 100). Stanley is wrong.

Although the Lomans never go into business together, they discover that there is a huge difference. From Happy's stealing other executives' fiancees to Biff's stealing the high school football, the box full of basketballs, the lumber and cement from the neighborhood, the suit in Kansas City, and Bill Oliver's fountain pen, the question of stealing deepens to encompass not only social crimes but fundamental private issues: the stealing of one's very identity, the loss of the self, the abrogation of responsibility. Inheritors of Willy's sins from the past, Happy and Biff find themselves fated to perpetuate the values instilled by their father in the present and future. Biff and Happy are flawed extensions of Willy and Linda, the genetic lineage carried on with devastating efficiency and symmetry. For throughout Miller presents characters who carry within them modern versions of an Aristotelian fatal flaw, the moral fissure, the *hubris*, that foretells their tragedy. Willy trains his sons well. Minor errors must be heaped upon larger sins, extending a terrible replicating process and ensuring that a tragic parental heritage will be passed on to all descendants. For each character, there is no escape from this family's tabooed ancestral history. Biff, especially, feels the tragic inevitability of his biological and spiritual fate. Problems of guilt and innocence haunt him, as do the relations between private life and social processes.

So one of the central problems Miller embeds in the script is that, though the Lomans know they have transgressed social law in their petty thievery and personal deceits, they seldom take the necessary first steps toward self-disclosure and, more significantly, self-knowledge. For the Lomans, Truth kills. Until the last twenty-four hours in Willy's life, neither Biff nor anyone else faces facts. The Real has long been devalued, deformed, defleshed. Illusion and its relation to familial bonds and the larger (in Rousseau's sense of the term) social contract have been conveniently twisted into the appearance of Truth. In brief, the Lomans remain co-conspirators, master builders of their illusory world.

Even Linda, who knows that "only the shallowness of the water" (p. 59) saved Willy from suicide the year before, and that Willy has "been trying to kill himself" (p. 58) recently, contributes to the truth-illusion matrix. If Linda casts herself as supportive wife, she is also a complex figure who plays a central role within the family dynamics. This became more apparent when Miller directed the play in Beijing, where he emphasized Linda's centrality. She was "'in action,'" Miller says. "She's not just sitting around. She's the one who knows from the beginning of the play that Willy's trying to kill himself. She's got the vital information." He pinpoints Linda's predicament, one underscoring the impossibility of her life: "Linda sustains the illusion because that's the only way Willy can be sustained. At the same time any cure or change is impossible in Willy. Ironically, she's helping to guarantee that Willy will never recover from his illusion. She has to support it; she has no alternative, given his nature and hers."[13] Hence Linda each morning takes the rubber pipe from the hot water heater—only to replace it each night when Willy returns home. "Ashamed," fearful that she might "insult him" (*Death of a Salesman*, p. 60), and not knowing how to deal with such a stubborn husband, Linda weds herself to an illusory world. To deny the crisis is to live, perhaps, another day. Illusions appear so suffused within the psychodynamics and vocabulary of the family that the Lomans, we realize, have slipped years ago into a psychotic denial, hoping all along that outer events will somehow right themselves—and their lives. Nothing could be further from the truth. Minutes before Willy kills himself, Biff screams to his father, "We never told the truth for ten minutes in this house!"—an insight immediately confirmed in Happy's lie: "We always told the truth!" (p. 131).

It would be misleading to claim that Manny Newman was the sole model for Willy Loman. Miller drew on multiple models and incidents, both fictional and historical. While "making preliminary sketches of scenes and ideas for a salesman play," Miller decided on the name Loman. "'Loman,'" Miller reports, "had the sound of reality, of someone who had actually lived, even if I had never known anyone by that name" (*Timebends*, p. 177). But one cold winter afternoon, while walking to the subway in New York City, the playwright noticed a film that was currently showing, one that had influenced his own aesthetic imagination years earlier. The film was Fritz Lang's *The Testament of Dr. Mabuse*. A key character's name in the film: Lohmann. Miller also provides a corrective to two generations of those scholars who reduced Willy's surname to a too obvious allusion. "In later years I found it discouraging to observe the confidence with which some commentators of *Death of a Salesman* smirked at the heavy-handed symbolism of 'Low-man.' What the name really meant to me was a terror-stricken man calling into the void for help that will never come" (*Timebends*, p. 179).

Surely there were many sources for Willy and the other characters. Miller drew upon his literary forebears as well as his own personal experiences during the Great Depression, which he has often called a moral catastrophe. Desperate American salesmen trying to fuel the Dynamo fascinated him. In Manny Newman's salesman friend, Miller saw the contours of hopeless heroism:

> Like any traveling salesman, he had to my mind a kind of intrepid valor that withstood the inevitable putdowns, the scoreless attempts to sell. In a sense, these men lived like artists, like actors whose product is first of all themselves, forever imagining triumphs in a world that either ignores them or denies their presence altogether. But just often enough to keep the game going one of them makes it and swings to the moon on a thread of dreams unwinding out of himself. (*Timebends*, p. 127)

In Manny Newman, Miller located similar patterns. After a chance meeting at the Colonial Theatre in Boston, Miller saw Manny, who had just watched *All My Sons*. He was weeping. "I could see his grim hotel room behind him, the long trip up from New York in his little car, the hopeless hope of the day's business" (*Timebends*, p. 132).

Toward a New Poetics

The influence of Miller's encounters with family and cinema had yet a deeper influence on *Death of a Salesman*. More than merely providing a model of character development, Manny Newman inspired Miller to theatricalize plot and narrative in wholly new forms. When Miller called out to Manny in the lobby of the Colonial Theatre, a distracted Manny ignored Miller's greeting and simply replied, "'Buddy is doing very well'" (*Timebends*, pp. 130–31). The lack of transition between Miller's "'Manny!'" and Manny's reference to Buddy, his eldest son who Miller describes in Biff-like terms, triggered the possibility of a new dramatic method. The absence of conversational transition, Miller writes, stuck in my mind; it was a signal to me of the new form that until now I had only tentatively imagined could exist. I had not the slightest idea of writing about a salesman then, totally absorbed as I was in my present production. But how wonderful, I thought, to do a play without transitions at all, dialogue that would simply leap from bone to bone of a skeleton that would not for an instant cease being added to, an organism as strictly economic as a leaf, as trim as an ant. (*Timebends*, p. 131)

Animating the transitions would be Miller's daring use of time. *Death of a Salesman*, after all, ignores the linear, chronocentric unfolding of time. To be sure, the action takes place during the last twenty-four hours of Willy's life, but the drama privileges the time of Willy's inner awareness. Time filters through daydreams. Miller conflates time. And it is a time that measures the intensity of felt experience, not the monotony of nine-to-five routines. In *Timebends*, Miller describes his intention to write

> a play that would do to an audience what Manny had done to me in our surprising meeting—cut through time like a knife through a layer cake or a road through a mountain revealing its geologic layers, and instead of one incident in one time-frame succeeding another, display past and present concurrently, with neither one ever coming to a stop.
>
> The past, I saw, is a formality, merely a dimmer present, for everything we are is at every moment alive in us. How fantastic a play would be that did not still the mind's simultaneity, did not allow a man to "forget" and turned him to see present through past and past through present, a form that in itself, quite apart from its content and meaning, would be inescapable as a psychological process and as a collecting point for all that his life in society had poured into him. This little man walking into the street had all my youth inside him, it seemed. And I suppose because I was more conscious than he, I had in some sense already created him. (*Timebends*, p. 131)

Miller wanted, to borrow Tom Wolfe's metaphor from *The Right Stuff*, to push the envelope, to reinvent the nature of theatricality itself. He wanted a play whose very ontology would be even more inventive than that achieved by some of his American predecessors, such as O'Neill in the early sea plays, in *The Hairy Ape* and *The Emperor Jones*, or Elmer Rice in *The Adding Machine*, works that challenged the prevailing American realistic theatre. Miller wanted to formulate a dramatic structure that would allow the play textually and theatrically to capture the simultaneity of the human mind as that mind registers outer experience through its own inner subjectivity.

Furthermore, Miller was not satisfied with merely drawing upon his uncles, other salesmen, and such notable portraits of American salesmen as seen in O'Neill's *Marco Millions* and *The Iceman Cometh*, or, in a more general sense, the plight of the American worker as reflected in Clifford Odets's *Awake and Sing!* and *Waiting for Lefty*. This hardly implies that Miller strays from social commitment. Indeed, more than any American playwright, Miller embeds a moral optimism and social seriousness in every play. This was as true for the earlier plays, from *The Golden Years* and *All My Sons* through *The Price* and *The American Clock*, as it is for his work in the 1990s, *The Ride Down Mount Morgan*, *The Last Yankee*, and *Broken Glass*. Such key theatre essays as "Tragedy and the Common Man" (1949), Introduction to *Collected Plays* (1957), and "About Theatre Language" (1994) highlight the civic function of Miller's artistry. He is an ethicist. His entire theatre stands as a critique of the *republica*. But in *Death of a Salesman* he wanted to refurbish the presentation of his moral and social commitment in a new form.

Miller sought nothing less than a new poetics. The notion of creating a sense of simultaneity, a dramatic process by which he could bend time, became increasingly important. He had worked carefully to achieve the success of the realistic *All My Sons*, which in 1994 he identified as his "most Ibsen-influenced play."[14] Yet even as he was beginning to enjoy the economic freedoms and entitlements from royalties generated by his first Broadway success, Miller tested new possibilities. As he put it, "*All My Sons* had exhausted my lifelong interest in the

Greco-Ibsen form" (*Timebends*, p. 144). This seems to be a curious remark for a thirty-two-year-old with only two Broadway productions to his credit, but it clearly indicates that his artistic instincts prompted dramaturgic revolution. He came of age as a young dramatist when "we thought it [the realism of Broadway] the perfect style for an unchallenging, simpleminded linear middle-class conformist view of life."[15] Even today some directors and audiences have difficulty when the playwright strays too far from mimesis. "They can't stand a metaphor," Miller told the editor of this volume:

> Metaphor is dangerous, ambiguous; it leaves people slightly mystified and the conscience of the American theatre is that of an intelligent business man. He is a realistic, intelligent, even sensitive person, but he ain't interested in metaphors. He wants to know who's on first and this has made for a very strong realistic tradition, not just in the theatre but in the novel, the movies, and so on. But as soon as you begin to stretch that into a metaphoric area, they get uneasy.[16]

And so, during his apprenticeship years, Miller grappled with the social power and aesthetic limitations of realism. "My own first playwriting attempt was purely mimetic, a realistic play about my own family. . . . I came out of the thirties unsure whether there could be a viable counterform to the realism around me."[17] Miller felt that "the problem with *All My Sons* was not that it was too realistic but that it left too little space and time for the wordless darkness that underlies all verbal truth" (*Timebends*, p. 144). For *Death of a Salesman*, photographic realism simply could not reflect the interior subjectivity he was seeking. He needed a play that exteriorized the "logic of the imagination."[18] One key to the greatness of *Death of a Salesman*, therefore, concerns its dramatic form as that form refracts the time of Willy Loman's experience."[19]

A Poetic Language

Just as Miller searched for a unique dramatic form and use of time, so he sought out a unique grammar of expression. He needed a language that would expose, in theatrical and psychological terms, the inside of Willy's head. Above all, he wanted a language that would present the simultaneity of Willy's thought processes and daydreams. A child of American dramatic realism, a playwright influenced by the social theories and dramatic practices of the eminently realistic Henrik Ibsen, Miller felt compelled to reformulate language in *Death of a Salesman*. Although Joseph A. Hynes claims the play's language seems highly sentimental,[20] and Harold Bloom that while "Miller is by no means a bad writer . . . he is scarcely an eloquent master of language,"[21] the playwright may be viewed as one of the most gifted and radical sculptors of language in American drama.

Interestingly, Tennessee Williams, not Ibsen or Shaw, liberated Miller. After Kazan took Miller to see *A Streetcar Named Desire* in New Haven, he was inspired to work even more precisely with his language. Seeing *Streetcar* "strengthened" Miller. It was a play that opened "one specific door," one that did not deal so much with "the story or characters or direction, but [with] words and their liberation, [with] the joy of the writer in writing them, the radiant eloquence of its composition, [that] moved me more than all its pathos. It formed a bridge . . . to the whole tradition of unashamed word-joy . . . we had . . . turned our backs on" (*Timebends*, p. 182). The beneficiary of this word-joy would be Willy Loman:

> With *Streetcar*, Tennessee has printed a license to speak at full throat, and it helped strengthen me as I turned to Willy Loman, a salesman always full of words, and better yet, a man who could never cease trying, like Adam, to name himself and the world's wonders. I had known all along that this play could not be encompassed by conventional realism, and for one integral reason: in Willy the past was as alive as what was happening at the moment, sometimes even crashing in to completely overwhelm his mind. I

> wanted precisely the same fluidity in the form, and now it was clear to me that this must be primarily verbal. The language would of course have to be recognizably his to begin with, but it seemed possible now to infiltrate it with a kind of superconsciousness. (*Timebends*, p. 182)

If Williams formed a bridge, whose foundation was the word, Miller suddenly crossed this creative bridge more confidently and entered fresh imaginative terrain. As in *After the Fall* and *The Ride Down Mount Morgan*, Miller sought in *Death of a Salesman* the verbal equivalents for his characters' troubled inner selves, a search that led him away from the realism of Ibsen, O'Casey, (the later) O'Neill, Odets, and Hellman and toward a new dramatic expression. He was also enormously attracted by what Williams called the "plastic theater."[22] The use of lights, music, sets, and other nonverbal expressions that would complement the textual version of the play became central kinesic forces in production. This willingness to open up his theatre to more than a merely language-grounded realism allowed Miller to create a lyric drama, a more poetic theatre, a more interiorized realism. Stage symbol, scenic image, body language were to assume important roles, roles accentuating the conflicts that the Lomans articulated to audiences through language.

Death of a Salesman works because of its linguistic simplicity. Miller had discovered his verbal *métier*. For, on one level, the play is exceedingly realistic, its language wrested from the American idiolect of clichés, its characters instantly recognizable to any theatregoer, its intertextual and extratheatrical references derived from the stuff of American popular culture of the day. References to Studebakers and Chevys, Ebbets Field and Red Grange, B. F. Goodrich and Thomas Edison immediately established personal correspondences and cultural signifiers for each member of the audience. Surely the irony of Biff, captain and quarterback of the *All-Scholastic* (my emphasis) Championship Team of the City of New York, failing math and never graduating, touched the nerve of parents whose sons were (whether they liked it or not) inculcated with athletics in the United States. World War II now over, it was time once again to release the furies on the gridiron. Adonises always beat Anemics.

Yet for all its linguistic simplicity, Miller interfolds a voracious repartee throughout *Death of a Salesman*. Miller's is a militant script. Nor is such voracity limited to Willy; all the characters have absorbed an assertive or even violent vocabulary. Willy hopes his boys can "lick the civilized world" (*Death of a Salesman*, p. 64), though Biff screams, "screw the business world!" (p. 61). Willy threatens to "whip" Biff, though he brags to Ben that his boys would "go into the jaws of hell for me" (p. 52). Biff claims that Willy "always wiped the floor with" Linda (p. 55), and Howard says to Willy, "If I had a spot I'd slam you right in" (p. 80). The infantile Happy brags that he "can outbox, outrun, and outlift anybody in that store" and resents the fact that he has "to take orders from those common, petty sons-of-bitches" (p. 24); he also wonders if he has "an overdeveloped sense of competition" (p. 25) and, near the end of Act Two, orders from the restaurant giant lobsters "with the claws" (p. 99), a fitting dinner for a man who, leering at Miss Forsythe, blathers, "I got radar or something" (p. 100). Only Happy, staring at his father's grave, could utter such banalities as "I'm staying right in this city, and I'm gonna beat this racket! . . . [Willy] fought it out here, and this is where I'm gonna win it for him" (pp. 138–39). In Boston, the Woman refers to herself as a football, one who has just been booted out of an illicit affair with Willy (pp. 119–20). Willy reflects in his last daydream, ". . . and when you hit, hit low, and hit hard" (p. 135), a reflection meant for Biff but which actually foreshadows his own suicide moments later. The ever-supportive Linda turns acerbic after her boys abandon Willy at the restaurant. She lambastes Happy and his "lousy rotten whores!" (p. 124) and orders Biff to clean up the scattered flowers she has just knocked to the floor: "Pick up this stuff, I'm not your maid any more. Pick it up, you bum, you!" (p. 124). Miller even anthropomorphizes some consumer objects through vigorous language: "That goddam Studebaker! [it's . . .] on its last legs." The refrigerator consumes belts "like a goddam maniac" (p. 73). And Howard's dictaphone, a symbolic reminder of how far Willy lags behind his own technological era, talks to Willy, who has no idea of how to turn off the newfangled invention. The taped voice of Howard's son spinning out of control foregrounds, of course, Willy's own life, which is spinning out of control. After all, Willy does not fit in with the industrialized world; he is more at home in a pastoral world, one in which he can use his hands to build a porch or plant seeds in a garden.

Miller's vigorous repartee—the rapidity and intensity with which actors deliver their lines—gains theatrical momentum through its imagistic referents. These are death-saturated dialogues. Willy launches the tragic trajectory of the play at the very start when admitting, "I'm tired to the death" (p. 13), which becomes a haunting monody throughout the play: "I'm so tired" (p. 68), he says to Linda at the end of Act One. Miller extends the death motif when a rested Willy opens Act Two by saying he slept "like a dead one" (p. 71), and Willy repeats the refrain minutes later when confiding to Howard, "I'm just a little tired" (p. 80). In a comment prefiguring his own demise, Willy wishes Howard's father, Frank, the best in the grave—"may he rest in peace" (p. 80). Linda knows that Willy's old friends are "all dead, retired" (p. 57). Schoolchildren "nearly died laughing!" at Biff's Birnbaum imitation (p. 118). Miller describes the music that has "*died away*" (p. 88). As the play reaches its climax, Biff utters, "Forget I'm alive" (p. 129) and Willy tells his son, "Then hang yourself! For spite, hang yourself!" (p. 132).

Death allusions permeate the script. Willy complains that builders "massacred the neighborhood" (p. 17). He boasts he "knocked 'em cold in Providence, slaughtered 'em in Boston" (p. 33), and that he will "knock 'em dead next week" (p. 36). Charley says, "My New England man comes back and he's bleedin', they murdered him up there" (p. 51); Willy calls business "murderous" p. 51). Although Bernard's language, in its reasoned cadences, plays counterpoint to the Lomans' outbursts, his most revealing lines describe Biff's return from Boston, the half-hour fist-fight they had, and how they kept "punching each other down the cellar, and crying right through it. I've often thought of how strange it was that I knew he'd given up his life" (p. 94). Near the end of Act Two, Willy says to Biff, "You're trying to put a knife in me—don't think I don't know what you're doing!" (p. 130). Images of fire abound, too. Not surprisingly, Willy is right when he talks about the woods burning. From the angry glow of orange to the Woman thinking there is a fire in the hotel, from the fire-engine red Chevy to Willy's being fired, from Biff's burning his sneaker in the furnace to his pleas that his father burn his phony dream, Miller's language suggests conflagration.

Despite whatever (anti)heroic attributes we ascribe to Willy, he is a figure savagely divided against himself. He emerges as a competitive man whose vision of entrepreneurial spirit, which has devolved into a series of self-deceiving gestures, too often fuels pride. He is a man who contradicts himself. However, given Willy's *physis* (what the ancient Greeks by the time of Sophocles conceived of as one's authentic nature), it could not have been otherwise. At all costs, Willy must leave his thumbprint on the world.[23] He must constantly name and re-name himself. Forever doomed to linger in the margins, Willy locates his essential self within the epicenter of the business world: "Go to Filene's, go to the Hub, go to Slattery's, Boston. Call out the name Willy Loman and see what happens! Big shot!" (*Death of a Salesman*, p. 62). But his pride descends to arrogance, and from arrogance to ignorance, an ignorance fostered by a competitive American business work ethic. Hence *Death of a Salesman*, many critics suggest, is a critique of a capitalist society that brutalizes the unsuccessful. In Marxist terms, Willy completes the brutalization process by reducing himself to a commodity, an object, a thing, which enables him to make the greatest and last sale of his entire professional life: the sale of his very existence for the insurance payment. The play exposes, for the ideologue, the inadequacies of a bourgeois America. This at least was the dominant view expressed by critics after the play's successful runs at the Pushkin Theatre in Leningrad and the Vakhtangov Theatre in Moscow during the summer of

1959. Since the Cold War was in full force, such a response seems predictable enough. However, while the sociopolitical textures of the play undeniably manifest themselves throughout, *Death of a Salesman* gains its power from other sources.

Death of a Salesman goes well beyond the level of oversimplified social protest (and a play to be used in the service of a particular ideology) because it concerns the fundamental practical and metaphysical question: what does it mean to be fulfilled in one's very existence? This question underpins the play's greatness, reinforces its philosophic largeness. For in Miller's cosmology, Willy Loman is much more than a neurotic malady, or, as Biff argues, "a hard-working drummer who landed in the ash can like all the rest of them!" (p. 132). Unquestionably the allure of wealth and fulfillment entice Willy Loman to dream, and to die. But a felt poignancy filled the Morosco Theatre on 10 February 1949 when Lee J. Cobb as Willy confides to Howard:

> We've got quite a little streak of self-reliance in our family. I thought I'd go out with my older brother and try to locate him, and maybe settle in the North with the old man. And I was almost decided to go, when I met a salesman in the Parker House. His name was Dave Singleman. And he was eighty-four years old, and he'd drummed merchandise in thirty-one states. And old Dave, he'd go up to his room, y'understand, put on his green velvet slippers—I'll never forget—and pick up his phone and call the buyers, and without ever leaving his room, at the age of eighty-four, he made his living. And when I saw that, I realized that selling was the greatest career a man could want.
>
> (p. 81)

No matter that Howard will fire Willy momentarily, or that Willy, like Dave Singleman, will soon die "the death of a salesman" (p. 81). For many, Willy Loman's aspirations have a ring of truth to them, grounded though they may be in a romanticized vision of an American Dream, one that ultimately certifies death.

Willy invites the audience to enter "the inside of his head," the original working title of the play. In effect, the audience becomes privy to the crisis within Willy and to the philosophic complexity of *Death of a Salesman*. Thus when Willy continues, "'Cause what could be more satisfying than to be able to go, at the age of eighty-four, into twenty or thirty different cities, and pick up a phone, and be remembered and loved and helped by so many different people?" (p. 81), he confirms what Linda knows. "So attention must be paid. He's not to be allowed to fall into his grave like an old dog. Attention, attention must be finally paid to such a person" (p. 56). Willy Loman's real condition lies in his insecurity in the universe, his profound sense of being unfulfilled, and in his inability to observe his own emotional speed limits. No question Willy exaggerates, cheats, and lies, charges which he is ill equipped to refute but well suited to deny. But when he screams to Biff, "I am not a dime a dozen! I am Willy Loman, and you are Biff Loman!" (p. 132), is he not laying claim, not only to his dignity and individual worth but also to every person's worthiness?

Undoubtedly Willy suffers from O'Neillean "pipe dreams," or Ibsenesque "vital lies." When convenient, or necessary, Willy confers upon illusions the status of objective reality. Yet he, in a sense, tragically knows at least part of himself. In telling rare occasions he locates his demythicized self without the rhetorical gallantries that mask his inadequacies. He admits that he is foolish to look at and that he babbles too much; he acknowledges that he feels temporary about himself. Strange thoughts bother him. He asks the grown Bernard for advice. Adding to Willy's paradoxical nature are those moments in which he mixes self-disclosure with external fact: "You'll [Happy] retire me for life on seventy goddam dollars a week? And your women and your car and your apartment, and you'll retire me for life! Christ's sake, I couldn't get past Yonkers today! Where are you guys, where are you? The woods are burning! I can't drive a car!" (p. 41). Miller occasionally bestows upon Willy a capacity for self-knowledge within the marketplace, as evident during the scene in Howard's office: "I put thirty-four years into this firm, Howard, and now I can't pay my insurance! You can't eat the orange and throw the peel away—a man is not a piece of fruit!" (p. 82). Willy knows America is no isocracy in which all people have equal power. Adding to Willy's tragic stature are those singular moments when he honestly assesses his overall predicament, as seen, for instance, when he meets his sons in the restaurant: "I'm not interested in stories about the past or any crap of that kind because the woods are burning, boys, you understand? There's a big blaze going on all around. I was fired today" (p. 107). Such insights make Willy more than a misfit or an oversimplified Everyman. Rather, they enhance his tragic stature precisely because they reveal to the audience Willy's capacity to distinguish reality from chimera; that the majority of his other remarks make such distinctions less clear only adds to the sense of tragic loss. Thus audiences find in Willy traces of the past tragic figures who populated the stages of Shaw, Ibsen, and Shakespeare and, backtracking to the primal origins of Western dramatic heritage, of Sophocles and Euripides. This is why Arthur Miller, I believe, is to the second half of twentieth-century American drama what Eugene O'Neill was to the first half: our supreme tragedian.

Coda

Half a century later, the significance of *Death of a Salesman* has only increased. As Miller remarks, "People tell me that *Death of a Salesman* is more pertinent now than then. The suppression of the individual by placing him below the imperious needs of society or technology seems to have manufactured more Willys in the world. But again, it is far more primitive than that. Like many myths and classical dramas, it is a story about violence within a family."[24]

If we live in a world which, indeed, manufactures more Willys, it is easy to understand why theatregoers today continue to be moved the way 1949 audiences were. From an ecological point of view, Willy's ravings about overpopulation, builders massacring elms to construct apartment complexes, and "Bricks and windows, windows and bricks" (*Death of a Salesman*, p. 17) resonate for twenty-first century audiences in London, Beijing, and any major city in the United States. From an economic perspective, Willy's struggles to pay the mortgage and, above all, his insurance, resonate for theatregoers who themselves increasingly feel the financial pressures exacted upon them by an increasingly capitalist, or at least Westernized, world. On a domestic level, global audiences respond to the play's exploration of the primal family unit and the way in which Miller presents the dynamics of the relationship between husband and wife, and parents and children. In a country where social security is more a lie of the mind than political fact, Willy's being fired after working thirty-four years with the firm annihilates Emersonian notions of self-reliance. Willy exists in a world that increasingly detaches itself from him, reminding him daily of his own insignificance. Whether driving 700 miles only to be denied a sale or meeting his sons for dinner only to be abandoned by them, Willy knows that he will reap more profits in one masterstroke—his suicide—than in all the sales he closed in a lifetime. As he points out to Ben, "Does it take more guts to stand here the rest of my life ringing up a zero?" (p. 126). Willy, exhausted after dealing with feelings of innocence and guilt, protection and betrayal, and celebration and loss, reasons "you end up worth more dead than alive" (p. 98). The Lomans, in sum, have become inextricably linked to various enabling American mythologies—and pathologies. This is precisely why *Death of a Salesman* outlines the collective and essentially moral anxieties of a nation as those anxieties, occupying the interstice of the Real and the Illusion, affect the individual.[25]

The funeral scene confirms Willy's ultimate fall. If the Requiem provides a sense of closure for Willy and for the audience, the surviving Lomans continue voicing their competing narratives. Happy blathers on, pointlessly. Biff, despite heroic efforts to face facts, still carries on an Oedipal resistance to his father. Willy, he insists, bought into the wrong dreams and did not know himself. Were the play to end with

Biff's lines, maybe "the secret we and Miller thereby deny is that we hate Willy because he represents everything we want to deny about ourselves."[26] But Miller doesn't end the play there, and I am not convinced he allows us to hate Willy. Charley's important "nobody dast blame this man" speech, perhaps, places Willy's fate in a broader social and philosophical context. Charley refers to the utter precariousness of human existence when that life comes face to face with emptiness. Questions of hate, spite, and so on continue to reverberate, but as distant echoes. Willy was, indeed, riding out there on a smile and a shoeshine, without a spiritual insurance policy that would have allowed his dreams to exist in equipoise with reality. Since he lived most of his life on the fault lines of the "earthquake" to which Charley refers (*Death of a Salesman*, p. 138), he could only survive with the hopeless hope of "a salesman" who's "got to dream, boy" (p. 138). If intellectually such a reading seems forced, it makes perfect sense theatrically. And, for Miller and most theatregoers, this is all that matters.

Despite the carnivalesque world of the Lomans, Miller provides a resolution of sorts. This resolution may be best understood in the context of the playwright's intellectual position, which reveals itself through his moral optimism. From *The Golden Years* through *Broken Glass*, Miller's poetics emphasize the primacy of the individual's social duty and the importance of familial love. Implicit in all the major plays is Miller's belief in the unifying force of love that creates the possibility for social revolt in the polis and personal insight within the family. These essentializing forces, which elude the Lomans, only increase the play's sense of tragic loss. The poetics of Arthur Miller are informed with a sense of charity and love which the Lomans can never adequately express. This is why Linda, sobbing quietly as the curtain falls, can only contemplate what could, or should, have been.

From *The Cambridge Companion to Arthur Miller*, ed. Christopher Bigsby (Cambridge: Cambridge University Press, 1997): 60-85. Copyright © 1997 by Cambridge University Press. Reprinted by permission of Cambridge University Press.

Notes

1. Arthur Miller, *Death of a Salesman* (New York: Viking Press, 1976), p. 17.

2. Linda Kintz, "The Sociosymbolic Work of Family in *Death of a Salesman*," in Matthew C. Roudané (ed.), *Approaches to Teaching Miller's Death of a Salesman* (New York: The Modern Language Association of America, 1995), p. 106. See also in this same volume Susan Harris Smith, "Contextualizing *Death of a Salesman* as an American Play," pp. 27–32, and Janet N. Balakian, "Beyond the Male Locker Room: *Death of a Salesman* from a Feminist Perspective," pp. 115–24. For other useful essays debating feminist issues in the play, see Charlotte Canning, "Is This Play About Women?: A Feminist Reading of *Death of a Salesman*," in Steven R. Centola, *The Achievement of Arthur Miller* (Dallas: Contemporary Research Associates, 1995), pp. 69–76; Gayle Austin, "The Exchange of Women and Male Homosocial Desire in Arthur Miller's *Death of a Salesman* and Lillian Hellman's *Another Part of the Forest*," in June Schlueter (ed.), *Feminist Rereadings of Modern American Drama* (Rutherford, NJ: Fairleigh Dickinson University Press, 1989), pp. 59–66; and Kay Stanton, "Women and the American Dream of *Death of a Salesman*," in *Feminist Rereadings*, pp. 67–102.

3. Brenda Murphy, *Miller: Death of a Salesman* (Cambridge: Cambridge University Press, 1995) P. 70.

4. "David Mamet," in Christopher Bigsby (ed.), *Arthur Miller and Company* (London: Methuen, 1990), p. 64.

5. "Dustin Hoffman," in Bigsby, *Arthur Miller and Company*, pp. 70–71.

6. Christopher Bigsby, *Modern American Drama, 1945–1990* (Cambridge: Cambridge University Press, 1992), p. 89.

7. Murphy, *Miller: Death of a Salesman*, p. 106.

8. Matthew C. Roudané, "An Interview with Arthur Miller," in Roudané (ed.), *Conversations with Arthur Miller* (Jackson: University Press of Mississippi, 1987), pp. 360–61.

9. Arthur Miller, "Tragedy and the Common Man," *New York Times*, 27 February 1949, section II, pp. 1, 3.

10. Arthur Miller, *Timebends* (New York: Grove Press, 1987), p. 190.

11. The physiological and psychological correspondences linking Manny Newman and Willy Loman seem equally compelling. "Manny Newman was cute and ugly, a Pan risen out of the earth, a bantam with a lisp, sunken brown eyes, a lumpy, pendulous nose, dark brown skin, and gnarled arms," Miller recalls (*Timebends*, p. 122). Physiologically, traces of Manny may be found in Willy, who confides to Linda that he is foolish-looking. F. H. Stewarts, a salesman, mockingly calls Willy a walrus. More important, Manny was also, like Willy, "a competitor, at all times, in all things, and at every moment" (*Timebends*, p. 122).

Although Miller only spent a few hours with Manny Newman during his lifetime, he nonetheless proved to be one of the pivotal figures upon whom Miller based Willy Loman. In describing Newman, Miller could very well be talking about Willy: "he was so absurd, so completely isolated from the ordinary laws of gravity, so elaborate in his fantastic inventions, and despite his ugliness so lyrically in love with fame and fortune and their inevitable descent on his family, that he possessed my imagination until I knew more or less precisely how he would react to any sign or word or idea" (*Timebends*, p. 123).

The coalescence of fiction and fact reaches its most poignant expression through the emotion of a profound sadness both Willy and Manny shared. During that fateful night in Boston, the Woman says to Willy, "You are the saddest, self-centredest soul I ever did see-saw" (*Death of a Salesman*, p. 116). Of Manny Newman Miller would write, "his unpredictable manipulations of fact freed my mind to lope and skip among fantasies of my own, but always underneath was the river of his sadness" (*Timebends*, p. 123). And director Elia Kazan, after reading a working draft of the script in 1948, telephoned Miller and in an "alarmingly somber" voice said, "My God, it's so sad" (*Timebends*, p. 185). Sadness, however, must be masked at all costs. Appearance counts. Hence there was a "competitiveness that drugged" Manny Newman's mind (*Timebends*, p. 124), the same competitive personality that would energize as it immobilized Willy Loman. Caught in a naturalistic world that reduces him to an insignificant speck in the universe, Willy and his soaring inner spirits are tempered by an outer deterministic environment: "There's more people! That's what's ruining this country! Population is getting out of control. The competition is maddening!" (*Death of a Salesman*, pp. 17–18). It was Manny Newman's and Willy Loman's "romance of hope" (*Timebends*, p. 126), then, that would partially define the trajectory of their lives.

12. Miller's conversation with Manny Newman's son was also a galvanizing, revelatory moment because it helped the playwright clarify the contradictory nature of Willy Loman. When he heard that Manny wanted "a business for the boys," Miller realized that this conventional, mundane wish was a shot of "electricity that switched all the random iron filings in my mind in one direction. A hopelessly distracted Manny was transformed into a man with purpose: he had been trying to make a gift that would crown all those striving years; all those lies he told, all his imaginings and crazy exaggerations, even the almost military discipline he had laid on his boys, were in this instant given form and point. To be sure, a business expressed his own egotism, but love, too" (*Timebends*, p. 130). Miller's reminiscence of Manny Newman found its theatrical corollary within Willy Loman; here Miller describes the Real, his uncle, but what follows even more accurately externalizes the fictional Willy Loman: "That homely, ridiculous little man had after all never ceased to struggle for a certain victory, the only kind open to him in this society—selling to achieve his lost self as a man with his name and his sons' names on a business of his own" (*Timebends*, p. 130).

Miller acknowledges that another salesman, a friend of his uncle, "was more vivid to me than even Manny." This salesman, unmarried and fitted with a wooden leg, differed in temperament from Manny Newman, his "reflective air" giving rise to an observation that arrested Miller. "'You've changed, haven't you?' he said. 'You've gotten serious.'" For a young man soon to turn craft into art, the salesman's observation gave Miller "the dignity of a history of my own," and, more important, the courage to follow artistic instincts within a meritocracy that valorizes a business as sacrament, ethic and ethos. "If ever I knew that salesman's name I forgot it long ago, but not his few interested words that helped crack the shell of suffocating subjectivity surrounding my existence" (*Timebends*, pp. 126–27).

13. Roudané, "Interview," p. 370.

14. Arthur Miller, "Ibsen and the Drama of Today," in James McFarland (ed.), *The Cambridge Companion to Ibsen* (Cambridge: Cambridge University Press, 1994) p. 232.

15. Arthur Miller, "About Theatre Language," in Miller, *The Last Yankee* (New York: Penguin, 1994), p. 81.

16. Unpublished interview with Arthur Miller, conducted by Christopher Bigsby, 1994.

17. Miller, "About Theatre Language," pp. 81, 84.

18. Bigsby, *Modern American Drama*, p. 90.

19. Miller elaborates on the use of form and time in the play:

> The form of *Death of a Salesman* was an attempt, as much as anything else, to convey the bending of time. There are two or three sorts of time in that play. One is social time; one is psychic time, the way we remember things; and the third is the sense of time created by the play and shared by the audience. When I directed *Salesman* in China, which was the first time I had attempted to direct it from scratch, I became aware all over again that the play is taking place in the Greek unity of twenty-four hours; and yet, it is dealing with material that goes back probably twenty-five years. And it almost goes forward through Ben, who is dead. So *time* was an obsession for me at the moment, and I wanted a way of presenting it so that it became the *fiber* of the play, rather than being something that somebody comments about. In fact, there is very little comment verbally in *Salesman* about time. I also wanted a form that could sustain in itself the way we deal with crises, which is not to deal with them. After all, there is a lot of comedy in *Salesman*; people forget it because it is so dark by the end of the play. But if you stand behind the audience you hear a lot of laughter. It's a deadly ironical laughter most of the time, but it is a species of laughter. The comedy is really a way for Willy and others to put off the evil day, which is the thing we all do. I wanted that to *happen* and not be something talked *about*. I wanted the feeling to come across rather than a set of speeches about how we delay dealing with issues. I wanted a play, that is, that had almost a biological life of its own. It would be as incontrovertible as the musculature of the human body. Everything connecting with everything else, all of it working according to plan. No excesses. Nothing explaining itself; all of it simply inevitable, as one structure, as one corpus. All of those feelings of a society falling to pieces which I had, still have, of being unable to deal with it, which we all know now. All of this, however, presented not with speeches in *Salesman*, but by putting together pieces of Willy's life, so that what we were deducing about it was the speech; what we were making of it was the moral of it; what it was doing to us rather than a romantic speech about facing death and living a fruitless life. All of these elements and many more went into the form of *Death of a Salesman*. All this could never have been contained in the form of *All My Sons*.
> (Roudané, "Interview," pp. 363–64)

20. Joseph A. Hynes, "'Attention, Attention Must Be Paid. . . ,'" *College English* 23 (1961): 576.

21. Harold Bloom, "Introduction," in Bloom (ed.), *Modern Critical Interpretations: Arthur Miller's Death of a Salesman* (New York: Chelsea House, 1988), p. 1.

22. Tennessee Williams, "Production Notes," *The Glass Menagerie*, in *The Theatre of Tennessee Williams*, vol. 1 (New York: New Directions, 1970), pp. 131–34.

23. For an informative discussion linking Arthur Miller, Willy Loman, and the function of art, see Bigsby's interview with Miller in *Arthur Miller and Company*, p. 233.

24. Roudané, "Interview," p. 361.

25. For excellent discussions of the public/private dialectic in Miller, see C.W.E. Bigsby, *A Critical Introduction to Twentieth-Century American Drama*, vol. 11 (Cambridge: Cambridge University Press, 1984), pp. 135–248; Bigsby, *Modern American Drama*, pp. 72–125; Bigsby, "Introduction to the Revised Edition," *The Portable Arthur Miller* (New York: Penguin, 1995) pp. xxv–xli; Robert A. Martin, "Arthur Miller: Public Issues, Private Tensions," in Matthew C. Roudané (ed.), *Public Issues, Private Tensions: Contemporary American Drama* (New York: AMS Press, 1993), pp. 65–75; Martin, "The Nature of Tragedy in Arthur Miller's *Death of a Salesman*," *South Atlantic Review* 61 (1996): 97–106; Bernard F. Dukore, *Death of a Salesman and The Crucible: Text and Performance* (London: Macmillan, 1989), pp. 116–20, 33–39, 45–56; Thomas P. Adler, *American Drama, 1940–1960: A Critical History* (New York: Twayne, 1994), pp. 62–83; June Schlueter and James K. Flanagan, *Arthur Miller* (New York: Frederick Ungar, 1987), pp. 56–66; Janet N. Balakian, "*Salesman*: Private Tensions Raised to a Poetic Social Level," in Centola, *The Achievement of Arthur Miller*, pp. 59–68; *Platform Papers: 7. Arthur Miller* (London: Royal National Theatre, 1995), pp. 3–36; and Matthew C. Roudané, "Arthur Miller and His Influence on Contemporary American Drama," *American Drama* 6 (1996) 1–13.

26. Walter A. Davis, *Get the Guests: Psychoanalysis, Modern American Drama, and the Audience* (Madison: University of Wisconsin Press, 1994), p. 144.

'Death of a Salesman'

Christopher Bigsby

The idea for *Death of a Salesman* had long been in Miller's mind. At seventeen he had written a story called 'In Memoriam', in which a Jewish salesman goes to his death. At university he jotted down some ideas about a man called Willy Loman and then again, immediately after university, wrote a striking stream-of-consciousness story, never published, about a salesman whose hopes have come to nothing and who goes to his death under the wheels of a subway car.

Though he would explain the play's origin by reference to a family member whose extravagant plans for his sons came to nothing, there is a more personal genesis for this play about a believer in the American dream who struggles with a knowledge of his failure. The play is not about Miller's father but one incident had brought home to him what it was to be a believer confronted with daily evidence of his own incapacities. When the family business had collapsed, Isidore Miller struggled to keep his dignity, starting new companies, looking for business. One day he was forced to borrow money for the subway from his son. It was a critical moment in their relationship as it was also a sudden and personal reminder of where America had failed so many of those who believed in the inevitability of success in a country which presented itself as specially blessed.

Even thus reduced in his present circumstances and future hopes, his father had still wanted his son to follow in his footsteps. When a young Arthur Miller explained his plans for college his father regarded this as a betrayal. It was not simply that where he had failed his son might succeed but that in succeeding he would justify that father who had abandoned one country for another on the promise of success. Love, pride, ambition, somehow braided together in that moment. Isidore Miller's identity had become invested in his company and if that had collapsed what was he unless he could see his son go on to do what he had not? It was necessary that his son should stay. For a teenage Arthur Miller it was necessary that he should leave. There was betrayal on both sides and there was love on both sides. Isadore's shamefaced request for money for the subway was evidence of his vulnerability, of a shift in the power relationship between father and son. It was also a reminder, however, that the governing principles of the culture were under strain, that promises had been broken, false values inculcated.

Death of a Salesman is as much about the public as the private world but, to Miller, this is a false distinction. Willy Loman in particular has absorbed the values of his society until they seem part of what he wishes to see as his own definition. His is a salesman, the epitome of a society built on social performance and wedded to the idea of a transforming future. By the same token, however, those who saw this play at the time, and in the over fifty years since that first production, have connected to it less through its comments on a culture wedded to a myth than through characters whose hopes and illusions seem instantly recognisable and archetypal. Willy Loman is a man who wishes his reality to come into line with his hopes, a man desperate to leave his mark on the world through his own endeavours and through those of his children. Though he seems to seek death, what he fears above all is that he will go before he has justified himself in his own eyes and there are few, from New York to Beijing, who do not understand the urgency of that need.

When the play begins, Biff Loman has been summoned home because his mother knows that her husband's life is at risk. He has begun to plan his suicide. Who else but the sons can rescue him? To return, however, is to threaten the peace which Biff has managed to secure for himself on the other side of the anarchy bequeathed by his father. Brought up to expect success, to take what he wants, he has spent time in jail. His brother Happy, meanwhile, has turned into a self-deceiving womaniser who believes in nothing but his own pleasure, getting nowhere but, seemingly like his father, contenting himself with illusions. But there is more to Willy Loman. He is tempted by suicide not because he fails to understand his situation but because he does. It is for that reason that he tracks back through his life in memory, restlessly searching for the moment when he betrayed life or it betrayed him. In that sense it is Willy Loman who constructs much of the play as he returns to a time which had once seemed golden but had, in some way he cannot understand, carried the seeds of his current dismay.

Where he remains illusioned is in his conviction that his death can win what his life cannot. His life insurance will gift his sons the success that has eluded them and him. Meanwhile, by his side is a woman who offers a redemption he is too blind to see. Raised in a world in which appearance mattered more than substance, the world of a salesman in which clothes must be spotless and a smile always on the lips, he fails to recognise something as intangible as her love.

* * *

Over the years Miller has offered a number of intriguing interpretations of *Death of a Salesman*. It is about 'the paradoxes of being alive in a technological civilization';[1] it is about 'the alienation brought by technological advance . . . the price we pay for progress'.[2] It is 'a story about violence within the family', about 'the suppression of the individual by placing him below the imperious needs of . . . society'.[3] It is 'a play about a man who kills himself because he isn't liked'.[4] It expresses 'all those feelings of a society falling to pieces which I had',[5] feelings that, to him, are one of the reasons for the play's continuing popularity. But the observation that goes most directly to the heart of the play is contained in a comment made in relation to the production he directed in China in 1983: '*Death of a Salesman*, really, is a love story between a man and his son, and in a crazy way between both of them and America'.[6]

Turn to the notebooks that he kept when writing the play and you find the extent to which the relationship between Willy and his son is central.[7] There are repeated notes about the magnetic force that paradoxically pulls them together and thrusts them apart: 'He is hounded by and is hounding Willy with guilt', he reminds himself; 'Raise the conflict in Biff between wanting NY success and hating Willy. This is the climax'; 'Biff wants to save him, and at the same time to free himself'. He is angry 'at Willy's weakness, helplessness, and at W's love for him'; 'Biff's conflict is that to tell the truth would be to diminish himself in his own eyes. To admit his fault. His confusion, then, is not didactic, or directed to Willy's elucidation or salvation, but toward a surgical break which he knows in his heart W could never accept. His motive, then, is to destroy W, free himself'. The essence of the drama is contained within these tensions. In a brief passage of dialogue, not to appear in the final play, he simultaneously identifies the dilemma of both men and the essence of his dramatic method:

> B: Don't believe the myth—if at first you don't succeed, try try again. Sometimes it's better to walk away.
>
> W: Just walk away.
>
> B: Yes.
>
> W: But if you can't walk away.
>
> B: Then . . . nobody can help you.

The truth is that neither man can walk away, though Biff will, it seems, do so at the end of the play, stepping out of the drama into a projected, if historically suspect, future. They are wedded to their dreams and they are held together by a complex of emotions they can barely understand, not least because they consist of contrarieties—love/hate, vengeance/redemption, ambition/despair. Father and son are a divided self. Their identities are ineluctably intertwined. For Willy Loman, Biff is his justification and vindication. In refusing to embrace his father's dreams he is, thus, denying him fulfilment, expiation, that sense of identity that comes from passing the torch from generation to generation. For Biff, his father stands between himself and his life. He is the past that has to be transcended, the falsehood that must be rejected, but also the debt that must be discharged.

There is a terrible rhythm to the play as the two men are drawn together and thrust apart, both acting out of a sense of love and yet both aware that the avenue to that love is occluded by guilt, by weaknesses in themselves. The past is the burden they bear in a play in which the past threatens at every moment to break through into an increasingly desperate present. There is a race on, a race for Willy's life and Biff's soul. If they could acknowledge their wrong paths, offer each other the absolution they seek, all might be well, but they cannot. And, for Miller, as he implied in his notebook entry, drama is born out of a situation in which the individual cannot walk away.

Biff and his father see the world differently. When Biff, in lines of dialogue that Miller scrawled in the *Salesman* notebook, announces that his ambition is merely to be happy, Willy replies, 'To enjoy yourself is not ambition. A tramp has that. Ambition is *things*. A man must want *things*! You're lost. You are a lost boy. And I know why now. Because you hate me you turned your back on all your promise. For spite, for spite of me, because I wanted you magnificent'. Elements of this are retained in the final play but Willy's materialism is not so much stated as embodied in his lament over the failure of the consumer goods he has acquired. Beyond that, the irony is that he lacks precisely the 'things' he thought he valued. His dilemma is that of a culture that proposes as a national mission the pursuit of happiness and then confuses this with material possessions, as did the Founding Fathers who debated whether happiness and property were synonymous. No wonder that Linda trumpets the fact that they have repaid their mortgage as if this was in some way the objective towards which their lives had been directed. The fact is that whatever Willy Loman says he is not content with things. He wants, above all, to be well liked, a condition he confuses with success.

Biff and Willy wrestle one another for their existence. Biff is Willy's ace in the hole, his last desperate throw, the proof that he was right, after all, that tomorrow things will change for the better and thus offer a retrospective grace to the past. Willy, meanwhile, is Biff's flawed model, the man who seemed to sanction his hunger for success and popularity, a hunger suddenly stilled by a moment of revelation. Over the years, neither has been able to let go of the other because to do so would be to let go of a dream that, however tainted, still has the glitter of possibility, except that now Biff has begun to understand that there is something wrong, something profoundly inadequate about a vision so at odds with his instincts.

As he says to Willy, in a speech included in the notebook but not the final play, 'You think I'm mad at you because of the woman, don't you. I am, but I'm madder because you bitched up my life, because I can't tear you out of my heart, because I keep trying to do something for you, to succeed for you'. He still feels the need to shine in his father's eyes, though all his instincts now rebel against the notion that the ends justify the means. He, after all, was encouraged as a young man to cut corners, to steal lumber from the nearby building site and basketballs when he wanted to practise. In truth, Miller indicates in his notes, 'Biff is not bright enough to make a businessman. He wants everything too fast'. As he was to have said, 'It took me a long time to understand. When I finished school I was given to understand that if a fella wants it, he'll rise in the firm. I stayed . . . 2 years as shipping clerk and nothing ever happened'.

He returns, now, partly out of a surviving sense of duty towards Willy and partly to resolve his conflict with him, to announce that he has finally broken with the false values offered to him as his inheritance. Two people are fighting for survival, in the sense of sustaining a sense of themselves. Willy desperately needs Biff to embrace him and his dream. As Miller observes in his notebook, he needs the affection and success of his sons 'to destroy his failure'. Biff, by contrast, desperately needs to cut the link between himself and Willy. This is the motor force of the play. There can be only one winner and whoever wins will also have lost. As Miller explained to the actor playing the role in the Beijing production: 'your love for him binds you; but you want it to free you to be your own man'. Willy, however, is unable to offer such grace because 'he would have to turn away from his own values'.[8]

Once returned, though, Biff is enrolled in the conspiracy to save Willy's life. The question which confronts him now is whether that life will be saved by making Willy face up to the reality of his life or by substantiating his illusions. To do the latter, however, would be to work against his own needs. The price of saving Willy may thus, potentially, be the loss of his own freedom and autonomy. Meanwhile the tension underlying this central conflict derives from the fact that, as Miller has said, 'the story of Salesman is absurdly simple! It is about a salesman and it's his last day on the earth'.[9]

Part of the plan to save Willy lies in the scheme for Biff and Happy to go into business together. Biff is to return to his former boss and solicit funds. It was never a credible proposition. Indeed it is one more evidence of the unreal world in which the Loman family have taken up residence. It is one more lie to pile on those that have corroded the links between them. And when Biff, at the interview, chooses to steal the pen of the man on whom his future supposedly depends, we have Miller's assurance, in a handwritten note in his notebook, that the thefts he has committed since catching his father in a Boston hotel room with another woman, are, at least subconsciously, indirect acts of vengeance. As he reminds himself, 'It is necessary to (1) Reveal to W that Biff stole to queer himself, and did it to hurt W. (2) And that he did it because of the Woman and all the disillusionment it implied'.

So it is that while humbling himself by soliciting money, in order to give his father the hope he lacks, he simultaneously subverts the action. Beyond that, Miller notes that 'Biff's telling of the theft must suggest the Dream', for the private actions, the personal betrayals, are always to be rooted in a broader truth.

In like manner, the two boys rendezvous with their father in a restaurant only to desert him. Biff, we are told in the notebook, 'left out of guilt, pity, and inability to open himself to W.—Hap out of shame'. The ebb and flow of their affections is an echo of the contradictions that litter Willy's language no less than his behaviour. They are their father's sons and that is the source of their and his dilemma.

Yet for all their abandonment of him, Biff, at least, 'still wants that evidence of W's love. Still does not want to be abandoned by him. And now this is necessary'. He resolves to cut them both free by telling the truth, returning to the house to force a confrontation: 'He has returned here', Miller notes, 'to disillusion W. forever, to set him upon a new path, and thus release himself from responsibility for W. and what he knows is going to happen to him,—or half fears will'. There is, in other words, still a profound ambiguity in his motives. He simultaneously wants to set Willy on a new path, and to absolve himself of responsibility for the death which he now feels is imminent.

However, if by disillusioning his father he will be liberating him to take a new path why does he at the same time see this gesture as freeing himself of culpability for his impending suicide? It is precisely this doubleness of motive, this fluctuating sense of moral duty, this ambiguous commitment to freedom and responsibility that characterises both men. If neither cared for, if neither loved the other there would be no problem. Neither would feel guilt, neither would feel a sense of obligation, a debt that must be discharged. As Biff remarks, in a scene amended in the final version, 'I've got an obligation. . . . What's happened to him is my fault. I realized that in the restaurant. I guess that's why I couldn't bear to stay. It's always the same—just when the truth has to be told I run away. . . . I don't want anything to happen to him . . . and I know it's me, it's me that's driving him'. As he adds in a note, 'What Biff wants is to be released. But Willy's guilt requires him to help him'. The irony is that when Willy at last acknowledges his son's love for him it merely strengthens his belief that he should bequeath him his dream, speeds him on his way to death: 'Through [Biff's] confession of his having *used* W's betrayal, W sees his basic love, and is resolved to suicide'.

* * *

Miller may, in his own words, be 'a confirmed and deliberate radical',[10] but *Death of a Salesman* is not an attack on American values. It is, however, an exploration of the betrayal of those values and the cost of this in human terms. Willy Loman's American dream is drained of transcendence. It is a faith in the supremacy of the material over the spiritual. There is, though, another side to Willy, a side represented by the sense of insufficiency that sends him searching through his memories looking for the origin of failure, looking for expiation. It is a side, too, represented by his son Biff, who has inherited this aspect of his sensibility, as Happy has inherited the other. Biff is drawn to nature, to working with his hands. He has a sense of poetry, an awareness that life means more than the dollars he earns. Willy has that, too. The problem is that he thinks it is irrelevant to the imperatives of his society and hence of his life which, to him, derives its meaning from that society.

Next door, however, in the form of Charley and Bernard, is another version of the dream, a version turning not on self-delusion and an amoral drive for success but on hard work and charity. What Miller attacks, then, is not the American Dream of Thomas Jefferson and Benjamin Franklin, but the dream as interpreted and pursued by those for whom ambition replaces human need and the trinkets of what Miller called the 'new American Empire in the making' are taken as tokens of true value. When, on the play's opening night, a woman called *Death of a Salesman* a 'time bomb under American capitalism', his response was to hope that it was, 'or at least under the bullshit of capitalism, this pseudo life that thought to touch the clouds by standing on top of a refrigerator, waving a paid-up mortgage at the moon, victorious at last' (*T.* 184). But the play goes beyond such particularities.

Charley is described by Miller as 'gruff, ignorant, and peasant-like'.[11] In talking of Howard Smith, who played the part in the first Broadway production, he identifies those qualities common to actor and character alike. He was, he says, 'a hard-headed, realistic, decent man; slightly dense, perhaps, but filled with human worth'.[12] Trying to explain Charley to a somewhat bewildered Chinese actor, when he was directing the play in Beijing in 1983, he suggested that he was motivated in part by his deep affection for Linda, for which his kindness is a kind of sublimation, but beyond that by a kind of envy 'for Willy's imagination, the condiments with which he sprinkles his life as contrasted with the blandness of Charley's more rational existence. Charley', he added, 'can laugh at Willy as a fool, but he is never bored with him'.[13] There is, then, something in Willy Loman, confused, infuriating, resentful, baffled though he is, that nonetheless raises him above the level of those who never question, are undisturbed by dreams of possibility, who rest content with the routines of a life never burnished with a transcendent hope.

In choosing a salesman for his central character Miller was identifying an icon of his society seized on equally by other writers before and since, not least because a salesman always trades in hope, a brighter future. In The Gilded Age Mark Twain sees the salesman as a trickster, literally selling America to the gullible. In Theodore Dreiser's *Sister Carrie*, he is a man who values appearance above substance and relies for his sexual success on sustaining that appearance. Sinclair Lewis chose a realtor as the key to his satire of American values as, decades later, John Updike chose a car salesman in his Rabbit Angstrom books. The central figure in Eugene O'Neill's *The Iceman Cometh* is a salesman, as is Stanley Kowalski in Tennessee Williams's *A Streetcar Named Desire* and Rubin Flood in William Inge's *The Dark at the Top of the Stairs*. David Mamet's *Glengarry Glen Ross* featured real estate salesmen. But what did Hickey sell, in *The Iceman Cometh*? He sold the same thing as Willy Loman, a dream of tomorrow, a world transformed, only to discover that meaning resides somewhere closer to home.

Willy's real creative energy goes into work on his house ('He was a happy man with a batch of cement'). But that is not something he can sell. What, then, does he sell? There were those who thought that a vital question, including Mary McCarthy, Robert Brustein and Rhoda Koenig (for whom his failure to offer this answer was a certain sign of the play's insignificance). But as Miller himself replied, he sells what a salesman always has to sell, himself. As Charley insists, 'The only thing you got in this world is what you can sell'. As a salesman he has got to get by on a smile and a shoeshine. He has to charm. He is a performer, a confidence man who must never lack confidence. His error is to confuse the role he plays with the person he wishes to be. The irony is that he, a salesman, has bought the pitch made to him by his society. He believes that advertisements tell the truth and is baffled when reality fails to match their claims. He believes the promises that America made to itself—that in this greatest country on earth success is an inevitability.

A salesman is a middle man. He is a means serving something beyond himself, an agent whose function is a factor of his own lost freedom. He is involved in transactions and the risk is that such transactions will begin to define his life, that the market which shapes his dreams and that of others, and in which he is implicated, will deprive him of the dignity he seeks and the significance for which he yearns. One of the questions that Miller's play seems to raise is that identified by the writer and salesman Earl Shorris, in his book *A Nation of Salesmen*: 'If America is a nation of salesmen, who are we, each and all of us together, and are we the people and the nation we hoped to be?'[14] For Shorris,

> when the market dictates the imagination and the act, the dream life as well as the day life of men, the true meaning of dignity comes clear. Kant did not pin his ethics on decorum; by dignity he meant 'free'. He could not tolerate man as a means, in the grasp of others, even in the grasp of God. He begins with man, with possibility; that is what is meant by freedom. . . . The surrender of freedom is the sadness of the age . . . human beings enter into an agreement in which everything exists as part of a transaction. A man is interchangeable with a thing; he no longer determines his own worth; a price can be put on him. Man has lost his humanity.[15]

However, in trying to explain to Ying Ruocheng, who played the part of Willy in the Beijing production, the force of Willy's elegy for the way of life of a salesman, Miller offers an intriguing reading of his sense of the world in which Willy had moved and the meaning of being a salesman:

> Of course, I said, he is romanticizing as he always does, but there is something real underlying his feeling. In the era he is talking about, the buyers for the stores he sold to were either the owners themselves or had held their jobs for many years and knew him. You know there was actually a man called Filene (the Boston department store named in *Salesman*), a man called Gimbel, R. H. Macy—and, for that matter, Louis Chevrolet, Buick, Olds, Ford, Firestone . . . these were actual human beings at one time, and if Willy did not really deal with them in person, their reality was part of his reality, and their beginnings in poverty and their rise in the world were the pantheon that circled his mind. The era of the salesman as mere order-taker whose canned pitch has been made for him on television and who has no options as what to say or charge, this was not yet the case in his time.[16]

The salesman, in the 1920s, was, he insists,

> a vital force in building the trade and commercial network of the country. The salesman needed little or no education, but an engaging personality and a faith in the inevitability of next week's upswing. Every salesman knew some other man who had hit it big, opened his own business, and died respected and rich. The myth of the salesman exemplified the open ranks of a society where practically overnight a man could leap to the head of the line.[17]

Ironically, the closest equivalent he could think of in the present was the actor who constantly lives in the hope and expectation of sudden fame, after no more than a year or two of training. Marlon Brando, after all, was a star at twenty-three. 'Willy believes in just that kind of quick, smashing beginning. And so his sons are never trained, have no patience with the process of foregoing and delaying the slaking of whatever thirst is on them at the moment. They are narcissists'.[18] This is the process that leads Happy into his pointless womanising and Biff to a prison cell. A deferred future is intolerable; it must be collapsed into the present. The contemporary equivalent of Willy's desire to be well liked is the wish to be famous, though not now for anything in particular. Fame is not so much the spur as the point of living, the substitution of seeming for being.

Death of a Salesman ends with the word 'free'. The irony ricochets back through the text. Willy Loman, in thrall to the constructed dreams of a country whose business is business, of a culture whose myths colonise the individual imagination, reshaping desires to serve a national destiny, becomes no more than a product, the product he must sell if he is to enter the promised land. He does, indeed, lose his freedom and his dignity. He can envisage no life outside the terms of the contract he has signed to subordinate himself to his function. The death in the play is not that of Willy Loman but of a salesman. His dignity is, indeed, destroyed as he puts a price on himself, in his encounter with his employer lowering his salary step by step in an inverse bargaining session ('If I could take home—well, sixty-five dollars a week . . . fifty dollars . . . forty dollars'),[19] and this in a play in which dollar sums recur as if they were, indeed, a measure of a man. 'I'm one dollar an hour',[20] says Biff, 'I'm a dime a dozen, and so are you!'[21]

Like Faulkner's Joe Christmas in *Light in August*, Willy Loman is a man who never finds out who he is. He believes that the image he sees reflected in the eyes of those before whom he performs is real, and, as Timothy B. Spears points out in *100 Years on the Road*, the metaphor of acting abounds in the literature of salesmanship. Thus James Knox, in *Salesmanship and Business Efficiency* (1912), had remarked that a salesman, like an actor, 'speaks the thoughts of other men; he persuades by his manner of speaking, his manner of acting, and by some indescribable force of his own personality which he is able to embody forth as real'.[22]

As a salesman, Willy stages a performance for buyers, for his sons, for the father who deserted him, the brother he admired. Gradually, he loses his audience, first the buyers, then his son, then his boss. He walks on to the stage, no longer confident he can perform the role he believes is synonymous with his self, no longer sure that anyone will care. He lives a temporary life, a life of cars, trains, offices, hotel rooms. The rhythm of his existence is determined by timetables, appointments, sales targets.

Whatever the salesman needs, Willy seems to lack. He is deeply un-self-confident. He fears he is laughed at, that there is something about him that offends. The play is set at a time when America was beginning to boom, when supply had difficulty catching up with demand. Salesmen hardly needed to sell, simply taking orders from those happily escaping from wartime austerity. Yet the year he proudly quotes as his most successful is 1928, twenty years earlier and, not incidentally, the year before the Crash (the year that triumph turned to disaster for Miller's father, Isidore). This is a man who kills his loneliness in a Boston hotel with a woman whose attraction seems to lie less in her sexuality than in the access she can grant to the buyer, the consolation she offers for his sense of failure, a woman herself not without a degree of desperation.

What does she see in him? She, Miller explains, 'is a lonely woman . . . who genuinely likes Willy and his line of gab and his pathos, and so she sees him for dinner perhaps twice a month and they talk and "behave like husband and wife for a night"' She might, he adds, 'have a similar relationship to a couple of other salesmen from time to time'.[23] Her laughter, which wells up and breaks through Willy's consciousness, is not, then, without a degree of self-mockery as she simultaneously acknowledges Willy's pathos and kills her own loneliness with a man whose humour comes from a deep sense of worthlessness for ever at battle with a desperate need to be acknowledged. It is a scene, however, that turns on what Miller has called an 'hallucinatory surrealism',[24] which had, he felt, got lost in all productions until, in Beijing, he found himself confronted with an actress who came out of an entirely different tradition of acting. This sent him back to the text and the realisation that he and other directors had tried to impose a realistic style on to dialogue that was, he now perceived, patently neither realistic nor a dialogue.

> THE WOMAN:
> Whyn't you have another drink, honey, and stop being so damn self-centred?
> WILLY: I'm so lonely.
> THE WOMAN:
> You know you ruined me, Willy.[25]

As it now seemed to him, they were not so much talking to each other as 'stating their dream-like, disjointed, and intensely compressed positions'.[26] And, of course, it is the nature of much of Willy's ostensible dialogue in the play that it is in fact a discussion with himself, an externalised account of his internal interrogation. Since he conducts these internal conversations in the presence of others, however, there is a surreal quality to many of the interchanges in a play whose sub-title is 'Certain Private Conversations'. The privacy is that provided by Willy's mind.

Why, though, given his state of mind, given the failure of his sales figures to match the importance of his territory, has the company kept him on, allowed him to represent them until he effectively precipitates his own dismissal? It is not entirely clear. He may, indeed, have once had a genuine relationship with the father of his current employer, but the downward spiral has been underway for some time. It seems that Howard, the former boss's son, has barely noticed him, wrapped up, as he is, in his own concerns, unwilling, it seems, to tackle the issue of an employee who, anyway, has only a few years before retirement. Willy is fired, in the end, not because a hard-nosed employer wants to eat the fruit and throw away the peel but because Willy cannot even sell himself. His pitch to Howard is a disaster.

When Charley says to him, 'The only thing you got in this world is what you can sell. And the funny thing is that you're a salesman, and you don't know that',[27] he simultaneously reveals his own complicity in the reductive processes at work in the culture and the basis of Willy's double failure, as a salesman and as a man who has surrendered freedom and dignity to a fantasy. When Willy replies 'I've always tried to think otherwise', however, it is not a plea for genuine human values but a statement of his belief that 'if a man was impressive, and well liked, that nothing—'. He breaks off, never completing the thought, but this is a significant exchange for if it exposes Willy's faith in appearance, it also reveals the extent to which Charley, deeply humane in his response to Willy, nonetheless subscribes to a reductive view of society and the individual.

Henry James, writing in 1904, had reacted against salesmen as agents of an intrusive commercialism, regarding them as in essence confidence men. He also, though, saw them as 'victims and martyrs, creatures touchingly, tragically doomed' by the business culture they represented but which also left them as solitary figures in the social landscape.[28] There is more than something of this about Willy Loman.

Willy wishes to believe in an identity separate from his actions, a self born out of a desire whose intensity he thought sufficient to bring him into being. He is Willy Loman, he shouts, fearing that that name contains nothing more than its own negation. As Erich Fromm has said, speaking of the dilemma of modern man, there is nothing of which we are more ashamed than of not being ourselves, but our avenue to that self lies through our participation in a cycle of production and consumption. We sell a commodity and become a commodity:

> we feel that we can acquire everything material or immaterial by buying it, and thus things become ours independently of any creative effort of our own in relation to them. In the same way we regard our personal qualities and the result of our efforts as commodities that can be sold for money, prestige, power. . . . Thereby man misses the only satisfaction that can give

> him real happiness—the experience of the activity of the present moment—and chases after a phantom that leaves him disappointed as soon as he believes he has caught it—the illusory happiness called success.[29]

That had been Willy Loman's fate. Balancing his sense of a life spiralling down, for which his memories of the past are the available evidence, is an equal and opposite belief in a redemptive future. What is missing is the present moment in which alone some consolation is available from those who value him for what he is and not what he might become.

Willy Loman has lost his contact with the natural world, the west of his youth and the tree-lined idyll of his middle age. He can do no more now than sow seeds on barren ground. He has also lost touch with those around him. In that, too, as it seems to Fromm, writing in another book, *The Art of Loving*, he is a representative figure: 'Modern man is alienated from himself, from his fellow men, and from nature. He has been transformed into a commodity, experiences his life forces as an investment which must bring him the maximum profit obtainable under existing market conditions.'[30] Despairing of realising this investment, he turns to the only place he can, his children. As Fromm observes,

> When a person feels that he has not been able to make sense of his own life, he tries to make sense of it in terms of the life of his children. But one is bound to fail within oneself and for the children. The former because the problem of existence can be solved by each one only for himself, and not by proxy; the latter because one lacks in the very qualities which one needs to guide the children in their own search for an answer.[31]

When Willy advised Biff not to tell jokes when trying to close a deal with a prospective employer he was, unknowingly, repeating a piece of advice offered at the beginning of the century by George Horace Lorimer in *Letters from a Self-Made Merchant to His Son*. What was conscious on his part, however, was the desire to pass to his son not merely the often contradictory advice he had picked up along the way, but the very values that would drive him to the point of self-destruction. He sees not death but justification, not simply an inheritance to fuel the dream he bequeathed to his son, but the funeral which, like that of Dave Singleman, the old drummer who had in part inspired his life as a salesman, would attract his peers, be the final evidence that he was, indeed, well liked.

There is no crime in *Death of a Salesman* and hence no ultimate culpability (beyond guilt for sexual betrayal), only a baffled man and his sons trying to find their way through a world of images, dazzling dreams and fantasies, in the knowledge that they have failed by the standards they have chosen to believe are fundamental. Willy has, as Biff alone understands, all the wrong dreams but, as Charley observes, they go with the territory. They are the dreams of a salesman reaching for the clouds, smiling desperately in the hope that people will smile back. Needing love and respect he is blind to those who offer it, dedicated as he is to the eternal American quest of a transformed tomorrow. What else can he do, then, but climb back into his car and drive off to a death that at last will bring the reward he has chased so determinedly, a reward that will expiate his sense of guilt, justify his life, and hand on to another generation the burden of belief that has corroded his soul but to which he has clung until the end?

He is engaged in an argument with himself, an exploration of the anxiety that has already come so close to destroying him. He invokes figures from his past to respond to that anxiety, take part in that dialogue. Their voices sound out, contrapuntally or in harmony. This inner orchestra is itself a product and exemplary of his state of mind. From the first flute music through the admonishing tone of Uncle Ben and the reassurances of Linda's voice, he hears the score of his emotional life, listening for the false note, acknowledging the discord, hoping for consonance within the dissonance.

As Miller observes in his notebook, 'It is the combination of guilt (of failure), hate and love—all in conflict that he resolves by "accomplishing" a 20,000 dollar death'. To the end he is a salesman. When he explains his plans to Ben, conjured up precisely to give him licence, to ratify his decision, he is making a sales pitch and since Ben is a figment of his imagination he is, in effect, making the pitch to himself. His death is the bargain on offer. It will solve all his problems. It will not only justify his life, it will also redeem his son. In a line of dialogue from the notebook he has Willy say, 'My boy is a thief—with 20,000 he'll stop it'. But beyond that, also from the notebook, he insists that with 20,000 to his name, 'Nobody will say I didn't accomplish something. . . . A little something must be left at the end'.

The insurance policy, now in its period of grace, is, he says, 'the only thing I bought that didn't break'. On the same page on which these lines appear Miller tried out *Period of Grace* as a possible title and, indeed, it is not without its force in a play in which the central character is living on borrowed time in search of grace, forgiveness and benediction.

* * *

Miller has explained that the association of his character's last name with the common man—Loman/Low man—was purely coincidental. Yet there is plainly a sense in which Willy does represent if not the average man then one dazzled by a national dream of becoming and possession. He is a man who attaches his life to a myth which proposes a life without limits but who finds himself trapped in a shrinking physical, social and psychological space. As played by Dustin Hoffman, his physical stature suggests someone intimidated and oppressed by the sheer scale of his problems and a world slipping out of his control. As played by Lee J. Cobb or Brian Dennehy, the sight of a large man humbled adds pathos as his physical strength and commanding presence is negated by a helplessness he cannot acknowledge.

Willy Loman's sales trips into the New England territory are ironic versions of a mythic experience in which the frontiersman simultaneously took possession of a country and a selfhood in challenging the physical world and encountering the new. The rhetoric survives: the reality does not. Knocking them dead in Boston is no longer an account of frontier challenges but of commercial success, access to which is controlled not by the threat of the wild but by secretaries to be cajoled, bribed or seduced. The great adventure is now no more than nights spent in seedy hotels and the constant humiliations suffered at the hands of those for whom profit prevails over human relationships. He had failed to go into the literal frontier with his brother, Ben, restrained by his own timidity but also by commitments not without a human legitimacy. By way of substitute, he invests his sales trips with the language of western venturing.

Willy Loman, desperately driving the highways of New York and New England, is at the end of a historical process that once saw men blaze trails into the heart of the unknown and of a utopia that promised a new identity and a new hope. His exhaustion reflects an entropy that infects more than just himself. Biff and Happy are no less bewildered by the loss of energy than their father. Linda's horizons seem never to have extended beyond the domestic limits of a house once located in the heart of the country and now already something of an anachronism in what seems no more than a cloying suburbia.

Charley is apparently at peace with his own limitations and achievements but for all his humanity is more prosaic than Willy, whose glimpses of lost horizons and adherence to flawed promises nonetheless charge his life with significance. As with his father, there is no doubt as to Bernard's success or humanity, a success, moreover, rooted securely in the Puritan ethic whose essence eludes Willy Loman, who believes that he bought into it by virtue of his American identity and by his purchase of consumer goods which seemed conspicuous evidence of his achievement. Bernard's journey to Washington to plead before the Supreme Court may not make him a twentieth-century frontiersman but it does locate him in a tradition which would take him back to Benjamin Franklin and the Founding Fathers rather than Horatio Alger Jr. There is a causality to his success. Nor does it owe anything to his father who prides himself on his hands-off approach to parenthood. At the same time, we never glimpse Bernard's sense of the cause which his upward mobility might serve. An honest and talented striver, he moves onwards with a certain grace and humanity but remains closed to us and therefore an uncertain paradigm of the Dream.

Certainly, Bernard's success seems a mystery to Willy. Why, after all, did Biff not follow a similar path? His gold-helmeted son was to have a golden future but ended up doing no more than steal a gold pen. Biff has spent time in jail, but why would he not when his father encouraged him to regard theft as evidence of initiative and schoolwork as an irrelevance in a society which he believed valued appearance over substance? Getting by on a smile and a shoeshine himself, how could a boy with such good looks and a fortuitous talent for sport fail?

Willy oscillates between awareness and denial. He discounts what he has but has no clear idea what he wants. What would success be for Willy Loman? Would it be to achieve fame as a salesman, like Dave Singleman, still working at eighty but apparently with no life beyond salesmanship, alone in a hotel room, taking orders? Is it to be well liked? Well liked for what? For himself or as a means to an end? He is discontented but unclear as to the real source of his discontent, beyond a troubled sense of guilt with respect to a son he had hoped would resolve his own sense of failure.

* * *

In the 1999 production, which began at Chicago's Goodman Theatre before moving to New York, two concentric revolves swung characters and scenes into vision as they were prompted by Willy's memory and imagination. Like the 1996 National Theatre production, which also deployed a revolve, these offered a correlative for Willy's mental process, a Proustian recall triggered by a word, a thought, a gesture. Time, for Willy, is like the sea, advancing and retreating, with concealed currents, disturbing eddies that threaten his equanimity.

The revolves also served suddenly to separate those who a moment before were together, an implied comment on the fragility of the connection between those who seem so close, so dependent on one another for the meanings of their lives. By the same token, the discontinuities within the self stand suddenly exposed. Past, present and projected future co-exist, are pulled apart, and reassemble as Willy tries to fit the jigsaw of his life together in such a way as to offer him the satisfaction or simply consolation he seeks. But the fractures, the disruptions, the sudden disturbing epiphanies slowly edge him towards the logic that will lead him to trade his life for the success he sought but never achieved. It is quite as if that life were indeed a consumer product, subject to the same attrition as had afflicted his car and refrigerator, but which is finally redeemable in one last unimpeachable transaction. In his own mind, at least, he will emerge as the consummate salesman he wished to be. And what greater salesman could there be than one who sold his own life and thereby retrospectively redeemed it, while purging himself of guilt and leaving an inheritance of hope to those whose evident despair has been a dagger pointing at his heart.

Linda Loman's first line, in Robert Falls's 1999 production, was amplified, not because of Broadway's accommodation to the nature of American actor-training, which favours the inward over the projected emotion, but because thereby we enter the play as we do the distorted world of a dream, and the dream is a central trope of the play.

At the end, in the Requiem which Miller regarded as the 'quietly sanctified end of the song',[32] Elizabeth Franz, as Linda Loman, lies on Willy's grave, arms outstretched like a nun prostrating herself before a mystery, and the truth is that, for all her everyday common sense, life does remain a mystery to her. Husband and sons are like strangers whose lives she can never fully grasp. She lacks Willy's flawed vision, the poetry whose rhythm both Willy and Biff hear, though only faintly in a world driven not so much by a dream of avarice as by the idea of striving and becoming. When Biff ran out onto the football field the crowd shouted his name, deafening him to the quieter voice of his own self-doubt. Willy's memories of the business for which he has worked throughout his life is that it had once been a family, connected at a human level. But this is now blotted out by the mechanical sounds of a wire recorder he feels powerless to stop, as he stands in his boss's office while that fantasy of familial loyalty is destroyed with a casual disregard.

Nietzsche saw the modern age as concerned with Becoming rather than Being and in this sense Willy Loman can stand as an exemplary figure. He is never at rest, a traveller for other reasons than his job. He leans into the future—like his own country—as if only in some deferred utopian moment could meaning cohere and the grace of true freedom be born. His is a pending life. He is on hold, waiting to hear the good news of his imminent arrival in the promised land of possibility. He holds his breath in awe of the promise, dying for want of the air he should breathe in a shared present. The irony is that, staring through the windshield towards the future, he increasingly finds himself looking into the rear-view mirror, suddenly struck by the irony that the meaning of his life might exist in the past. It is guilt that draws him back, but the greater irony is that he might, after all, have missed the epiphany for which he has waited an entire life.

* * *

Writing to Stephen Marino, in April 1999, apologising for his absence from a conference to be held in Brooklyn where *Salesman* is surely set, he said, 'I did a lot of wandering about in the neighborhood a long time ago, and now there you are talking about the work I was never sure I'd get done. We are forever unknowingly walking over the threads of others' memories, entangling our own with theirs. The transiency is all . . . in America, anyway'.[33] That transiency is a vital element of *Death of a Salesman*, as it would be fifty years later of *Mr. Peters' Connections*.

The world is changing. Willy's memories no longer mean anything to his employer. The past seemingly exists to mock him. His horizons have shrunk in almost every respect. He is still waiting for revelation and redemption even as his grasp on the real slackens. The apparent fixities of the social world are revealed as contingent. Yesterday's new technology becomes today's obsolete product. The rural becomes the urban; bright hopes fade into regrets. Yet his memories, specific to himself, are those of a culture attempting to live mythically, to retain the language if not the substance of frontier individualism and a dream of the new.

In that same letter Miller speaks of being discontented, if also secretly envious of, the products of Broadway as he began his career. What they failed to reach, it seemed to him, was 'the spirit'. Their realism was too immediate, too committed to appearance, to exposing the mechanisms but not the essence of human life. 'I recall thinking', he explained,

> that all the important things were between the lines, in the silences, the gestures, the stuff above or below the level of speech. For a while I even thought to study music, which is the art of silences hedged about by sound. Music begins *Salesman*, and not by accident; we are to hear Willy before we see him and before he speaks. He was there in the hollow of the flute, the wind, the air announcing his arrival and his doom.

The music was to express the past which he thought to transcend but to which he and his son Biff are both drawn. It is a problematic past, speaking of his own abandonment and of the betrayal that has so disabled him in his relationship with his son, but it is a past in which father and son can meet in that both value a pre-modern world. Both are most themselves when they work with their hands. At the same time, there is a melancholy to the flute that speaks both to a lost world and to the elegiac mood of a play which concerns a man's last day of life.

Subsequent productions, including the fiftieth anniversary one, abandoned the original music. The latter settled for a jazz-influenced score by Richard Woodbury which, if anything, stressed the modern over the romantic, the urban over the rural. It reflected what disturbed rather than seduced a Willy Loman caught between his own instinctive rhythms and those offered to him by a society on the make, moving on, sweeping the tracks behind it. Nonetheless, the music remained a crucial counterpoint to his mood, a commentary on a man who hears a different drummer but believes his destiny is to keep step with a society resolutely marching towards a promised revelation. For Miller, the music was 'powerful', offering 'a post-romantic view'.

Struck by the play's survival, not only in America but throughout the world (a Japanese actor reportedly played the role for thirty years, finally abandoning it at the age of ninety, only for it to be taken over by his son: a Norwegian audience returned a second night to find out how what they took to be a saga would finally end), Miller confessed that it made him wonder,

> whether we are all forever being hunted, pursued by one or another sloganized meaning, one or other packaged view of life and death which in our weakness we surrender to when in the privacy of our midnights what we most long to find is the freedom to be and believe everything. Maybe that is what Willy does, since he is all mood, all feeling, a naked branch of an old tree swaying in the wind. Willy moves with the air and from one moment to the next, one feeling to the next, and in a sense believes everything at once . . . that he is loved, that he is contemptible; that he is lost, that he has conquered; that he is afraid, that nothing frightens him and that everything does, and on and on and on. It may be that he has escaped the categories simply because he is a human, and too self-absorbed to be embarrassed by being one. Whatever else you may say about him, he is unmistakably himself . . . even including the times when he wishes he wasn't.[34]

For Miller, Willy had been in search of his immortal soul. That he chose to look in the wrong place stained his search with irony. It did not, however, invalidate it.

The play ends with a Requiem. Elia Kazan's wife Molly suggested that it could be dispensed with, as she did the character of Ben. Few audiences would agree. We never hear the sound of the car crash. As it speeds off so, Miller instructs, 'the music crashes down in a frenzy of sound, which becomes the soft pulsation of a single cello string'. This, in turn, gives way to a dead march. Leaves begin to appear, as if past and present had collapsed into mythic time. The characters move slowly and in silence.

In the version he first drafted in his notebook, people had turned out in numbers for the funeral. As Linda exclaims, 'Wasn't it wonderful that so many people came?' 'Yeah', replies Charley, 'he had a lot of friends'. He was, it seems, well liked, after all. He simply 'worried too much about it', because 'he was so small', adds Linda. In truth, as Miller quickly realised, the essence of Willy is that, as he suspected, he has no friends and, outside of his tortured family, was not well liked. In the final version no one has come to his funeral but the family and his next-door neighbours Charley and Bernard. In that sense he is close kin to Jay Gatsby, another believer in the dream, who died alone, who died still believing in the green light of possibility.

In the first draft Biff draws a social conclusion from his father's death: 'He lived to pay his debts. . . . Look . . . the whole cemetery is filled with them. All good customers who drove themselves into the dirt trying to buy a character that would fit them'. This disappears in the final version, his exemplary status sufficiently established to render such remarks redundant. What is retained, though in modified form, is Biff's observation that, 'He didn't know who he was . . . He had the wrong dream; it was so [text illegible] for him he had to win it with his life. The pity of it is, that he was happy only on certain Sundays, with a warm sun on his back, and a trowel in his hand, some good wet cement, and something to build. That's who he really was'.

What is also retained is Charley's lament for the salesman, though it appears in the notebook in verse, its opening line, 'A salesman doesn't build anything', offering a counterpoint to Biff's remark, that 'A man who doesn't build anything must be liked'.

The play ends, as it had begun, with the sound of a flute while the leaves dissolve and the surrounding apartment buildings come into sharp focus. Time bends back on itself, a life now complete. Biff is presumably about to light out for the territory, following the sound of the flute. But that rural world was where the first act of betrayal occurred, as it did in the original Eden. Perhaps, as Fitzgerald has Carraway say in *The Great Gatsby*, this had been a story about the west, after all. The west, in this case, is that towards which Biff will go, as it was once the place where Willy's salesman father deserted his family (in pursuit of diamonds in Alaska where, Ben suggests in the notebook: 'Father could make more in a year than most men do in a lifetime'). It was where Uncle Ben began his capitalist enterprise, an enterprise which Willy believed first he and then Biff would match and whose suspect nature would have been underlined in the 1999 production had the Watergate 'plumber' G. Gordon Liddy played the part, a piece of casting seriously considered.

Again in the notebook, we are told that 'Willy both feels deserted by father and worships his "greatness"'. 'All I've got', he says, 'is my boys'. And there, of course, is the irony for as a note explains, '. . . the desertion of his sons, loss of their love, with his father's desertion . . . equals proof that he bungled his life'. 'Have flute play', Miller indicates, when Willy puts these pieces together in his mind, the flute that plays at the beginning and then at the end as Willy rides to what he believes to be glory and what Biff alone understands to be nothing more than an empty and dangerous dream.

Willy goes on quests, like some medieval knight, riding forth to justify himself while at the same time his Platonic paradigm for the salesman-warrior is a man in carpet slippers, smoking a cigarette with a telephone in his hand. The maiden in distress in the Boston hotel was, in the notebooks, to have been a hooker but is now a blowsy secretary with a laugh that echoes in his mind and down the years as a reminder of his insignificance. His is a story threaded through with irony.

Death lies at the end of tragedy like the ultimate promise of form. It offers a retrospective grace, flooding contingency with a meaning that can only come from its apparent dissolution. Willy Loman is hardly a tragic hero. He dies with a smile, not relishing an irony or accepting a fate but driving to redemption, as he assumes, deeply self-deceived, bright with the conviction that he has completed the ultimate deal with the Mephistopheles of American utopianism.

Willy Loman dies in the machine that has carried him daily deeper into despair and yet which is the ambiguous symbol of his culture, on the move into the future yet itself always in thrall to entropy. Tragedy is a subjective victory won in the face of an objective defeat. Willy, it seems, is defeated in his very self. There is almost no subjectivity not compromised by internalising the assumptions of the world he believes himself to be seizing, the world he imagines to contain the meaning of his life. When he calls out his name there is no echo because there is no longer any substantial reality to reflect it back to him.

He cannot live in a world not energised by the imagination. He goes gently into the night precisely because his death is drained of the tragic, no matter what Miller may have chosen to believe. He dies in hope. He dies radiant with unexamined optimism, almost an absurd hero finding meaning in his conspiracy with death, purpose in the purposeless. He never does close the gap between what he wishes to be and what he is.

The tragic hero is a thinker dismayed at where thought has taken him, a man betrayed by actions that accomplish nothing but their own undoing, who nonetheless discovers a truth lost somewhere between thought and its realisation. The tragic hero dies in a moment of transcendent truth, all illusion flown. Oedipus learns a terrible truth and stares it in the face. Macbeth understands that he is no more than a man. Lear unbuttons to an unaccommodated man, shedding self-deceit along with kingship. Hamlet, through a play, learns the power of seeming and understands a truth that hastens him to his death. Willy, by contrast, is blinded with the sun of a false epiphany.

Camus said of the absurd man that he was always longing for tomorrow, where everything in him ought to reject it. Willy thought time his friend until he was suddenly aware of it as an enemy. Camus spoke of the fact that no code of ethics and no effort are justifiable a priori in the face of the cruel mathematics that command the human condition. Willy is aware of that mathematics.

At the end of the century, in a play that would look back through the century, Mr Peters (in *Mr. Peters' Connections*, Miller's 1998 play) would confront that same disturbing human economy, watching the meaning he had spent a lifetime constructing unwind itself, no more than a series of images unspooling in the face of a gathering night. Willy Loman sees those same pictures, replays them trying to detect the logic that has brought him to this moment of bewilderment.

So long as the mind keeps silent in 'the motionless world of its hopes', Camus remarked, nostalgia could seemingly offer a secure foundation. But with its first move, he warned, this world would crack and tumble. Willy's world has done no less. The memories that flood his mind, far from offering the reassuring structure of nostalgia, underscore the irony which increasingly disables him as he recalls, and re-experiences, 'the feelings and joys of his great moment, decades ago, when through Biff he felt he was within inches of some fabled victory over life's ignominious leveling'.[35]

For Samuel Beckett's 'Let's go. (*they do not move*)', Miller offers, 'The trouble is he's lazy', 'There's one thing about Biff—he's not lazy'. Willy is caught in contradictions because the world fails to come into line with his desires and because there is an irony in welcoming a future that in fact conceals the truth of dissolution and finality. It is that tension which is the source of an absurdity that he attempts to resist by succumbing to it, dying while still denying the finality of death. Even in the face of death, he insists, there is still a tomorrow. In part that is the tomorrow of the American dream, of a culture that instructs its citizens to pursue happiness, as if it were a destination and not a condition, but in part it is final evidence of that absurdity which is a product of a refusal to acknowledge the fundamental condition of existence and the need to discover meaning as though it would become apparent in some final revelation.

What Willy Loman finally seeks is not success but immortality. He wishes to pass something more than an inheritance to his sons. He wants to live in and through them, which is why he offers a death with such equanimity. It is Biff's declaration of love, as Willy interprets it, that enables and justifies his decision to trade his life for an insurance policy. But what he has insured/ensured is, he believes, precisely that life will continue.

For Miguel de Unamuno (referring, as Miller is prone to do, to the figure of Cain), man is prepared to sacrifice not only his life but his happiness for the sake of his name. Is it pride, he asks himself, which drives the desire for immortality, to leave an 'ineradicable name'? No, he replies, it is a terror of extinction, just as it is a fear of poverty that drives a poor man to seek for money. Willy Loman had striven for success because of his fear of failure. He dies for the sake of his name—the name he shouts out in desperation—for fear of leaving no trace of his having existed. He wants to live in the divine memory. And since the world he inhabits seems to offer no transcendence, no consoling God, he tries to write his name in flesh. The irony is that his sons are bequeathed absurdity.

This is not to say that Miller is somehow a version of Beckett. He, himself, after all, would resist such a suggestion. But where in his essays he saw a contrast between himself and a playwright who seemed to him so different, perhaps there is, after all, a point of contact as well as contrast. Beckett's ironies are puritanically severe, though their expression contradicts that severity. Beckett lifts his characters out of a social environment, isolates them in a featureless world, for the most part strips them of a past unless that be the echoing repetition of *Krapp's Last Tape*. Miller, on the other hand, creates dense social worlds, characters whose choices are real and who are capable of decisions which define them. Nonetheless, in Willy Loman he comes close to creating an absurd hero whose very hope is the source of his absurdity. It is Biff's understanding of this, however, that deflects the absurd logic.

Where, then, does that leave us with respect to Willy Loman who

Miller wished to see as a tragic hero? Perhaps the best summary was that which he offered to a group of Chinese actors struggling with an alien play about a dying salesmen. They were, he felt, still acting and not being. The key, he explained to them, was indeed, love, that between a man and his son and between both of them and the culture which they embraced and from which they urgently needed to separate themselves. But there was something else, too,

> not admiration, necessarily, but a kind of visceral recognition that in his fumbling and often ridiculous way he is trying to lift up a belief in immense human possibilities. People can't stand him, often, they flee from him, but they miss him when he isn't there. Perhaps it is that he hasn't a cynical bone in his body, he is a walking believer, the bearer of a flame whose going-out would leave us flat, with merely what the past has given us. He is forever signaling to a future that he cannot describe and will not live to see, but he is in love with all the same.[36]

For Miller, the ironies at the heart of the absurd are simply too implacable. This, after all, was a play written out of pity. Willy Loman's faith in human possibilities has taken wholly the wrong form but Miller was himself not ready to surrender his own faith in a redemptive future even if, like Biff, he increasingly defined it in terms of a past in which the individual had not yet been alienated from the products of his labour, from the natural world and from those others who constituted a functioning community dependent on a mutuality of needs and satisfactions.

* * *

Death of a Salesman is, as Tyrone Guthrie understood, a long poem by Willy Loman. For much of the play it is he who hears the voices, shapes the rhythms, creates the rhymes. He turns experience into metaphor, bringing together discrete moments to forge new meanings which then dissolve. When he dies we leave his consciousness for a stripped-down stage and people whose words are baffled approximations for the man whose world we have seen from the inside.

There is, as Miller has said, a space between the Requiem and the play. It was not only Molly Kazan but also some directors who thought it should be cut. But to Miller it is crucial as a moment when the contradictions are stilled, the false hopes laid aside, and we no longer see the world through the eyes of a man who never knew who he was, or what he might be, apart from the flickering images projected by a society at risk of subsuming the spiritual in the material. And though Happy rededicates himself to Willy's false dreams, his is a voice that now lacks social resonance. Biff, alone, draws the necessary conclusions from the death of a man he loved but from whom he had to separate himself, Biff the man who 'returned for Willy's blessing without which he cannot find himself as a man', a fact which was unplanned by Miller, but, as he once remarked, 'there it is'.

Writing to a director in 1975, Miller explained his sense of this moment:

> The people are in the mood of that kind of death-shock which moves us to what one might call an emblematic feeling—one wants to utter something to leave in the grave, a summing up.
>
> So they are not quite talking to one another. Yet the death has drawn them together, each in his own separate relation to the dead man.
>
> There is nothing overwrought or self-conscious or pompous about such a thing, it is as common as a funeral, and there is no reason to fear self-consciousness. We hire clergymen to say a few words. Silence seems inhuman at such moments. Here they are their own clergymen, that's all.
>
> They should stand in a group. There is no viable image now; instead there is a kind of timorousness. There is no reason to be afraid of it. Before rehearsals Kazan feared this scene too but when he saw the piling up of feeling in the last twenty minutes he ceased disputing its validity. It says something we want to hear, it sends Willy off and somehow helps us to believe everything all over again.[37]

Willy Loman's last ride takes him out of time and into myth, where he will be immune to decay. The future, to which he had looked for resolution, but that so tormented him, will now be dissolved. His family and neighbours gather together at the end, suddenly freed, no longer projections of his troubled mind, as if surrendered by him as a final act of grace. They now walk forth released from their roles, like actors whose pretence is at last laid aside, liberated from the story in which they have been contained.

The man who feared he meant so little and whose ending is attended by so few, was, we see, central after all. Why else do these people feel a sense of loss, regret and, in Linda's case, desolation? Tomorrow she will live in an empty house. The mortgage will have been paid but no longer will there be the smell of shaving soap or the sound of a man talking to himself as if arguing the case for his own existence. That very emptiness is a measure of the man. He failed his family. He was guilty of betrayal and subsisted on denial. Yet he was the centre of their world. Linda has the key to the play at the very beginning. She has found the evidence that he intends to kill himself. Her battle is now lost. The irony is that Willy believed that his was won.

'We're free . . . We're free', cries Linda, as the hard towers of modernity rise up and the stage is slowly shrouded in darkness. The silence that invariably seems to follow this moment in the theatre—a silence that disturbed Miller when the play was first staged and he waited to judge the nature and extent of the applause—is surely an expression of the audience's unwillingness to break the moment, to step out of the unresolved tension with which they have been confronted as a man slips away from life mourned only by those who lacked the power to stop him. Ironically, it is, finally, the absence of Willy Loman that is the measure of the man. There may be only this handful of mourners at his grave but the audience is added to that number. The play edges towards silence with only the flute music now audible, as the surrounding apartment buildings come into sharp focus. America's past and present are thus brought together, as they had been in Willy's mind, a reminder of utopian dreams lost somewhere in their materialisation. Like Fitzgerald's Gatsby, Willy 'believed in the green light, the orgastic future that year by year recedes before us. It eluded us then, but that's no matter—tomorrow we will run faster, stretch our arms further. . . . And one fine morning—So we beat on, boats against the current, borne back ceaselessly into the past'.[38]

Willy Loman's vision of the future, too, lay behind him, as it does for a country that weds the idea of progress to a myth of innocence and endlessly renewed beginnings. To see life as destiny is a form of nostalgia and that is Willy's plight. He seemingly yearns for tomorrow but is repelled by all evidence of the modern—high-rise apartments, wire recorders—which lie outside his control. The problem is that the future holds the certainty of dissolution. The lesson is to hand. His refrigerator, his car, are disassembling themselves before his eyes and so, he knows, is he.

Only the past can shape the future as he wishes. Only the past is uninfected with decay. His destiny is thus contained in the flute music with which he entered the world, his world and that of the play. He is drawn back to that day when his son, an extension of himself, climbed some ultimate mountain to perfection in a ball game that shines golden in his mythic memory.

On rereading the play in 1958, Miller noted that while Biff confessed that he was nothing, Willy insisted on his name. 'I like Willy better', Miller observed. Biff, it seemed to him, had settled for failure. Willy set his face against it.

It is a curious comment for the fact is that Biff only thought himself a failure when accepting his father's measure of meaning. Released from a corrosive fantasy he reclaims an identity rooted in the real. Willy insists on his name but is blind to the fact that he has drained it of individuation. Yet there is, indeed, something about Willy Loman that is compelling, something that justifies Miller's retrospective embrace of this failed man inhabiting an unreal world. He may dream the wrong dreams and fail to understand the redemption he is offered by those who care more for him than he appears to care for them, but he retains the capacity for wonder.

In an article Miller wrote a year after the play's opening, he anticipated that a time would come 'when they will look back at us astonished that we saw something holy in the competition for the means of existence'. He had not, it seems, forgotten the language at least of the pre-war years, but the real force of the play lay elsewhere. The 'tragedy of Willy Loman', he said, derived from the fact that he gave his life, or sold it, in order to justify the waste of it. 'It is', he said,

> the tragedy of a man who did believe that he alone was not meeting the qualifications laid down for mankind by those clean-shaven frontiersmen who inhabit the peaks of broadcasting and advertising offices. From those forests of canned goods high up near the sky, he heard the thundering command to succeed as it ricocheted down the newspaper-lined canyons of his city, heard not a human voice, but a wind of a voice to which no human can reply in kind, except to stare in the mirror of failure.[39]

In 1992, Miller wondered why he was still capable of being reduced to tears by this drama of an aging salesman with the wrong dreams when 'he is such a damned fool'. But in the end what audiences responded to then as now was not a damned fool but the portrait of a man desperate to make sense of his life while aware of his failure to do so. What compelled was the drama of a man blind to the love of those who watched dismayed as he sacrificed himself to an idea, the false promise of a golden future.

From *Arthur Miller: A Critical Study* (Cambridge: Cambridge University Press, 2005): 100-123. Copyright © 2005 by Cambridge University Press. Reprinted by permission of Cambridge University Press.

Notes

1. Arthur Miller, *The Theater Essays of Arthur Miller*, ed. Robert A. Martin and Steven R. Centola (New York, 1996), p. 419.

2. *Ibid.*, p. 136.

3. *Ibid.*, p. 420.

4. Matthew Roudané, *Conversations with Arthur Miller* (London, 1987), p. 17.

5. Martin and Centola, eds., *Theater Essays*, p. 423.

6. Arthur Miller, *'Salesman' in Beijing* (London, 1984), p. 49.

7. *Death of a Salesman* notebook held at the Harry Ransom Center, University of Texas at Austin.

8. Miller, *'Salesman' in Beijing*, p. 79.

9. Martin and Centola, eds., *Theater Essays*, p. 423.

10. Roudané, *Conversations with Arthur Miller*, p. 17.

11. Miller, *'Salesman' in Beijing*, p. 14.

12. *Ibid.*, p. 22.

13. *Ibid.*, p. 50.

14. Earl Shorris, *A Nation of Salesmen: The Tyranny of the Market and the Subversion of Culture* (New York, 1994), pp. 10–11.

15. *Ibid.*, p. 331.

16. Miller, *'Salesman' in Beijing*, p. 90.

17. *Ibid.*, p. 130.

18. *Ibid.*

19. Arthur Miller, *Death of a Salesman* (New York, 1998), pp. 59–61.

20. *Ibid.*, p. 106.

21. *Ibid.*, p. 105.

22. Timothy B. Spears, *100 Years on the Road* (New Haven, 1995), p. 219.

23. Miller, *'Salesman' in Beijing*, p. 151.

24. *Ibid.*, p. 151.

25. Miller, *Death of a Salesman*, p. 91.

26. Miller, *'Salesman' in Beijing*, p. 152.

27. Miller, *Death of a Salesman*, p. 75.

28. Quoted in Spears, *100 Years on the Road*, pp. 424–429.

29. Erich Fromm, *Fear of Freedom* (London, 1942), p. 226.

30. Erich Fromm, *The Art of Loving* (London, 1957), p. 74.

31. *Ibid.*, p. 86

32. Miller, *'Salesman' in Beijing*, p. 78.

33. Letter to Stephen Marino.

34. *Ibid.*

35. Miller, *'Salesman' in Beijing*, p. 49.

36. *Ibid.*

37. Arthur Miller, Letter to 'George', 6 June 1975, in Arthur Miller's private papers.

38. F. Scott Fitzgerald, *The Great Gatsby* (Harmondsworth, 1950), p. 188.

39. Arthur Miller, *New York Times*, 5 February 1950.

RESOURCES

Chronology of Arthur Miller's Life

1915	Arthur Asher Miller born on October 17 in Harlem, New York City, to Isidore and Augusta Miller. Second of three children.
1929	Father's business is struggling, which forces the family to move to Brooklyn.
1933	Graduates from high school. Rejected from Cornell University and the University of Michigan. Writes his first short story, "In Memoriam," depicting an aging salesman. Reapplies to the University of Michigan and is granted a conditional acceptance.
1934	Enters University of Michigan to study journalism. Reporter and night editor on student paper, *The Michigan Daily*. Studies playwriting under Professor Kenneth T. Rowe.
1936	First play, *No Villain*, is produced and receives the University of Michigan's Avery Hopwood Award.
1937	His play *Honors at Dawn* receives Hopwood Award. Receives the Theatre Guild's Bureau of New Plays Award for *They Too Arise*, a revision of *No Villain*.
1938	Graduates with a B.A. in English. Joins the Federal Theatre Project in New York City to write radio plays and scripts.
1939	Writes radio plays for CBS and NBC.
1940	Travels to North Carolina to collect dialect speech for the folk division of the Library of Congress. Marries Mary Grace Slattery.
1941	Works various odd jobs. Writes radio plays over next few years, including *The Pussycat and the Expert Plumber Who Was a Man* and *William Ireland's Confession*.
1944	Daughter, Jane, is born. First Broadway production, *The Man Who Had All the Luck*, closes after four performances but receives the Theatre Guild National Award.

1945	*Focus* (novel) published.
1947	Son, Robert, is born. *All My Sons* opens on Broadway, earning Miller a New York Drama Critics' Circle Award. Becomes involved in a variety of anti-Fascist and pro-Communist activities. Buys farmhouse in Roxbury, Connecticut, as a vacation home.
1949	*Death of a Salesman* opens on Broadway, under the direction of Elia Kazan and starring Lee J. Cobb in the title role. Receives the Pulitzer Prize and the New York Drama Critics' Circle Award. Miller publishes first of his many theatrical and political essays.
1950	Adaptation of Henrik Ibsen's *An Enemy of the People* premieres, but closes after thirty-six performances.
1951	Meets Marilyn Monroe for the first time. First film production of *Death of a Salesman*, with Fredric March, for Columbia Pictures.
1952	Visits the Historical Society "Witch Museum" in Salem to conduct research for *The Crucible.*
1953	*The Crucible* opens on Broadway. Wins Antoinette Perry and Donaldson awards for Best Play.
1954	Denied passport by State Department to attend opening of *The Crucible* in Brussels because of his alleged support of the Communist movement.
1955	The one-act *A View from the Bridge* premieres in a joint bill with *A Memory of Two Mondays*. The House Committee on Un-American Activities (HUAC) pressures city officials to withdraw permission for Miller to make a film he has been planning about New York juvenile delinquency.
1956	Divorces Mary Slattery; marries Marilyn Monroe. Subpoenaed to appear before HUAC for attending Communist meetings and refuses to name names of others attending meeting organized by Communist sympathizers.
1957	*Collected Plays* published. Indicted on charge of contempt of Congress for refusing to name names to HUAC.

1958	United States Court of Appeals overturns his contempt of Congress conviction. Elected to the National Institute of Arts and Letters. Filming begins of Miller's *The Misfits*, starring Marilyn Monroe.
1959	Receives the Gold Medal for Drama from the National Institute of Arts and Letters.
1961	*The Misfits* is released in theaters. Miller divorces Monroe.
1962	Marries Austrian photographer Ingeborg Morath. Monroe dies.
1963	Daughter, Rebecca, is born.
1964	*After the Fall* and *Incident at Vichy* open in New York.
1965	Elected president of International P.E.N., the worldwide literary organization.
1967	*I Don't Need You Anymore* (short stories) published.
1968	*The Price* opens on Broadway.
1969	Publishes *In Russia* (travel journals), with photographs by Inge Morath.
1970	One-act plays *Fame* and *The Reason Why* produced. Miller's works are banned in the Soviet Union as a result of his work to free dissident writers.
1971	*The Portable Arthur Miller* is published. *The Price* and *A Memory of Two Mondays* appear on television.
1972	*The Creation of the World and Other Business* opens on Broadway, but closes after twenty performances.
1974	*After the Fall* appears on television.
1975	Revival of *Death of a Salesman* in New York.

1977	*In the Country* published (reportage with Inge Morath). *The Archbishop's Ceiling* premieres in Washington, D.C.
1978	*The Theater Essays of Arthur Miller*, edited by Robert A. Martin, published. Miller visits China.
1979	*Chinese Encounters* published (reportage with Inge Morath).
1980	*The American Clock* opens in New York; closes after only twelve performances.
1981	*Collected Plays, Volume II* published.
1982	One-acts *Elegy for a Lady* and *Some Kind of Love Story* are produced under the title *2 by A.M.* in Connecticut.
1983	Directs *Death of a Salesman* at the People's Art Theater in Beijing, the People's Republic of China.
1984	*Death of a Salesman* revived on Broadway, starring Dustin Hoffman. Miller receives Kennedy Center Honors for his lifetime achievement.
1985	*Death of a Salesman* with Dustin Hoffman airs on CBS; earns ten Emmy nominations and takes home three awards.
1987	Publishes *Timebends: A Life* (autobiography). *All My Sons* appears on television.
1990	Revival of *The Crucible* in New York and London. *Danger: Memory!* produced in New York.
1992	*Homely Girl* (novella) published.
1994	*Broken Glass* opens at the Booth Theatre on Broadway, earning Miller another Tony Award for best play.
1995	Receives William Inge Festival Award for distinguished achievement in American theater. *Plain Girl* is published in England.

1996	Receives the Edward Albee Last Frontier Playwright Award. Critically acclaimed film adaptation of *The Crucible* is released, starring Winona Ryder and Daniel Day Lewis.
1998	Major revival of *A View from the Bridge* wins two Tony Awards. Miller is named Distinguished Inaugural Senior Fellow of the American Academy in Berlin.
1999	*Death of a Salesman* revived on Broadway for the play's fiftieth anniversary; wins Tony for Best Revival of a Play.
2000	*The Ride Down Mount Morgan* appears again on Broadway, also a revival of *The Price*. Major eighty-fifth birthday celebrations for Miller held at University of Michigan and at the Arthur Miller Center in England. *Echoes Down the Corridor* is published (collected essays from 1944 to 2000).
2001	Miller is named Jefferson Lecturer by the National Endowment for the Humanities and receives the John H. Finley Award for Exemplary Service to New York City.
2002	Miller's wife Inge Morath dies. *Resurrection Blues* premieres. Miller receives the International Spanish Award, Premio Príncipe de Asturias de las Letras.
2003	Awarded the Jerusalem Prize.
2004	His last play, *Finishing the Picture*, premieres at Chicago's Goodman Theatre. Miller announces he is planning to marry thirty-four-year-old artist Agnes Barley.
2005	At the age of eighty-nine, Miller dies of congestive heart failure in his Connecticut home on February 10. Memorial services are held in Roxbury and New York.

Works by Arthur Miller

Drama

Honors at Dawn, pr. 1936
No Villain, pr. 1937
The Golden Years, wr. 1940, pr. 1987, pb. 2000
The Man Who Had All the Luck, pr. 1944, pb. 1989
All My Sons, pr., pb. 1947
Death of a Salesman, pr., pb. 1949
An Enemy of the People, pr. 1950, pb. 1951 (adaptation of Henrik Ibsen's play)
The Crucible, pr., pb. 1953
A Memory of Two Mondays, pr., pb. 1955
A View from the Bridge, pr., pb. 1955 (one-act version)
A View from the Bridge, pr. 1956, pb. 1957 (two-act version)
Collected Plays, pb. 1957 (includes *All My Sons*, *Death of a Salesman*, *The Crucible*, *A Memory of Two Mondays*, and *A View from the Bridge*)
After the Fall, pr., pb. 1964
Incident at Vichy, pr. 1964, pb. 1965
The Price, pr., pb. 1968
Fame, pr. 1970
The Reason Why, pr. 1970
The Creation of the World and Other Business, pr. 1972, pb. 1973
The Archbishop's Ceiling, pr. 1977, pb. 1984
The American Clock, pr. 1980, pb. 1982
Arthur Miller's Collected Plays, Volume II, pb. 1981 (includes *The Misfits*, *After the Fall*, *Incident at Vichy*, *The Price*, *The Creation of the World and Other Business*, and *Playing for Time*)
2 by A.M., 1982 (includes one-acts *Elegy for a Lady* and *Some Kind of Love Story*)
Two-Way Mirror, pb. 1984
Danger: Memory!, pb. 1986, pr. 1987
Plays, pb. 1988-1995 (5 volumes)
The Last Yankee, pb. 1991, pr. 1993
The Ride Down Mount Morgan, pr., pb. 1991
Broken Glass, pr., pb. 1994
Mr. Peters' Connections, pr. 1998, pb. 1999
Resurrection Blues, pr. 2002
Finishing the Picture, pr. 2004

Long Fiction

Focus, 1945
The Misfits, 1961

Short Fiction

I Don't Need You Any More, 1967
Homely Girl, a Life: And Other Stories, 1992 (in the U.K. as *Plain Girl*, 1995)
Presence, 2007

Screenplays

The Misfits, 1961
Everybody Wins, 1990
The Crucible, 1996 (adaptation of his play)

Teleplay

Playing for Time, 1980

Nonfiction

Situation Normal, 1944
In Russia, 1969 (photo essay; with Inge Morath)
In the Country, 1977 (photo essay; with Morath)
The Theater Essays of Arthur Miller, 1978 (revised and expanded, 1996; Robert A. Martin, editor)
Chinese Encounters, 1979 (photo essay; with Morath)
"Salesman" in Beijing, 1984
Conversations with Arthur Miller, 1987 (Matthew C. Roudané, editor)
Spain, 1987
Timebends: A Life, 1987
Arthur Miller and Company, 1990 (Christopher Bigsby, editor)
Echoes Down the Corridor: Collected Essays, 1947-2000, 2000
The Crucible in History, and Other Essays, 2000
On Politics and the Art of Acting, 2001

Bibliography

Aarnes, William. "Tragic Form and the Possibility of Meaning in *Death of a Salesman*." *Furman Studies* 29 (December 1983): 57–80.

August, Eugene R. "*Death of a Salesman*: A Men's Studies Approach." *Western Ohio Journal* 7, no. 1 (1986): 53–71.

Austin, Gayle. "The Exchange of Women and Male Homosocial Desire in Arthur Miller's *Death of a Salesman* and Lillian Hellman's *Another Part of the Forest*." From *Feminist Rereadings of Modern American Drama*. Ed. June Schlueter. Rutherford, NJ: Fairleigh Dickinson University Press, 1989: 59–66.

Balakian, Jan. "Beyond the Male Locker Room: *Death of a Salesman* from a Feminist Perspective." From *Approaches to Teaching Miller's Death of a Salesman*. Ed. Matthew C. Roudané. New York: Modern Language Association of America, 1995.

Bigsby, C.W.E. *Arthur Miller: A Critical Study*. Cambridge, England: Cambridge University Press, 2005.

____________, ed. *The Cambridge Companion to Arthur Miller*. New York: Cambridge University Press, 1997.

Bloom, Harold, ed. *Arthur Miller*. New York: Chelsea House, 1987.

____________, ed. *Willy Loman*. New York: Chelsea House, 1990.

Brater, Enoch. *Arthur Miller: A Playwright's Life and Works*. New York: Thames and Hudson, 2005.

____________. *Arthur Miller's Global Theatre*. Ann Arbor: University of Michigan Press, 2007.

____________, ed. *Arthur Miller's America: Theater and Culture in a Time of Change*. Ann Arbor: University of Michigan Press, 2005.

Brucher, Richard T. "Willy Loman and the Soul of the New Machine: Technology and the Common Man." *Journal of American Studies* 17 (1983): 325–36.

Cohn, Ruby. "The Articulate Victims of Arthur Miller." From *Dialogue in American Drama*. Bloomington: Indiana University Press, 1971: 68–96.

Corrigan, Robert W., ed. *Arthur Miller: A Collection of Critical Essays*. Englewood Cliffs, NJ: Prentice-Hall, 1969.

Davis, Walter A. "All in the Family: *Death of a Salesman*." From *Get the Guests: Psychoanalysis, Modern American Drama, and the Audience*. Madison: University of Wisconsin Press, 1994: 103–46.

Foster, Richard J. "Confusion and Tragedy: The Failure of Miller's *Salesman*." From *Two Modern American Tragedies: Reviews and Criticism of Death of a Salesman and A Streetcar Named Desire*. Ed. John D. Hurrell. New York: Scribner's, 1961: 82–88.

Gordon, Lois. "*Death of a Salesman*: An Appreciation." From *The Forties: Fiction,*

Poetry, Drama. Ed. Warren French. DeLand, FL: Everett/Edwards, 1969: 273–83.

Gottfried, Martin. *Arthur Miller: His Life and Work*. Cambridge, MA: Da Capo Press, 2003.

Griffin, Alice. *Understanding Arthur Miller*. Columbia: University of South Carolina Press, 1996.

Hadomi, Leah. "Fantasy and Reality: Dramatic Rhythm in *Death of a Salesman*." *Modern Drama* 31 (1988): 157–74.

Harshbarger, Karl. *The Burning Jungle: An Analysis of Arthur Miller's Death of a Salesman*. Washington, DC: University Press of America, 1978.

Hayman, Ronald. *Arthur Miller*. London: Heinemann, 1970.

Huftel, Sheila. *Arthur Miller: The Burning Glass*. New York: The Citadel Press, 1965.

Hurrell, John D., ed. *Two Modern American Tragedies: Reviews and Criticism of "Death of a Salesman" and "A Streetcar Named Desire."* New York: Scribner's, 1961.

Koon, Helene Wickham, ed. *Twentieth Century Interpretations of Death of a Salesman: A Collection of Critical Essays*. Englewood Cliffs, NJ: Prentice-Hall, 1983.

Malpede, Karen. "Everybody's Father." *Michigan Quarterly Review* 37, no. 4 (Fall 1998): 609–10.

Marino, Stephen A. *A Language Study of Arthur Miller's Plays: The Poetic in the Colloquial*. Lewiston, NY: Mellen Press, 2002.

____________, ed. *"The Salesman Has a Birthday": Essays Celebrating the Fiftieth Anniversary of Arthur Miller's Death of a Salesman*. Lanham, MD: University Press of America, 2000.

Martin, Robert A., ed. *Arthur Miller: New Perspectives*. Englewood Cliffs, NJ: Prentice-Hall, 1982.

Martine, James J. "The Nature of Tragedy in Arthur Miller's *Death of a Salesman*." *South Atlantic Review* 61, no. 4 (Fall 1996): 97–106.

____________, ed. *Critical Essays on Arthur Miller*. Boston: G. K. Hall, 1979.

Mielziner, Jo. "Designing a Play: *Death of a Salesman*." From *Designing for the Theater*. New York: Bramhall House, 1965: 23–63.

Mitchell, Giles. "Living and Dying for the Ideal: A Study of Willy Loman's Narcissism." *Psychoanalytic Review* 77 (1990): 391–407.

Moss, Leonard. *Arthur Miller*. New York: Twayne, 1980.

Murphy, Brenda. *Miller: Death of a Salesman*. Cambridge: Cambridge University Press, 1995.

Murphy, Brenda, and Susan C. W. Abbotson, eds. *Understanding "Death of a Salesman": A Student Casebook to Issues, Sources, and Historical Documents*. Westport, CT: Greenwood Press, 1999.

Nilsen, Helge Normann. "From *Honors at Dawn* to *Death of a Salesman*: Marxism and the Early Plays of Arthur Miller." *English Studies: A Journal of English Language and Literature* 75, no. 2 (March 1994): 146–56.

Oates, Joyce Carol. "Arthur Miller's *Death of a Salesman*: A Celebration." (Fall 1998). http://jco.usfca.edu/arthurmiller.html. Celestial Timepiece: A Joyce Carol Oates Home Page. (August 30, 2007).

Otten, Terry. *The Temptation of Innocence in the Dramas of Arthur Miller*. Columbia: University of Missouri Press, 2002.

Rich, Frank. "Theater: Hoffman, 'Death of a Salesman.'" *The New York Times*, March 30, 1984.

Roudané, Matthew C., ed. *Approaches to Teaching Miller's Death of a Salesman*. New York: Modern Language Association of America, 1995.

___________, ed. *Conversations with Arthur Miller*. Jackson: University of Mississippi Press, 1987.

Savran, David. *Communists, Cowboys, and Queers: The Politics of Masculinity in the Work of Arthur Miller and Tennessee Williams*. Minneapolis: University of Minnesota Press, 1992.

Schlueter, June, and James K. Flanagan. *Arthur Miller*. New York: Ungar, 1987.

Spears, Timothy. *100 Years on the Road: The Traveling Salesman in American Culture*. New Haven: Yale University Press, 1995.

Welland, Dennis. *Miller: A Study of His Plays*. London: Methuen, 1979.

Wilson, Robert N. "Arthur Miller: The Salesman and Society." From *The Writer as Social Seer*. Chapel Hill: University of North Carolina Press, 1979: 56–71.

Zeinneddine, Nada. *Because It Is My Name: Problems of Identity Experienced by Women, Artists, and Breadwinners in the Plays of Henrik Ibsen, Tennessee Williams, and Arthur Miller*. Braunton, Devon: Merlin Books, 1991.

CRITICAL INSIGHTS

About the Editor

Brenda Murphy is Board of Trustees Distinguished Professor of English at the University of Connecticut. Her scholarly work, spanning more than thirty years, reflects her interest in placing American drama, theater, and performance in the broader context of American literature and culture. She has written numerous articles about American playwrights and other writers, but her most significant work is in the ten books she has authored on the American theater.

Among Murphy's books are *The Provincetown Players and the Culture of Modernity* (2005), *O'Neill: Long Day's Journey Into Night* (2001), *Congressional Theatre: Dramatizing McCarthyism on Stage, Film, and Television* (1999), *Miller: Death of a Salesman* (1995), *Tennessee Williams and Elia Kazan: A Collaboration in the Theatre* (1992), *American Realism and American Drama, 1880-1940* (1987), and, as editor, *Twentieth Century American Drama: Critical Concepts in Literary and Cultural Studies* (2006) and the *Cambridge Companion to American Women Playwrights* (1999). She has been recognized as breaking new ground through her synthesis of the study of the play as literary text and the play as performance in her books on Tennessee Williams, Arthur Miller, and Eugene O'Neill. *Congressional Theatre*, her study of the theater's response to the House Committee on Un-American Activities in the 1950s, was honored by the American Society for Theatre Research in 1999 for outstanding research in theater history and cognate studies.

Professor Murphy has been active in a number of international professional organizations throughout her career. She serves on the editorial boards of several journals and book series and on the boards of several societies that promote the study of American playwrights, and has served as President of the American Theatre and Drama Society and The Eugene O'Neill Society. Her research has been supported by grants from the National Endowment for the Humanities, the American Council for Learned Societies, the National Humanities Center, and other sources.

About *The Paris Review*

The Paris Review is America's preeminent literary quarterly, dedicated to discovering and publishing the best new voices in fiction, nonfiction, and poetry. The magazine was founded in Paris in 1953 by the young American writers Peter Matthiessen and Doc Humes, and edited there and in New York for its first fifty years by George Plimpton. Over the decades, the *Review* has introduced readers to the earliest writings of Jack Kerouac, Philip Roth, T. C. Boyle, V. S. Naipaul, Ha Jin, Jay McInerney, and Mona Simpson, and published numerous now classic works, including Roth's *Good-*

bye, Columbus, Donald Barthelme's *Alice*, Jim Carroll's *Basketball Diaries*, and selections from Samuel Beckett's *Molloy* (his first publication in English). The first chapter of Jeffrey Eugenides's *The Virgin Suicides* appeared in the *Review*'s pages, as well as stories by Edward P. Jones, Rick Moody, David Foster Wallace, Denis Johnson, Jim Shepard, Jim Crace, Lorrie Moore, Jeanette Winterson, and Ann Patchett.

The Paris Review's renowned Writers at Work series of interviews, whose early installments include legendary conversations with E. M. Forster, William Faulkner, and Ernest Hemingway, is one of the landmarks of world literature. The interviews received a George Polk award and were nominated for a Pulitzer Prize. Among the more than three hundred interviewees are Robert Frost, Marianne Moore, W. H. Auden, Elizabeth Bishop, Susan Sontag, and Toni Morrison. Recent issues feature conversations with Salman Rushdie, Joan Didion, Stephen King, Norman Mailer, Kazuo Ishiguro and Umberto Eco. (A complete list of the interviews is available at www.theparisreview.org) In November 2008, Picador will publish the third of a four-volume series of anthologies of *Paris Review* interviews. The first two volumes have received acclaim. *The New York Times* called the Writers at Work series "the most remarkable and extensive interviewing project we possess."

The Paris Review is edited by Philip Gourevitch, who was named to the post in 2005, following the death of George Plimpton two years earlier. Under Gourevitch's leadership, the magazine's international distribution has expanded, paid subscriptions have risen 150 percent, and newsstand distribution has doubled. A new editorial team has published fiction by Andre Aciman, Damon Galgut, Mohsin Hamid, Gish Jen, Richard Price, Said Sayrafiezadeh and Alistair Morgan. Poetry editors Charles Simic, Meghan O'Rourke and Dan Chiasson have selected works by Billy Collins, Jesse Ball, Mary Jo Bang, Sharon Olds, and Mary Karr. Writing published in the magazine has been anthologized in *Best American Short Stories* 2006, 2007 and 2008, *Best American Poetry*, *Best Creative Non-Fiction*, the Pushcart Prize anthology, and *O. Henry Prize Stories*.

The magazine presents two annual awards. The Hadada Award for lifelong contribution to literature has recently been given to William Styron, Joan Didion, Norman Mailer and Peter Matthiessen in 2008. The Plimpton Prize for Fiction given to a new voice in fiction brought to national attention in the pages of *The Paris Review* was presented in 2007 to Benjamin Percy and to Jesse Ball in 2008.

The Paris Review won the 2007 National Magazine Award in photojournalism and the *Los Angeles Times* recently called *The Paris Review* "an American treasure with true international reach."

Since 1999 *The Paris Review* has been published by The Paris Review Foundation, Inc., a not-for-profit 501(c)(3) organization.

The Paris Review is available in digital form to libraries worldwide in selected academic databases exclusively from EBSCO Publishing. Libraries can contact EBSCO at 1-800-653-2726 for details. For more information on *The Paris Review* or to subscribe, please visit: www.theparisreview.org.

Contributors

Brenda Murphy is Board of Trustees Distinguished Professor of English at the University of Connecticut. Her books on Arthur Miller include *Miller: Death of a Salesman* in the Cambridge University Press series Plays in Performance and, with Susan Abbotson, the casebook *Understanding Death of a Salesman*, as well as a substantial portion of *Congressional Theatre: Dramatizing McCarthyism on Stage, Film, and Television*. She has published many articles on Miller and other American playwrights, as well as books such as *The Provincetown Players and the Culture of Modernity*, *O'Neill: Long Day's Journey Into Night*, *Tennessee Williams and Elia Kazan: A Collaboration in the Theatre*, *American Realism and American Drama, 1880-1940*, and, as editor, the *Cambridge Companion to American Women Playwrights*.

Carl Rollyson is Professor of Journalism, Baruch College, CUNY. He has published biographies of Marilyn Monroe, Lillian Hellman, Martha Gellhorn, Rebecca West, Susan Sontag, Jill Craigie, Marie Curie, and Norman Mailer. He is currently at work on a biography of Amy Lowell. His other publications include *Biography: A User's Guide* and *A Higher Form of Cannibalism? Adventures in the Art and Politics of Biography*. He is general editor of the Hollywood Legends series, published by University Press of Mississippi, and of several multivolume works for Salem Press, including *Critical Survey of Mystery and Detective Fiction*, *Critical Survey of Drama*, and *Critical Survey of Long Fiction*.

Elizabeth Gumport is an MFA candidate in fiction at Johns Hopkins University. Her writing has appeared in *n+1*, *Canteen*, and *Slate*.

Jon Dietrick is Assistant Professor of English at Babson College. His work has appeared in journals such as *American Drama*, *Twentieth Century Literature*, and the *Journal of International Women's Studies*.

Joshua E. Polster is Assistant Professor in the Performing Arts Department at Emerson College. He is a reviewer for *Choice Magazine*, and has contributed articles to *the Arthur Miller Journal*, *Law and Literature*, *Texas Theatre Journal*, and *Theatre Tours*. He has been the recipient of a Modern Language Quarterly grant and the Michael Quinn Prize. Dr. Polster has also served as the Assistant Director of the Nuffield Theatre in Southampton, England, the Assistant Artistic Administrator at the Goodman Theatre, and the Artistic Director of the Steep Theatre Company in Chicago.

Neil Heims is a writer and teacher living in Paris. His books include *Reading the Diary of Anne Frank* (2005), *Allen Ginsberg* (2005), and *J. R. R. Tolkien* (2004). He has also contributed numerous articles for literary publications including essays on William Blake, John Milton, William Shakespeare, and Arthur Miller.

Amy Sickels is an MFA graduate of Pennsylvania State University. Her fiction and essays have appeared or are forthcoming in *DoubleTake*, *Passages North*, *Bayou*, *The Madison Review*, *LIT*, *Natural Bridge*, and *The Greensboro Review*.

Chester E. Eisinger served as a Professor of English at Purdue University for 35 years where he was founder of the American Studies program. He contributed articles to numerous publications and covered a wide variety of literary topics. He was author of the book *Fiction of the Forties* (1963), and edited the volume *The 1940s: Profile of a Nation in Crisis* (1969).

Irving Jacobson taught at State University of New York, Syracuse. His essays appeared in well-regarded publications such as *American Literature* and *Studies in Short Fiction*, and *Agora: A Journal in the Humanities and Social Sciences*.

Kay Stanton is Professor of English at California State University, Fullerton. She has contributed chapters to a number of books including *Feminist Readings of Modern American Drama* (1989), *Ideological Approaches to Shakespeare* (1992), and *A Feminist Companion to Shakespeare* (2000).

Granger Babcock is Associate Dean of the Honors College at Louisiana State University. He is a contributor to *American Playwrights, 1880–1945: A Research and Production Sourcebook* (1994), and *New Readings in American Drama* (2002). He has also contributed articles to the *Journal of Dramatic Theory and Criticism* and *American Drama*.

Fred Ribkoff teaches English at Kwantlen Polytechnic University in British Columbia. He has published articles on the works of Daphne Marlatt and Arthur Miller.

Terry W. Thompson is Assistant Professor at Georgia Southern University. He has published articles on, among others, Mary Shelley, Herman Melville, Joseph Conrad, Henry James, M. R. James, Edith Wharton, H. G. Wells, James Dickey, and Bobbie Ann Mason.

Heather Cook Callow is a Professor at George Washington University. In addition to her writing on Miller, she has written extensively on James Joyce.

Lois Tyson is a Professor of English at Grand Valley State University. Her books include *Psychological Politics of the American Dream* (1994), *Learning for a Diverse World: Using Critical Theory to Read and Write about Literature* (2001), and *Critical Theory Today: A User-Friendly Guide* (2006).

Matthew C. Roudané is Professor and Chair of American Drama, Modern Drama, and American Literature at Georgia State University. He has taught as a Fulbright scholar, and has been the Editor of the *South Atlantic Review* since 1994. He has written and edited numerous books including *Understanding Edward Albee* (1987), *'Who's Afraid of Virginia Woolf?': Necessary Fictions, Terrifying Realities* (1990), *Approaches to Teaching Miller's 'Death of a Salesman'* (1995), *The Cambridge Companion to Tennessee Williams* (1997), *American Drama, 1960—Present: A Critical History* (1996), *The Cambridge Companion to Sam Shepard* (2002), and *Drama Essentials: An Anthology of Plays* (2008).

Christopher Bigsby is Professor of American Studies at the University of East Anglia. He has published over forty books and won numerous awards for his scholarship and teaching. Among his publications are *Confrontation and Commitment: A*

Study of Contemporary American Drama (1967), *Approaches to Popular Culture*, ed. (1976), *Tom Stoppard* (1976), *The Second Black Renaissance* (1980), *The Radical Imagination and the Liberal Tradition*, ed. (1982), *A Critical Introduction to 20th Century American Drama, 3 Vols.* (1982), *The Portable Arthur Miller* (1995), *The Cambridge History of American Theatre Vols. I-III, Beginnings to 1870* (1998–2000), *The Cambridge Companion to Modern American Culture*, ed. (2006), and *Remembering and Imagining the Holocaust: The Chain of Memory* (2006).

Acknowledgments

"Arthur Miller" by Carl Rollyson. From *Critical Survey of Drama, Second Revised Edition* (2003): 2346-2358. Copyright © by Salem Press, Inc. All rights reserved.

"The *Paris Review* Perspective" by Elizabeth Gumport. Copyright © 2008 by Elizabeth Gumport. Special appreciation goes to Christopher Cox and Nathaniel Rich, editors for *The Paris Review.*

"Focus on Arthur Miller's *Death of a Salesman*: The Wrong Dreams" by Chester E. Eisinger. From *American Dreams, American Nightmares*, ed. David Madden. Copyright © 1970 by David Madden. Reprinted by permission of David Madden.

"Family Dreams in *Death of a Salesman*" by Irving Jacobson. From *American Literature* 47, no. 2 (May 1975): pp. 247-258. Copyright © 1975 by Duke University Press. All rights reserved. Used by permission of the publisher.

"Women and the American Dream of *Death of a Salesman*" by Kay Stanton. From *Feminist Rereadings of Modern American Drama*, ed. June Schlueter. Copyright © 1989 by Associated University Presses. Reprinted by permission of Associated University Presses.

"'What's the Secret': Willy Loman as Desiring Machine" by Granger Babcock. From *American Drama* 2, no. 1 (Fall 1992): 59-83. Copyright © 1992 by the American Drama Institute. Reprinted by permission of the American Drama Institute.

"Shame, Guilt, Empathy, and the Search for Identity in Arthur Miller's *Death of a Salesman*" by Fred Ribkoff. From *Modern Drama* 43, no. 1 (Spring 2000): pp. 48-55. Special thanks to the Graduate Centre for the Study of Drama at the University of Toronto. Copyright © 2000 University of Toronto Press Inc. Reprinted by permission of University of Toronto Press Incorporated (www.utpjournals.com).

"The Ironic Hercules Reference in *Death of a Salesman*" by Terry W. Thompson. From *English Language Notes* 40, no. 4 (June 2003): pp. 73-77. Copyright © 2003 by *English Language Notes*. Reprinted by permission of *English Language Notes*.

"Masculine and Feminine in *Death of a Salesman*" by Heather Cook Callow. From *"The Salesman Has a Birthday": Essays Celebrating the Fiftieth Anniversary of Arthur Miller's* Death of a Salesman, ed. Stephen A. Marino. Copyright © 2000 by University Press of America. Reprinted by permission of University Press of America.

"The Psychological Politics of the American Dream: *Death of a Salesman* and the Case for an Existential Dialectics" by Lois Tyson. From *Essays in Literature* 19, no. 2 (Fall 1992): 260-278. Copyright © 1992 by Western Illinois University. Reprinted by permission of Western Illinois University.

"*Death of a Salesman* and the Poetics of Arthur Miller" by Matthew C. Roudané. From *The Cambridge Companion to Arthur Miller*, ed. Christopher Bigsby (Cambridge: Cambridge University Press, 1997): 60-85. Copyright © 1997 by Cambridge University Press. Reprinted by permission of Cambridge University Press.

'*Death of a Salesman*' by Christopher Bigsby. From *Arthur Miller: A Critical Study*. (Cambridge: Cambridge University Press, 2005): 100–123. Copyright © 2005 by Cambridge University Press. Reprinted by permission of Cambridge University Press.

Index